GENDERED BODIES

Feminist Perspectives

Judith Lorber
*Brooklyn College and
Graduate Center, CUNY*

Lisa Jean Moore
*State University of New York
at Purchase*

Roxbury Publishing Company
Los Angeles, California

Library of Congress Cataloging-in-Publication Data

Gendered bodies: feminist perspectives / Judith Lorber, Lisa Jean Moore.
   p. cm.
   Includes bibliographical references and index.
   ISBN 1-933220-41-4 (alk. paper)
   1. Body, Human—Social aspects. 2. Gender identity. 3. Sex differences. 4. Feminist theory. I. Lorber, Judith. II. Moore, Lisa Jean, 1967–

HM636.G46 2007
306.4—dc22   2006005528

Publisher: Claude Teweles
Managing Editor: Dawn VanDercreek
Production Editor: Monica K. Gomez
Copy Editor: Ann West
Typography: Jerry Lenihan
Cover Design: Marnie Kenney

Printed on acid-free paper in the United States of America. This book meets the standards for recycling of the Environmental Protection Agency.

ISBN 1-933220-41-4

ROXBURY PUBLISHING COMPANY
P.O. Box 491044
Los Angeles, California 90049-9044
Voice: (310) 473-3312 • Fax: (310) 473-4490
E-mail: roxbury@roxbury.net
Website: www.roxbury.net

For Judith's grandchildren, Conrad and Charlie

For Lisa's parents, Linda and Richard

Contents

About the Authors

Judith Lorber is Professor Emerita of Sociology and Women's Studies at Brooklyn College and The Graduate Center, City University of New York. She is the author of *Breaking the Bowls: Degendering and Feminist Change, Gender Inequality: Feminist Theories* and *Politics, Paradoxes of Gender, and Women Physicians: Careers, Status and Power.* She is co-editor of *Handbook of Gender Studies and Women's Studies, Revisioning Gender,* and *The Social Construction of Gender.*

***

Lisa Jean Moore is Coordinator of Gender Studies and Professor of Sociology and Women's Studies at the State University of New York at Purchase. She is the author of the forthcoming *Sperm Tales* and many articles on the social and cultural analysis of human bodies, particularly genital anatomy and semen. With Judith Lorber, she is the author of the second edition of *Gender and the Social Construction of Illness.*

Acknowledgements

Parts of this book were adapted from Judith Lorber and Lisa Jean Moore's *Gender and the Social Construction of Illness,* Second Edition, Walnut Creek, CA: AltaMira Press, and from Lisa Jean Moore, "Polishing the Pearl: Discoveries of the Clitoris," in *Sex and Society,* edited by Steven Seidman, Nancy Fischer, and Chet Meeks, London: Taylor and Francis, forthcoming.

We would like to thank the following for their guidance and assistance: Robyn Mierzwa, Michael Ortiz, and Natalie Rapp. We would also like to thank the anonymous reviewers for their helpful suggestions. ✦

Introduction

Key Terms and Issues

The human body has been an object of fascination from the beginning of the human species, judging from the little prehistoric statues we see in museums. In this book, we explore feminist contributions to contemporary social studies of the human body. We present the ways bodies are constructed in Western society, which is ordered by gender.

Although our focus is on gendered social constructions of bodies and their consequences, we show how racial constructions, economic and class issues, and the influence of sexual orientations intersect with gender to make the human body a social body. White people are privileged in the United States, so members of other racial and ethnic groups are under the burden of having to look and act "White" to improve their chances for a good job, admission to an elite school, or entry into a popular social circle. Latinas with plumper figures may go on extreme diets, and some Asians use cosmetic surgery to make their eyes look bigger. Lighter-skinned African American media stars and politicians experience greater social acceptance, which can lead to rifts within African American communities. Similarly, because homosexuals are so devalued, gay men and women in the public eye may choose to look "straight" in their appearance, even when they are open about their sexuality. Working-class women and men, who can't afford expensive beauty and fitness services, can't compete in appearance with toned, slim, surgically altered middle- and upper-class people.

These are some of the ways that social norms and expectations shape bodies. Other ways are stigmatizing fat people, disrespecting old people, making people with disabilities invisible, and assuming that

1

everyone is heterosexual. Although it is impossible to separate gender norms from those imposed by social class, racial, ethnic, religious, and sexual communities, in this book we will be foregrounding gender.

Gendered Societies

We live in a deeply gendered society, where work, family, and other major areas of life are organized by dividing people into two categories, "men" and "women," assigning them to different jobs and positions, and socializing them to do the work of their assigned category. The categorization of infants into "boys" and "girls" may originally be based on genitalia, but the systematic allocation of people into gendered positions is done through social processes.

Inequalities emerge through the distribution of privileges and rewards based on this allocation of social positions by gender, so that men's work is more prestigious and better paid than work done by women. Child care and domestic work are women's unpaid work for the family. Cultural and knowledge production reflects and legitimates gender divisions. The division of people by gender also permeates social relationships in friendships and other informal groups. In sum, we see ourselves and the world around us through the binary gender schema.

The division of society and our immediate social worlds by gender is so taken for granted that we rarely probe the processes that produce it. They are virtually invisible. Yet it is our actions and beliefs that construct the gendered social order. It is maintained by those who benefit from it, as well as those who are shortchanged by the resulting inequalities. Women and men, for the most part, go along with gendered norms for appropriate masculine and feminine behavior because their identities and self-esteem are built on meeting social expectations. A girl or woman who looks or acts masculine and a boy or man who looks or acts feminine are criticized, stigmatized, and sometimes ostracized.

In Western societies, most people are persuaded to accept gender inequalities by a belief that they emerge from the body. This belief claims that it is our "natural differences" that explain why men and women have different roles and positions in work organizations, politics, education systems, and the other main areas of society, and why men predominate in positions of power and authority. These "natural" explanations are reinforced by culture, the mass media, religions, and knowledge systems and erase the ways in which social processes produce gendered bodies and behavior.

Using feminist social construction theory, we argue that the differences between women and men are produced through social practices that encourage boys and girls to use their bodies and minds differently. Boys and men are expected to be assertive and rational; girls and women are expected to be compliant and nurturing. Gendered work organizations divide jobs into "women's work" and "men's work." Movies, television, and marketing focus women's lives on marriage and motherhood, men's lives on a wider range of physical and mental activities.

The socially produced gendered attributes and activities are differently valued and have different life outcomes. Boys' and men's bodies and behavior have a higher value in Western society and are intended to bring economic independence and political power. Girls' and women's bodies are often exploited sexually and maternally, and their behavior is intended to bring economic dependence and domestic harmony. These effects, we argue, are not natural to women and men but are socially produced through many of the processes described in this book.

Beliefs About Bodies

According to feminist theory, claims about bodies are part of the social arrangements and cultural beliefs that constitute the gendered social order. As a social institution, gender produces two categories of people, "men" and "women," with different characteristics, skills, personalities, and body types. These gendered attributes, which we call "manliness" or "masculinity" and "womanliness" or "femininity," are designed to fit people into adult social roles, such as "mother," "father," "nurse," or "construction worker."

Men's physical capabilities are, for the most part, considered superior to women's. Feminist theories have examined the contexts of this superiority in sports and physical labor. As bodies prone to illness and early death, as well as higher infant mortality rates and lower pain thresholds, men's are actually more fragile than women's, and feminist analysis has tried to tease the physiological from the social, cultural, and environmental in illness and death rates.

As some feminists argue, domination requires that the subordinate group be marked as different from the superior group. Thus, claims that women and men are physically different become fodder for the development and perpetuation of a gender hierarchy or a dominance system favoring men over women. Through the disciplines of science and medicine, socially constructed gendered body differences are recast as natural, physical, universal, transhistorical, and permanent facts. The common belief is that men's and women's bodies are different because they were born that way. We argue that male and female bodies are indeed different, but they are, for the most part, made that way by social practices and expectations of how girls and boys, women and men, should look and act.

Gendered Bodies

People experience their bodies, and these experiences produce different senses of self. Women's experiences of menstruation, pregnancy, childbirth, menopause, and breast cancer have been examined through critical feminist perspectives on science, medicine, and psychology, as have men's experiences of sexuality, impotence, and prostate cancer. In more specific contexts—sex selection, gene manipulation, ritual genital cutting, cosmetic surgery, rape, physical violence, sports, disabledness, and transgendering—feminist perspectives have grappled with cultural values and theories of power and control to analyze the complexities of these body-based phenomena.

The theme that runs through all of these topics is *gendered bodies.* Human bodies are not allowed to develop in all their diversity of shapes, sizes, and physical capabilities. Human bodies are not "natural"; they are socially produced under specific cultural circumstances. They are shaped by sociocultural ideals of what female and male bodies should look like and be capable of (and further shaped by national, racial ethnic, and social class ideals for each). Bodies are socially constructed for dominance and submission and are symbolic in different ways. Simple attributes, like height, become ways of signaling superiority and inferiority. We believe that men should be taller than women, and we make it so: If a woman in a heterosexual couple is taller than the man, she typically wears flat shoes and stands one step below him for photographs.

Feminism has increased awareness of how bodies are gendered by making visible the cultural and social dynamics that produce difference and dominance out of male and female bodies. Feminists have called into question many accepted "truths" about gender and bodies and have challenged the evidence on which dubious claims of men's physical superiority are based. In addition, the practice of feminism has the political aim of improving the status and treatment of women and girls by valuing women's bodies as much as men's bodies.

Key Definitions

Feminists have tried to develop a precise vocabulary for referring to the body. We use the following terms in this book:

Sex: Biological criteria for classification as female or male: chromosomes (XX for female, XY for male), hormones (estrogen for female, testosterone for male), genitalia (clitoris, vagina, and uterus for female; penis and scrotum for male), procreative organs (ovaries and uterus for female, testes for male).

Secondary sex characteristics: At puberty, in males, testosterone increases muscle size and mass, deepens the voice, and accelerates growth of facial and body hair. In females, estrogen produces breasts and menstruation, widens the pelvis, and increases the amount of body fat in hips, thighs, and buttocks.

Sex category: Self-identification and self-display as a female or male; the assumption is that identity and self-presentation are congruent with the sex assigned at birth, but they may not be.

Gender: Legal status as a woman or man, usually based on sex assigned at birth, but may be legally changed. Gender status produces patterns of social expectations for bodies, behavior, emotions, family and work roles. Gendered expectations can change over time both on individual and social levels.

Gender display: Presentation of self as a gendered person through the use of markers and symbols, such as clothing, hairstyles, jewelry. Managing interaction with others using attitudes and physical activities considered appropriate for one's sex category.

Sexuality and sexual identity: Attraction to and desire for a sexual object choice of one or both of the same or opposite sex or gender. Common identity terms are homosexual or gay and lesbian (same sex or gender), heterosexual (other sex or gender), bisexual (both sexes or genders), queer sexuality (fluidity and variety).

Intersexual: A person born with procreative or sexual anatomy that doesn't seem to fit the typical definitions of female or male—appearing genitally female but having mostly male-typical anatomy internally, or a girl (XX) born with a noticeably large clitoris or lacking a vaginal opening, or a boy (XY) born with a notably small penis or with a divided scrotum resembling female labia. A person born with mosaic genetics, so that some cells have XX chromosomes and some have XY. Intersex characteristics may not show up until puberty, or at attempts to conceive. Some intersexuals are not identified until an autopsy is done after death.

Transgender: Identification as someone who is challenging, questioning, or changing gender from that assigned at birth to a chosen gender—male-to-female (MtF), female-to-male (FtM), transitioning (between genders), gender queer (transgressive, challenging gender norms).

Heteronormativity: A social environment that assumes that a "normal" boy or girl will inevitably fall in love with or have sex with a person of the other sex or gender. Heterosexuality is taken for granted as the natural, default state, and homosexuality is seen as a deviant, abnormal state. The social pressures for compulsory heterosexuality are invisible.

Patriarchy: Originally, a social organization marked by the supremacy of the father in the clan or family, the legal dependence of wives and children, and the reckoning of descent and inheritance in the male line. Now, a belief system that presupposes the dominance of certain groups of men, the priority of high-status men's agendas and interests, and the acceptability of men's acquisition of a disproportionately large share of social and political power.

Plan of the Book

The intent of this book is to cover a broad spectrum of topics relating to the body, as a way of foregrounding the body in feminist social science theory. Although we understand feminism to be a theoretical and political movement composed of eclectic perspectives, feminist theories and activism have always considered the body as imperative, and some postmodern scholarship is entirely about the body and its problematics. Radical feminism has focused on sexual and procreative aspects of the female body and on the politics of menstruation and menopause. Feminist studies of men and masculinities have incorporated body studies through examining sports, violence, and media representations of men. There have been many liberal and poststructuralist feminist critiques of Western culture's emphasis on thinness, Caucasian beauty, and cosmetic surgery. Theoretically, feminism has analyzed the interplay among the physiological body, the sexual body, and the social body. In this book, the focus is on gendered aspects of how bodies are shaped, used, and abused, with an emphasis on how gendered body practices perpetuate and reinforce hierarchies of power.

The book starts with a review of theories of the body and then presents eight themes with feminist readings. The readings were chosen to show some of the feminist work on the topic and to present a range of examples of what is discussed more conceptually in the text. Each chapter has an alphabetic list of key concepts that are covered in the text, three readings, recommended books and articles, and internet sources. At the end of the book, we offer class exercises and a list of movies with somatic themes.

There are other aspects of gendered bodies than those presented in this book that could be covered. We have tried to choose topics that would be of most interest to college students in the United States. Although we present examples from other cultures, our focus is North America.

Chapter 1. Neither Nature nor Nurture reviews feminist critiques of theories of the gendered body and brain: loop-back systems in producing sex/gender differences, hormonal influences on women's and men's behavior, prenatal and genetic "hardwiring" of brain structure, evolutionary development, and another look at a nature-versus-nurture accidental experiment.

Chapter 2. "Are You My Mother? My Father?" shows how conception, procreation, pregnancy, and childbirth, assumed to be natural, are socially constructed as gendered. Particular issues covered are prenatal sex and genetic testing, new technologies, surrogacy, infertility, maternal responsibility and powerlessness in pregnancy and childbirth, the medicalization of "natural childbirth," the search for the male pill, and representations of the masculinity of sperm in children's facts-of-life books.

Chapter 3. Barbie and G.I. Joe focuses on how social expectations and self-regulatory behaviors lead to gendered body performances of children and to the production of masculinity, violence, and social empowerment in sports. Topics covered are the shape of the ideal body, gendered children's games, Title IX and gender equality in sports, steroids and sports, and sports and violence.

Chapter 4. Eve, Venus, and "Real Women" explores the combination of conformity, agency, and resistance evident in the social construction of women's bodies and examines the extent to which women can take control over the social definition of their bodies. The chapter discusses menstrual activism, the clitoris and female sexuality, ritual genital cutting, breast cancer and body image, eating disorders, and elective cosmetic surgeries.

Chapter 5. Adonis, Don Juan, and "Real Men" describes the social construction of the ideal Western male body and sexuality and also shows how, in different contexts, a variety of male bodies and sexualities are valorized. Particular issues covered are idealizations of male bodies; Black, gay, and urban variations; prostate cancer and men's gender identity; the quest for a male contraceptive pill; and the controversy over routine nonmedical circumcision of male infants.

Chapter 6. Ambiguous Bodies discusses the lives and politics of intersexed and transgendered people, whose "ambiguity" is constructed against a narrow view of "normality," and whose politics are organized around efforts to gain recognition and legitimacy. Topics covered are living on the boundaries of the sex/gender binaries, transgendering, intersexuality, and the politics of ambiguity.

Chapter 7. You Don't Need Arms and Legs to Sing discusses the continuum of physical functioning, the social construction of "disability," and the standpoint of those at the intersection of body function, gender, and sexual orientation. Topics covered are gendering and disabling, disability and gendered sexuality, community and isolation, and transcending the body.

Chapter 8. Political Bodies explores the gendered aspects of violence and violations of human bodies. Topics covered are men and women in the military and in prison, sexual torture, suicide bombers, sexual slavery, and prostitution.

Chapter 9. Social Bodies discusses how physical bodies become social bodies through community values and social status, the symbolic use of women's bodies by the three major world religions, and how knowledge of the body is determined by social contexts. Topics covered are the effect of disasters on bodies, body economics, religious bodies, and how *Our Bodies, Ourselves*, the groundbreaking North American women's health movement book, has been adapted to different cultural and national contexts. ✦

Chapter 1

Neither Nature nor Nurture

Theories of the Gendered Body

Key concepts: evolutionary adaptation, genes and gender, hormonal influences on behavior, loop-back systems, prenatal brain organization

Human bodies vary in many ways, but we tend to group them into contrasting types—attractive, repulsive; old, young; fat, thin; tall, short; strong, weak; and so on. When we first meet people, it is practically automatic to characterize their body types. Are they masculine or feminine? Upper class or lower class? White, African American, Latina, or Asian? The physical typologies are intertwined with social behavior—we think that physically attractive people have appealing personalities, that tallness conveys authority, that body strength is manly.

Generally, people assume that the physical traits of bodies produce an individual's social characteristics. But physical traits—genes, hormones, and anatomy—are also affected by behavior and environment. We are born with a skeletal type and the potential for physical functioning, but where we live, how much we exercise, what we eat, drink, and breathe, the traumas and illnesses we suffer, and the treatment and medications we are given all modify muscles, bones, and body shape throughout the life cycle. Diet is an obvious example—ethnic culture, social class, and available foods affect individual eating patterns. In the United States, among working-class communities, fattening fast foods are as near as the next McDonald's; the result is often childhood and adult obesity, high blood pressure, and diabetes.

We talk about "nature" versus "nurture" in the production of gendered bodies, but there is an interplay among the components we sum up as "nature and nurture." What is "nature" for humans is female and male procreative systems and secondary sex characteristics, hormones and genes, the evolution of human bodies, the structure of the human brain. What is "nurture" is personal life experiences, the social milieu of similarly located people, the culture of the society at a specific point in time, and the physical environment and its resources and hazards. As physical bodies, we are the result of all the "natural" and "nurtured" input working together and affecting each other, producing behavior that further changes bodies and brains in a *loop-back system.*

The loop-back system makes it difficult to separate the biological and social input into differences between girls and boys, women and men. A girl's choice of a career in elementary school teaching and a boy's selection of engineering are often attributed to hormones, brain organization, prehistoric human evolution, or genes. But you cannot omit socialization, family and peer pressure, the advice of school counselors, and the gender-typing of jobs.

A constant question of contemporary feminism has been the extent of women's and men's body and brain differences, and their origins and universality. If differences between women and men are "natural," there is not much to be done about altering them. Much could be done to insure that the differences are not used to legitimate unequal legal rights or discriminatory practices. Significantly though, there is constant debate over how equal women and men can be, given what seems to be a substantially wide and unbridgeable gap between female and male "natures."

The argument tends to come down to *sex differences* (biological, unchangeable) versus *gender differences* (social, changeable) as sources of women's and men's behavior and social positions. These views explain the social order in different ways. What are the determinants of who has power and authority, who produces knowledge and culture, who works at what, who nurtures, whose values prevail, and so on? Those arguing that *sex differences* naturally produce the social order tend not to see a need for change. Or else they feel that since the social order is the manifestation of biology and nature, it cannot be changed. Those arguing that differences between women's and men's behavior and social positions are produced and maintained by humans in a social order that perpetuates power inequities and hierarchies feel that it can—and should—be changed.

Many of those arguing that differences between women and men are caused by biology or evolution usually accept racial ethnic and social class differences as socially produced. But not so long ago, racial ethnic and social class differences were also seen as products of biological inheritance (then called "blood") or evolution (social Darwinism). Those who argue for the social origins of the differences between women's and men's behavior and positions in society note that both are modified by racial ethnic, social class, and other group differences.

For the most part, explanations of the origins of the differences between women and men tend to focus on one cause. Because so many of these biological explanations have become extremely popular, we will discuss each in turn in this chapter. Our contention is that social and cultural effects are equally important but are usually downplayed, and so we devote the rest of the book to how bodies get *socially constructed* as gendered.

Testosterone, Estrogen, and Gendered Behavior

A popular theory of sex/gender differences focuses on hormones—testosterone and estrogen. Increased levels of testosterone and estrogen shape male and female bodies at puberty. Testosterone increases muscle and bone size and mass, resulting in growth spurts in males. It thickens the vocal cords to deepen the voice and accelerates the growth of hair on the face and body. In females, estrogen produces breasts, pubic and underarm hair, ovulation, and menstruation. The pelvis widens, and the body gets rounder from the deposits of body fat in hips, thighs, and buttocks. These physical signs of maleness and femaleness are accompanied by sexual desires and wet dreams and by mood changes. The body changes and sexual urges are certainly distracting, but the changes in intellectual focus and academic accomplishment, particularly among adolescent girls and working-class boys, are much more the result of peer pressure and norms of femininity and masculinity (Leonard 2006).

Testosterone and estrogen are found in both women and men, and both are important for human development. But testosterone is the theorized source of aggression and machismo in men, and estrogen supposedly produces empathy and nurturance in women. There are certainly behavioral and emotional effects of hormones, but the pathway is not linear. There is a loop-back effect: Hormones can affect behavior and behavior can raise hormone levels. A familiar example is that aggression raises testosterone levels in men, and these raised levels in turn produce more aggressiveness.

Stress, for men, sets off a *fight-or-flight* response. A recent study of responses to stress found that adult women don't have a fight-or-flight response but rather a *tend-and-befriend* reaction. In situations provoking fear or anxiety, men are prone to standing and defending themselves physically or running away to protect themselves. Women often seek out support from other people, or they protectively look after their children. Since 1932, most of the subjects of the research on stress responses were men, so this alternative behavior was virtually unknown. Recent studies have revealed that the biological source of stress responses in men is testosterone; in women it is oxytocin, the same hormone that induces labor in childbirth and milk letdown in breast-feeding (Taylor et al. 2000).

There is also a social side to these differences in stress-response behavior. Women usually have children to protect, and so their responses may be psychologically or socially induced, and the high oxytocin levels may be an effect of maternal protectiveness rather than a cause of it—or there may be, more plausibly, a loop-back effect.

Female and Male Brains

Another popular argument for the biological source of gendered behavior is brain organization. *Organization theory,* which goes back to 1959, argues that the male brain is organized or "hardwired" for masculinity by prenatal androgens produced by the fetal testicles. The female brain is organized for subsequent feminine behavior by maternal and fetal estrogen input. Brain organization theory was widely adopted by psychologists and neuroendocrinologists and became textbook knowledge by the 1960s. It is still a widely used explanatory model for female and male behavior, even though it was found in the 1970s that "male" hormones had to be converted to "female" hormones before "masculinizing" the brain. Information about the hormonal "mixed bag" hit the newspapers as new knowledge in the 1990s, concurrent with now-accepted ideas of the overlap of masculinity and femininity.

Organization theory was popular with animal researchers because it provided a method for showing the effects of prenatal hormones on mature sexual behavior. Pregnant rats were administered large doses of testosterone or estrogen, which resulted in altered sexual behavior in the offspring. Female rats whose mothers had received testosterone mounted male rats, and male rats whose mothers had received estrogen presented themselves sexually to females; both are the opposite of nonaltered behavior. These results were extrapolated to human sexuality as a theory of the origin of homosexuality and by extension, used as an explanation of stereotypical and nonstereotypical gendered behavior, including skills and career choice. The theory of "brain sex" suppressed evidence of male-female behavioral overlaps in humans and in animals and did not allow for social factors in the gendering of human behavior. In fact, there was a great deal of effort to separate out the biological from the social causes of masculinity and femininity in the search for bedrock origins.

The problem here is that despite our constant contrasts and comparisons of boys and girls and men and women, human beings show a continuum of physiological and behavioral patterns that are not clearly and neatly divided into "female" and "male." The seemingly natural binary division of brain structure and behavior is a division imposed by researchers looking for differences between women and men. Similarities and overlaps are made invisible because researchers start with the assumption that there are two and only two clear-cut categories of different sorts of people, so they dismiss the in-between areas as aberrations. When researchers start with the variety of patterns they see and classify them into finer categories, and then run those categories against multiple social categories (combinations of racial ethnic groups, social classes, sexual orientations, and genders), they come up with many more than two contrasting sets of people. If people cannot be sorted into clear and separable sex groups, how can you validate sex differences in the structure of the brain and the sex-typed behavior they are supposed to produce?

Another problem with brain organization theory is that brain pathways do not get established once and forever prenatally or during infancy. Anne Fausto-Sterling cited research that shows that brain structures respond to behavior by laying down new neural pathways, which in turn affect behavior in a loop-back developmental pattern (2000, 195–232). Despite this evidence of changes in individual brains and behavior, theories of evolutionary psychology claim that there is a deeply embedded core of human behavior that was laid down in our primate ancestry and further ingrained by the food-gathering behavior of prehistoric humans.

Primates Are Us

A popular theory of the source of human behavior is that since we share 99 percent of our genes with our primate ancestors, we must act the way they do. Male primate behavior is usually invoked as an explanation for men's propensity for warfare (territorial defense) and sexual aggression (the alpha male has first pick of the females). But the behavior of gorillas, chimpanzees, baboons, and bonobos is very different. Bonobos, for instance, spend much of their time having sex and grooming each other, as a way of ensuring peaceful cooperation.

Another false idea about primates is that while they learn local skills, like how to crack nuts with stones, from each other (mostly from their mothers), their social behavior is genetically established and unchanging. An accidental experiment in changing male primate behavior occurred in a group of 62 baboons:

> Among a troop of savanna baboons in Kenya, a terrible outbreak of tuberculosis 20 years ago selectively killed off the biggest, nastiest and most despotic males, setting the stage for a social and behavioral transformation unlike any seen in this notoriously truculent primate. . . . The victims were all dominant adult males that had been strong and snarly enough to fight with a neighbor-

ing baboon troop over the spoils at a tourist lodge garbage dump, and were exposed there to meat tainted with bovine tuberculosis, which soon killed them. Left behind in the troop, designated the Forest Troop, were the 50 percent of males that had been too subordinate to try dump brawling, as well as all the females and their young. With that change in demographics came a cultural swing toward pacifism, a relaxing of the usually parlous baboon hierarchy, and a willingness to use affection and mutual grooming rather than threats, swipes and bites to foster a patriotic spirit.

Remarkably, the Forest Troop has maintained its genial style over two decades, even though the male survivors of the epidemic have since died or disappeared and been replaced by males from the outside. (As is the case for most primates, baboon females spend their lives in their natal home, while the males leave at puberty to seek their fortunes elsewhere.) The persistence of communal comity suggests that the resident baboons must somehow be instructing the immigrants in the unusual customs of the tribe. . . . Dr. Sapolsky, who is renowned for his study of the physiology of stress, said that the Forest Troop baboons probably felt as good as they acted. Hormone samples from the monkeys showed far less evidence of stress in even the lowest-ranking individuals, when contrasted with baboons living in more rancorous societies. (Angier 2004, F1-2)

If baboons can change so quickly, are humans really stuck in the Stone Age?

Hunters and Gatherers

The answer is, they are not. Another theory of evolutionary adaptation argues that if modern humans are not quasi-primates, we are children of our prehistoric ancestors. This theory of evolutionary adaptation spans hundreds of thousands of years, from when humans lived in tribes where women gathered plant food and men hunted for meat. Evolutionary psychology theory argues that the behaviors prehistoric humans required for survival are still ingrained in today's human genes. These survival adaptations are supposedly expressed in men's roaming, preditoriness, and sexual promiscuity and in women's nesting, nurturing, and sexual loyalty.

The theory of evolution is that bodies and behavior must be adaptive if a species is to survive. Success in survival involves living long enough to pass on one's genes, which will replicate successfully adapted bodies and behavior. Part of the evolutionary argument is that women have a "maternal instinct" and will put children before their careers, professions, politics, or artistic endeavors because motherhood and mothering continue the survival of the species. Voluntary childlessness or letting someone else take care of your children is thus considered "unnatural" and certainly "unwomanly."

This evolutionary theory of women's mothering assumes that it is universal and unchanging, that mothers never evolved. But feminist anthropologists show that in the past as in the present, maternal behavior is consciously strategic and socially adaptive to changing physical and social circumstances, not instinctual. Sarah Blaffer Hrdy, an anthropologist who has studied primates and written about human evolution, claims that the idea of a universal and unchanging "maternal instinct" downplays the varied and purposeful action of mothers as they adapt to changing physical and social environments. In *Mother Nature*, Blaffer Hrdy argues that prehistorically, historically, and in the present, "every female who becomes a mother does it her way" (1999, 79). A mother's goal is not so much to get the best man's genes to pass on as to ensure the survival of her best children—the healthiest, liveliest, and fattest—those with the best chance of living to adulthood. To do so, she may abandon, kill, or fail to feed sickly children, twins, or deformed infants. She will certainly recruit *alloparents* to help her care for and raise her children—older children, other women in her kin group and community, and fathers.

Just as mothering behavior adapts to changing environmental and social conditions, so does other human behavior. There is genetic evidence that as food production changed from hunting and gathering to farming and herding 10,000 to 12,000 years ago, humans adapted with new genes for resistance to malaria, lactose tolerance, salt sensitivity, skin pigmentation, bone structure, and brain development (Gross 2006; Voight et al. 2006). However, the changes at this time of major human social evolution were not just genetic—human cultures changed enormously from small, nomadic, foraging tribes to large settlements and cities. Writing evolved, roles were specialized and assigned to different categories of people, and ownership of land and herds created hierarchies. Hunting and gathering tribes are comparatively egalitarian, and women, as major food producers, have a high status. In the economic evolution of some human societies from foraging to agriculture, women lost status because they produced less of the food. Their main roles became child producers and child minders.

Genes and Gender

Now that the human genome has been mapped, and the effects of more and more genes have been isolated, the belief that "it's all in the genes" is a prevalent idea about physical and mental differences between women and men. Feminists have critiqued this belief for its underlying assumptions about the universality and immutability of masculine and feminine behavior, and particularly for its legitimation of men's dominance of women. Any introductory cultural anthropology text has descriptions of assertive women and passive men, of men weaving and women building houses, of women heads of families, and of kinship structures where children belong to the mother's tribe, not the father's. The dominant status of men has varied throughout history and varies today. Scandinavian countries are much more egalitarian when it comes to gender than fundamentalist Islamic countries, yet their women and men presumably have the same kinds of genes, hormones, brains, and evolutionary history.

In addition to the variation in women's and men's behavior cross-culturally and through time, the changes brought about through feminist activism in the last thirty-five years have modified what has seemed like genetically ingrained behavior. In January 2005, Lawrence Summers, the president of Harvard University, caused a furor when he said that the lack of women in science and engineering might be due as much to genetic differences as to social differences—discrimination and the difficulty of balancing demanding careers with family responsibilities. However, today many more women receive higher degrees in the science professions than they did thirty years ago. In 1970–71, women got 0.6 to 16.5 percent of the Ph.D.'s in the physical, biological, health, and computer sciences. In 2001–02, they got 15.5 to 63.3 percent of the Ph.D.'s in those same sciences (Cox and Alm 2005). Thirty years is too short a span for genetic changes, but it is the period of feminist protest against gender discrimination in higher education and the professions.

To say "it's all in the genes" ignores how genes work. Genes are proteins that turn body processes on or off. They are not one-time recipes for the production of bodies, minds, or behavior. Genes interact with the body's changes and with the physical and social environment in which the body lives. Genes may be triggers, but what sets them off are complex factors, and they don't work once but continue to interact with the body and environment. Furthermore, gendered behavior is complex; there couldn't be one gene for creating a gendered body or a gendered mind.

We need to think in terms of interactive developmental processes. Interactive models and biosocial perspectives did not emerge until the 1980s. They were, in part, a reflection of the work done in the sociology of the body, which argued for a continuous, lifelong, loop-back interchange of bodily, behavioral, environmental, and social structural factors:

> We take for granted that the bodies of a new-born, a twenty-year-old, and an eighty-year-old differ. Yet we persist in a static vision of anatomical sex. The changes that occur throughout the life cycle all happen as part of a biocultural system in which cells and culture mutually construct each other. For example, competitive athletics leads both athletes, and a larger public who emulate them, to reshape bodies through a process that is at once natural and artificial. Natural, because changing patterns of diet and exercise change our physiology and anatomy. Artificial, because cultural practices help us decide what look to aim for and how best to achieve it. Furthermore, disease, accident, or surgery—from the transformations undergone by surgical transsexuals, to the array of procedures (applied to secondary sexual characteristics) that include breast reduction or enlargement and penile enlargement—can modify our anatomic sex. We think of anatomy as constant, but it isn't. . . . The body and the circumstances in which it reproduces are not separable entities. (Fausto-Sterling 2000, 242–243)

A Nature-Versus-Nurture Controversy Revisited

In the 1970s, there was a case that seemed to be an ideal accidental experiment that could test whether nature or nurture had primacy in gender development. The penis of a baby boy who was an identical twin was destroyed in the course of a botched circumcision when he was 7 months old. The parents were advised to legally change the child's name and sex to "female" and to treat the child as a girl as much as possible. A vagina was surgically constructed when the child was 17 months old. The child was feminized with frilly dresses, hair ribbons, and jewelry, and the child's exuberant and dominant behavior was squelched:

> The girl had many tomboyish traits, such as abundant physical energy, a high level of activity, stubbornness, and being often the dominant one in a girls' group. Her mother tried to modify her tomboyishness: ". . . I teach her to be more polite and quiet. I always wanted those virtues. I never did manage, but I'm going to try to manage them to—my daughter—to be more quiet and ladylike." From the beginning the girl had been the dominant twin. By the age of three, her dominance over her brother was, as her mother described it, that of a mother hen. The boy in turn took up for his sister, if anyone threatened her. (Money and Ehrhardt 1972, 122)

You could argue that this child was a tomboy because of male genes, but the mother had also been a tomboy. Although the mother said she had learned feminine behavior poorly while she was growing up as a biological female, she insisted that her physically reconstructed daughter learn it well.

But when the child became a teenager and faced further surgery, lifelong hormone injections, and relegation to what had become a hated female status, the child rebelled and insisted on being returned to a male physical and social status (Colapinto 2000). He had testosterone injections and surgical construction of a penis. He married and became a stepfather to three children. This outcome seems to clinch the argument that nature trumps nurture. But this case can be read as the rejection of a devalued gender status as much as it can the inevitable emergence of bodily and psychological "hardwiring."

In an account of the case that favored the nature argument, the teenager was referred to as Joan/John. "Joan" was described as hating being a girl. Colapinto (1997, 68) quoted Joan's identical twin brother as saying,

> "When I say there was nothing feminine about Joan," Kevin laughs, "I mean there was nothing feminine. She walked like a guy. She talked about guy things, didn't give a crap about cleaning house, getting married, wearing

makeup. . . . We both wanted to play with guys, build forts and have snow-ball fights and play army." Enrolled in the Girl Scouts, Joan was miserable. "I remember making daisy chains and thinking, 'If this is the most exciting thing in Girl Scouts, forget it,' John says. "I kept thinking of the fun stuff my brother was doing in Cubs."

Is this rejection of conventional "girl things" the result of internal mascu-linization or the gender resistance of a rebellious child? Being a man is a pre-ferred status in many societies, so it is not surprising when those with ambig-uous genitalia prefer that gender identity (Herdt and Davidson 1988).

Joan might have been happier growing up in the pro-feminist 1980s and 1990s, playing sports and taking leadership roles. Given the surgery she had had as a child, she might have become an intersex activist. What actually happened to Joan/John and the twin brother is that they both committed suicide:

A Winnipeg man who was born a boy but raised as a girl in a famous nur-ture-versus-nature experiment has died at the age of 38. David Reimer, who shared his story in the pages of a book and on the TV show Oprah, took his own life last Tuesday. His mother, Janet Reimer, said she believes her son would still be here today had it not been for the devastating gender study that led to much emotional hardship. "He managed to have so much courage," Janet told The Sun yesterday. "I think he felt he had no options. It just kept building up and building up." . . .

David recently slumped into a depression after losing his job and separating from his wife. He was also still grieving the death of his twin brother two years earlier, their mother said. A cause of death was never confirmed but Janet suspects it might have been an overdose of medication which Brian required to treat schizophrenia. Daily, David would visit his brother's grave, placing fresh flowers and pulling weeds to keep it tidy. Just last week, David told his parents that things would get better soon but they never imagined he was planning to commit suicide.

Janet said she'll remember her son as "the most generous, loving soul that ever lived." . . . "He was so generous. He gave all he had." (Chalmers 2004)

This case can be seen as induced gender dysphoria and the child as an accidental transsexual. The "nature" argument is that the true sex won out, but too late, and suicide was the result. But the intact twin brother also had mental problems and also may have committed suicide. A disturbed family history, perhaps precipitated by the botched circumcision, for which the mother always felt guilty, was no doubt an element in both children's unhappiness. But more significant were the pressure and constraints of the Western sex/gender system of the mid-twentieth century. It dictated that a child without a penis could not be a boy, and that a girl had to be feminine—restrained, subdued, and dressed in frilly clothes. We are somewhat more open to a range of behavior for girls and women, but bodies are still circumscribed by rigid gender norms and expectations.

Critical Summary

Even though there is ample evidence to the contrary, beliefs about the biological essence of differences between girls and boys and women and men persist. For example, there has been experimental evidence since the 1930s that the so-called male and female hormones are equally important to the development of both females and males, and sex testing at sports competitions has shown that people with XY chromosomes can have female anatomy and physiology. Nonetheless, all of the research efforts in the twentieth century were geared to finding clear female-male differences, preferably with an easily identifiable physiological source. Before the intensive criticism by feminist scientists and social scientists, there was very little effort to document the *social* sources of masculinity and femininity in Western societies and their variety and fluidity.

Sex differences do matter in illness and aging. There is good evidence that the presence of the extra X chromosome in females provides protection against certain genetic diseases that is missing in males, since the smaller Y chromosome has fewer genes. There is also good evidence that estrogen is protective against certain illnesses, and that males and females experience the physical effects of aging differently. So there are certainly sex differences in illness risks, but the evidence for sex differences in intellectual and emotional capacities and behavior is much less solid. Lifetime experiences, such as gender socialization, gendered norms and expectations, differences in educational and job opportunities, economic status, and family responsibilities, have an enormous impact on men and women, and it is these social factors, we argue, that construct women and men as different in emotions, attitudes, and behavior.

In sum, while it is incorrect to say there is no prenatal "hardwiring" of human behavior through genetic predispositions, hormonal flooding of the fetus, brain development, or evolutionary adaptability, human brains and bodies respond significantly to their physical and social environments. Sex differences are modified by gendered norms and expectations, opportunities over the life cycle, and input from racial ethnic and social class differences. Sex differences are not fixed and unchangeable, nor do they have one cause.

If there isn't a simple or single answer to the question of whether differences between women and men are genetic, hormonal, evolutionary adaptations, or recently learned behavior, then there isn't a simple or single way of determining how much or how little can be changed by new social patterns. Rather than accepting whatever the status quo is for their time and place as natural and unchangeable, feminists have pushed for social changes. The results of feminist social change have shown that women's and men's bodies, brains, and behaviors are quite adaptable to these new social patterns.

References and Recommended Readings

Adair Gowaty, Patricia (ed.). 1996. *Feminism and Evolutionary Biology: Boundaries, Intersections and Frontiers*. New York: Chapman and Hall.

Angier, Natalie. 2004. "No Time for Bullies: Baboons Retool Their Culture." *New York Times*, 13 April, F1–2.

Birke, Lynda. 2000. *Feminism and the Biological Body*. New Brunswick, NJ: Rutgers University Press.

Blaffer Hrdy, Sarah. [1981] 1999. *The Woman That Never Evolved*. Cambridge, MA: Harvard University Press.

——. 1999. *Mother Nature: A History of Mothers, Infants, and Natural Selection*. New York: Pantheon.

Braidotti, Rosi. 1994. *Nomadic Subjects: Embodiment and Sexual Difference in Contemporary Feminist Theory*. New York: Columbia University Press.

Butler, Judith. 1993. *Bodies That Matter: On the Discursive Limits of "Sex."* New York: Routledge.

Carey, Benedict. 2006. "Searching for the Person in the Brain." *New York Times* Week in Review, 4 February, 1, 4.

Cealey Harrison, Wendy. 2006. "The Shadow and the Substance: The Sex/Gender Debate." In *Handbook of Gender and Women's Studies,* edited by Kathy Davis, Mary Evans, and Judith Lorber. London: Sage.

Cealey Harrison, Wendy, and John Hood-Williams. 2002. *Beyond Sex and Gender.* London: Sage.

Chalmers, Katie. 2004. "Sad End to Boy/Girl Life." *Winnipeg Sun/News,* 10 May. *www.canoe.ca/NewsStand/WinnipegSun/News/2004/05/10/pf-453481.html*

Colapinto, John. 1997. "The True Story of John/Joan." *Rolling Stone,* 11 December, 54–97.

———. 2000. *As Nature Made Him: The Boy Who Was Raised as a Girl.* New York: HarperCollins.

Cox, Michael W., and Richard Alm. 2005. "Scientists Are Made, Not Born." *New York Times,* 28 February, A19.

Fausto-Sterling, Anne. 1985. *Myths of Gender: Biological Theories About Women and Men.* New York: Basic Books.

———. 2000. *Sexing the Body: Gender Politics and the Construction of Sexuality.* New York: Basic Books.

———. 2005. "The Bare Bones of Sex: Part 1—Sex and Gender." *Signs: Journal of Women in Culture and Society* (hereafter, *Signs*) 30, 1491–1527.

Gross, Liza. 2006. "Clues to Our Past: Mining the Human Genome for Signs of Recent Selection." *PLoS Biology* 4 (3), 0001. DOI: *10.1371/journal.pbio.0040094*

Haraway, Donna. 1989. *Primate Visions.* New York: Routledge.

———. 1997. *Modest_Witness@Second_Millenium. FemaleMan©.Meets OncoMouse™: Feminism and Technoscience.* New York: Routledge.

Hausman, Bernice L. 2000. "Do Boys Have to Be Boys? Gender, Narrativity, and the John/Joan Case." *NWSA Journal* 12, 114–138.

Herdt, Gilbert, and Julian Davidson. 1988. "The Sambia 'Turnim-Man': Sociocultural and Clinical Aspects of Gender Formation in Male Pseudohermaphrodites With 5α-Reductase Deficiency in Papua, New Guinea." *Archives of Sexual Behavior* 17, 33–56.

Hubbard, Ruth. 1990. *The Politics of Women's Biology.* New Brunswick, NJ: Rutgers University Press.

Jacobus, Mary, Evelyn Fox Keller, and Sally Shuttleworth (eds.). 1990. *Body/Politics: Women and the Discourses of Science.* New York: Routledge.

Jordanova, Ludmilla. 1989. *Sexual Visions: Images of Gender in Science and Medicine Between the Eighteenth and Twentieth Centuries.* Madison: University of Wisconsin Press.

Kemper, Theodore D. 1990. *Social Structure and Testosterone: Explorations of the Socio-Bio-Social Chain.* New Brunswick, NJ: Rutgers University Press.

Leonard, Diana. 2006. "Gender, Change, and Education." In *Handbook of Gender and Women's Studies,* edited by Kathy Davis, Mary Evans, and Judith Lorber. London: Sage.

Lorber, Judith. 1993. "Believing Is Seeing: Biology as Ideology." *Gender & Society* 7, 568–581.

Money, John, and Anke A. Ehrhardt. 1972. *Man & Woman, Boy & Girl.* Baltimore, MD: Johns Hopkins University Press.

National Human Genome Research Institute. 2005. "Studies Expand Understanding of X Chromosome: NIH-Supported Research Sheds New Light on the Role of Sex Chromosomes in Health and Disease." *www.genome.gov/13514331*

Oudshoorn, Nelly. 1994. *Beyond the Natural Body: An Archeology of Sex Hormones.* New York: Routledge.

Roberts, Celia. 2000. "Biological Behavior? Hormones, Psychology, and Sex." *National Women's Association Journal* 12, 1–20.

———. 2002. "'A Matter of Embodied Fact': Sex Hormones and the History of Bodies." *Feminist Theory* 3, 7–26.

Rossi, Alice S. 1977. "A Biosocial Perspective on Parenting." *Daedalus* 106, 1–31.

Roughgarden, Joan. 2004. *Evolution's Rainbow: Diversity, Gender, and Sexuality in Nature and People.* Berkeley: University of California Press.

Sapolsky, Robert M., and Lisa J. Share. 2004. "A Pacific Culture Among Wild Baboons: Its Emergence and Transmission." *PLoS Biology* 2 (4), 0534–0541. DOI: *10.1371/journal.pbio.0020106*

Taylor, Shelley E. 2002. *The Tending Instinct: How Nurturing Is Essential to Who We Are and How We Live.* New York: Times Books, Henry Holt.

Taylor, Shelley E., Laura Cousino Klein, Brian P. Lewis, Tara L. Gruenewald et al. 2000. "Biobehavioral Responses to Stress in Females: Tend-and-Befriend, Not Fight-or-Flight." *Psychological Review* 107, 411–429.

Van den Wijngaard, Marianne. 1997. *Reinventing the Sexes: The Biomedical Construction of Femininity and Masculinity.* Bloomington: Indiana University Press.

Voight, Benjamin F., Sridhar Kudaravalli, Xiaoquan Wen, and Jonathan K. Pritchard. 2006. "A Map of Recent Positive Selection in the Human Genome." *PLoS Biol* 4 (3): 0446–0458. DOI: *10.1371/journal.pbio.0040072*

Wizemann, Theresa M., and Mary-Lou Pardue (eds.). 2001. *Exploring the Biological Contributions to Human Health: Does Sex Matter?* Washington, DC: National Academy Press.

Internet Sources

American Heart Association
www.americanheart.org/presenter.jhtml?identifier=2775

American Medical Association Women Physicians Congress on cholesterol and heart information for women
www.ama-assn.org/ama/pub/category/11005.html

Evolutionary Feminism
 www.evoyage.com/Evolutionary%20Feminism/WhatisEvoFeminism.htm
Gender Medicine
 www.gendermedjournal.com
Georgetown University Center for the Study of Sex Differences in
 Health, Aging, and Disease
 http://csd.georgetown.edu
International Journal of Men's Health and Gender
 www.jmhg.org
Partnership for Gender-Specific Medicine at Columbia University
 www.cumc.columbia.edu/dept/partnership/aboutus.html
Society for Women's Health Research
 www.womenshealthresearch.org
"Women's Health: Sex- and Gender-Based Differences in Health and Disease,"
 AMA Council of Scientific Affairs Report
 www.ama-assn.org/ama/pub/category/13607.html
WomenHeart: National Coalition for Women With Heart Disease
 www.womenheart.org
Women-Related Websites in Science/Technology
 http://research.umbc.edu/wmst/links_sci.html ✦

Chapter 2

'Are You My Mother? My Father?'

Gendering Procreation

Key concepts: genetic engineering, heteronormativity, the male pill, new technologies, patriarchal control over procreation, state and medical control of childbearing, surrogacy, valorization of sperm

One of the most significant contributions of feminist scholarship has been the ongoing analysis of human procreation.[1] From valuing the lived experiences of a pregnant woman to analyzing the proliferation of high-tech innovations for getting pregnant and the medicalization of childbirth, feminism offers critical insights into the social aspects of a seemingly natural process. Through feminist analyses, we are made aware of the ironies of human procreation: It occurs in female bodies yet is profoundly controlled by patriarchal government interests and individual men's prerogatives.

Women as a group and as individuals generally are not the power brokers when it comes to contraceptive research, abortion policies, access to and financing maternal and child health care, or labor and delivery practices. At the same time, since procreation takes place inside a woman's body, it has been historically and cross-culturally considered a woman's responsibility to manage all its dimensions: conception, contraception, prenatal care, breast-feeding, physical care of

29

infants and small children, emotional nurturance, and teaching children how to be proper members of their social group.

In addition to gendered power differences, human procreation provides a clear example of economic differences between industrialized and developing nations. The bodies of women of color and poor women have a history of being used for medical experimentation. The modern birth control movement, ushered in with the mass distribution of the pill, was enabled in part through pharmaceutical testing on poor and uneducated Puerto Rican women throughout the 1950s and 1960s. Unaware that they were part of an experiment, women residents of Humacao were enrolled in the study by U.S. doctors. These doctors needed to provide large-scale human trial data about the pill in order to receive FDA approval. These abuses of research subjects led to tighter rules of informed consent in human clinical trials.

The demographic trends of testing contraceptive devices, sterilization, access to prenatal care, and use of expensive technologies tell us that some mothers and babies are socially valued over others. Some countries have pronatal policies encouraging women to have children by restricting access to contraception and making abortion illegal. Other countries have population restriction policies, discouraging women from having more than one or at most two children. Patrilineal family demands for sons to carry on the male line lead to multiple childbirths or selective abortions of female fetuses. Poor countries have high rates of maternal and infant mortality; rich countries spend money developing age-defying fertility treatments. Is it fair that a postmenopausal 59-year-old grandmother can give birth to triplets while an otherwise healthy 20-year-old woman dies in childbirth?

In this chapter, we explore the intersections of human procreation and gendered bodies in four arenas. First, we discuss the way that prenatal sex testing demonstrates a societal preference for particular gendered bodies. Second, we show how new technologies and surrogacy underscore power differentials based on racial, class, and gender stratification. Third, we analyze the processes of pregnancy and childbirth as an illustration of the paradox of women's responsibility and powerlessness. Fourth, we discuss the search for the male pill and the valorization of sperm as examples of men's control over procreation.

Prenatal Sex Testing and Social Consequences

Gender, racial, and class dynamics imbue the questions of who is encouraged to procreate and who is prevented, and what types of human bodies should be born. There is ample evidence to suggest a tacit preference for rich, first-world, properly sexed and gendered, male, heterosexual, attractive, White, able-bodied, genetically enhanced babies (Mies 1994; Fogg-Davis 2001; Karsjens 2002). But how can this be guaranteed? Eugenics, meaning good genes, is the study of hereditary and genetic "improvement" of the human race by controlled selective breeding. Eugenics is today called social engineering.

Historically, eugenics has been practiced by preventing those who were regarded as having undesirable traits from passing them on to children. The Holocaust and Rwandan genocide of women, men, and children are two examples of the violent elimination of "inferior" genes by mass murder carried out by a supposedly physically and racially "superior" group. In addition to genocide, sterilization campaigns have been undertaken by governments to modify the gene pool. In the United States between 1907 and 1917, 16 states adopted laws advocating the sterilization of the dependent poor, criminals, the feeble-minded, and other people allegedly unfit to have children (Apple 1990, 397). In 1924, a U.S. Supreme Court decision said that state practices that routinely sterilized the "feeble minded" were constitutional. By 1937, 27 states had passed variations on such laws. Under these laws, women who were poor, Black, Puerto Rican, Chicana, Native American, or mentally retarded were sterilized either without their consent or with consent obtained under duress. For example, North Carolina's sterilization program concentrated on welfare recipients, most of whom were Black women (Schoen 2005). Often, women in active labor have been pressured to sign consent forms so that physicians could perform a tubal ligation or hysterectomy immediately after delivery. In many cases, the women spoke little or no English and did not understand what they were signing.

The advent of sonograms that show the sex of the fetus provided another way to control what kind of babies would be born. Until about twenty-five years ago, the first declaration made about a newly born infant was, "It's a girl!" or "It's a boy!" In many places in the world today, parents can decide to find out the sex at 16 to 19 weeks of pregnancy—at the now routinized first sonogram. Even earlier, embryos can be sorted by sex, and earlier still, sperm can be manipulated to favor X or Y chromosomes. The earlier the "sexing," the easier it is to abort fetuses of the "wrong" sex—usually female.

In addition, genetic engineering and prenatal genetic testing can be used to enhance or suppress desirable or undesirable traits in fetuses. Women's bodies are thus manipulated and increasingly under surveillance to create socially valued fetuses prior to the birth of these new human beings. With the innovation of each new prenatal testing technology, the stakes of pregnancy change for women and their bodies. Kristen Karlberg's article describes the ways that prenatal testing serves today's eugenics.

Shaping Babies: No, Not THAT Kind! Can I Try Again?
Kristen Karlberg
Beford Corners, New York

Kristen and John Magill adore all three of their daughters—11-year-old twins and a 5-year-old baby sister. But when they began to plan for their next—and last—child, the Magills really wanted a boy. "My husband is a 'Junior' and has a family business that he wants to continue in the family name," said Kristen, 37, of Grafton, Massachusetts. So the Magills combined a family trip to Disneyland in August with a stop at a Los Angeles fertility clinic that enables couples to pick the sex of their babies. Kristen is now expecting twin boys. "I'm excited," she said, "We always wanted a boy. We really wanted just one, but we'll be happy with two."(Stein 2004)

Pregnant Knowledge: I Can Find Out What?!

It used to be that a pregnant woman had to wait until birth to find out the sex of her child. Today many women are told the sex of their child during the pregnancy rather than at delivery, and some opt to find out at conception. The brave new world fantasy of being able to dictate what kind of child you want began with detecting genetic diseases and birth defects through prenatal testing and ultrasound technologies. But since the sex of the fetus is also evident in the chromosomes and on the sonograms, there is also a way of choosing sex.

The information about what "kind" of baby you will have is powerful and literally life-altering. This type of knowledge is negotiated by pregnant women and their families and reinterpreted to become family knowledge, with appropriate meanings and actions. The pregnant woman is socially responsible for the type of child she produces, so she must selectively reproduce, filtering out the undesirable fetuses through abortion.

The routinization and normalization of prenatal genetic testing and sex identification effectively transform the pregnancy and its potential product—a "perfect" baby—into a medical and genetic experience. Geneticization refers to the ways in which genetic technologies are increasingly used to manage problems of "health" (Lippman 1991). A fetus' sex is arguably not a "health" issue, but "diagnosing" sex is something many pregnant women and their partners and families wish to do during the pregnancy. The sex of a fetus can be visualized as early as 12 weeks gestation using ultrasound, and is commonly revealed during the routine 16-to-19-week sonogram most pregnant women undergo in the United States. Often one of the first questions a pregnant woman hears after, "When are you due?" is "Do you know what it is?"

Technologies are now available that design the sex of the fetus at conception. MicroSort ($2,800–$4,000 per attempt) is a patented technique where sperm carrying the X chromosome (female) are separated from sperm carrying the Y chromosome (male), resulting in a 74 percent pure sample of Y sperm and a 91 percent pure sample of X sperm. These samples are then used in artificial insemination of the woman to result in a child of the chosen sex. MicroSort only selects for sex, which the company calls "family balancing." The Genetics and IVF Institutes in Northern Virginia and Laguna Hills, California, who own the patent, are conducting a study seeking FDA approval. So far, several thousand couples have used the technique, resulting in more than 400 babies. Despite the documented preference for boys in developing countries, at this American company 75 percent of families have been seeking girls (Stein 2004).

Parents with a family history of inherited disorders and older parents often undergo genetic testing of the fetus. There are many different prenatal genetic testing technologies available today, amniocentesis being the most common. Amnio is conducted between 15 and 18 weeks of gestation by inserting a needle through the abdomen and into the uterus, withdrawing a small amount of amniotic fluid. The fluid is then cultured and examined to determine chromosomal makeup and, if indicated, the presence or absence of specific genes. Because amnio examines chromosomes, the sex is automatically "diagnosed" because it is dictated by the final pair of the 23 pairs of chromosomes in a human being. Chromosomal disorders, such as an absence of or extra chromosomes, are also easily detected. Down's syndrome is the most common chromosomal disorder, indicated by an extra chromosome 21.

What is often not clear to pregnant women is that genetic disorders, caused by the absence or presence of specific genes housed on chromosomes, are not automatically tested for with amniocentesis. Specific tests for specific genes must be ordered at the time the amnio is performed, and the genotypes of the biological parents must be previously obtained for comparison. When an amnio shows "normal" chromosomes, it does not guarantee a genetically "normal" child. More than 450 conditions can be diagnosed through amniocentesis, and with family pedigree and ethnicity information, about a dozen tests for genetic mutations are routinely offered to all applicable pregnant women (Harmon 2004).

In vitro fertilization, costing $10,000 to $20,000 per try, in conjunction with preimplantation genetic diagnosis (PGD), is another way to try to guarantee the sex and genetic makeup of the fetus. PGD, which costs $1,000 to $4,500 or more per attempt, depending on what is tested for, combines the benefit of finding out the sex of the embryo before implantation with examining it for chromosomal or specific genetic disorders. Embryos are created through in vitro fertilization, and when they reach the eight-cell stage, one cell is removed, cultured, and tested for chromosomal and, if indicated, genetic abnormalities. After the analysis is conducted on the available embryos, those with the desired sex and/or traits are implanted into the woman's uterus. PGD is banned for nonmedical use in Australia, Britain, Canada, France, Germany, India, Japan, and Switzerland (Stein 2004).

Genetic Bodies and Genetic Families: Everyone Has Something

Prenatal sex identification and prenatal genetic testing equate health with the desired sex and "normal" or "good" genes and designate the undesired sex and "deviant" or "bad" genes as illness. This process reduces individuals to their genes, just as the question, "Do you know what it is?" reduces the future baby to its sex. In this perspective, genetics is permeated with conceptions of normality and deviance, resulting in socially constructed "genetic bodies." Those being tested for deviations in genes or chromosomes become "genetic bodies" when they are found to have "bad" or "good" genes or the "right" or "wrong" sex chromosomes. This definition could encompass all individuals, because all bodies have potential genetic information discoverable through genetic testing.

Women's bodies are inherently multiply defined because of their capacity to produce other bodies through their own. The current constructions of flawed genomes and bodies are predominantly represented as dwelling within the female body, which is layered with gendered experiences and meanings. One of these gendered experiences is pregnancy. A pregnant woman's body is potentially two genetic bodies simultaneously—hers and the fetus's—and they both belong to a genetic family.

Genetics magnifies the links among blood relatives, even as the new reproductive technologies have the potential for severing biological from social parenting in ways that go beyond adoption. The traditional understanding of "parent" now has been generally subcategorized into "biological" and "social," with the "genetic" parent as a facet of the biological parent. If one blood relative possesses a genetic trait, it is extremely likely that another blood relation has that trait. Thus, the genetic body is not one's own when viewed through the lens of familial heredity. Genetic bodies belong to genetic families: those where a member has experienced some type of genetic testing that explicitly identifies genetic information about the family. A genetic family does not have to have a genetic anomaly to be "marked"; it must have merely been examined through the lens of genetics. Once this genetic information is "in the family," the genetic family will forever be marked by that genetic knowledge, be it benign or dangerous. A genetic family does not have to be blood-related to be affected by this information. Same-sex partners, adopted children, donor-egg and donor-sperm children are all implicated in the genetic family. The genetic family I refer to here is one fashioned by genetic technologies to produce the desired kind of family, be it composed of one boy and one girl, or with children free of genetic disease or a genetic condition, such as deafness.

The uniqueness of genetic families is their multiple social realities. They may be traditional and often nuclear in the blood and marital relation of members, yet they are technological and biomedical through obtaining genetic information. Genetic families also may be formed through donor insemination utilizing screening of the egg, sperm, or embryo, with no blood relations among members. No matter what their structure, genetic families are postmodern because they are defined through biotechnological capabilities, genetic linkages, or both.

Genetic Responsibility to Shape Families: It's Women's Work

Pregnant women are the center of genetic families. They are in the tenuous position of mediating the needs and desires of individual families in relation to the social acceptability and social demands of American society in the twenty-first century. The parental responsibility to produce a healthy child is taken very seriously today. It is assumed that a pregnant woman will undergo testing to guarantee genetic health. The genetic stigmatization of certain detectable genetic disorders can be viewed as a bridge to the potential label of genetic irresponsibility. Women who have children with Down's syndrome are queried as to whether they had a prenatal test to detect the disorder. The query implies that if they did not, they failed in their parental responsibilities to the future child. If they did, and kept the baby, they may be criticized for the added burden on their family or society.

Practice guidelines from the American College of Obstetricians and Gynecologists recommend that all pregnant women be offered or referred for genetic screening, and those over age 35 should be offered or referred for amniocentesis. If doctors do not provide information about testing to pregnant women, they can be held liable for births of children that parents argue would not exist if they could have detected the disorders prenatally and aborted the fetuses (Cleaver 2002; Marteau and Anionwu 1996).

These types of testing offer no cure for the "wrong" sex or genotype. If something undesirable is detected after the fetus is implanted in the uterus, the only way to prevent a baby with that genetic trait is to have an abortion. The assumption that defects can be repaired through surgery in utero is grossly mistaken. Fetal surgery is in clinical trials and currently available at four hospitals in the United States and for only four congenital malformations, all of which are detected through ultrasound and are not considered genetic conditions (Wilson 2002). Postnatal surgical repair is a viable option for many congenital malformations of the gastrointestinal tract, lungs, and heart, but genetic conditions are usually multifaceted syndromes and are not curable through surgeries.

The responsibility for what kind of fetus will develop into an acceptable baby to fit within a family lies primarily with the pregnant woman (Karlberg 2004). Pregnant women and their partners construct families through their shared meanings of genetic fitness or desired sex for that particular family. The American cultural hegemony of the nuclear family is a thing of the past. The unit "man, woman, child" is dismissed through biotechnological solutions and personal definitions for various groupings of kin, including same-sex parents.

What Is 'Normal?' Controversies and Conflicts

Shaping families, whether through prenatal genetic testing and ultrasound with abortion or through assisted reproductive technologies allowing choice of type of embryo to be inserted into the uterus, is a controversial issue. Sex selection is more clear-cut than selecting on genetic diagnoses, but both conjure images of "designer babies." Jeffrey Steinberg, director of The Fertility Institutes, which have offices in Las Vegas and Los Angeles that offer sex selection, says, "These are grown-up people expressing their reproductive choices. We cherish that in the United States. These people are really happy when they get what they want" (Stein 2004). Ralph Kazer, a Northwestern University fertility doctor, offers a contrasting opinion. He says, "My job is to help people make healthy babies, not help people design their babies. Gender is not a disease" (Stein 2004).

Research at the Genetics and Public Policy Center at Johns Hopkins University found that 60 percent of Americans are uncomfortable with sex selection for nonmedical reasons. (A medical reason would be a potentially lethal sex-linked trait.) What is disturbing about prenatal sex selection is that worldwide, the ratio of infant boys to girls is far off balance. The normal ratio of newborns is approximately 106 boys for every 100 girls. In China, the ratio is a numbing 119 boys to 100 girls, and in Korea, 110 boys to 100 girls (Carmichael 2004). In India in 1996, the ratio was 121 boys to 100 girls (Glenn 2004). The outcome of a gender-unbalanced society is that there are not enough adult women to partner with adult men, but some propose that a higher proportion of unpartnered men bodes more than a lack of heterosexual partners. Some social scientists suggest that crime and social disorder are more likely in societies with "surplus males" (Glenn 2004). The preference for boys worldwide makes the option of sex selection extremely disturbing in the light of the persistence of patriarchy and male dominance.

While prenatal sex selection is obviously not socially acceptable to many in the United States, the question of where to draw the line with genetic disorders is less clear. Prenatal genetic testing results often come in statistics, and numbers are confusing when trying to apply them to quality of life. Is a 40 percent chance of mental retardation too high? What about a 1/90 chance for Down's syndrome? Do you allow a baby to be born with a disorder that is "incompatible with life," like anencephaly (the brain does not develop)? Is a life expectancy of 35 for a baby born with cystic fibrosis too short? Would a person with achondroplasia (dwarfism) be accepted in the family? What if there is a family member with the disorder diagnosed in the fetus? Is a cleft palate severe enough to terminate? Is a missing limb reason to abort? The levels of acceptability vary by family, but time and again, in my research with pregnant women who had prenatal genetic testing, I heard, "I'm just grateful for the opportunity to find out and prevent it if I can" (Karlberg 2004).

Women's feelings about their experiences of pregnancy have been altered by prenatal genetic testing. Anxiety around the testing, both whether to have testing and what to do with the information it provides, has been extensively studied. The most notable finding is that women attempt to withhold attachment to the developing fetus until the results are available. Diane Beeson (1984) termed this "suspension of pregnancy," while Barbara Katz Rothman (1986) called it "the tentative pregnancy." Rayna Rapp's (1999) decade of ethnographic research in the prenatal genetic testing arena supports their findings. Studies that have examined women's experiences of a selective termination following a genetic diagnosis found that many women suffer severe emotional consequences, sometimes impacting on everyday activities and lasting as long as a year after the abortion (Beck Black 1994; Green and Statham 1996).

Pregnant women are at the forefront of the decision-making process, and they are the ones most implicated because being pregnant one day and not the next without a baby born involves questions about what happened. The answers to those questions are filtered through personal preferences and beliefs about abortion, religion, and disability, among others. Some argue that the mere availability of prenatal testing implies that the goal is to prevent births of children with disabilities. The yearning to have a child free of genetic abnormalities has been explored in a body of research that found that women who have had exposure to people living with a particular genetic disease are generally less inclined to consider abortion of a fetus with that disorder (Beeson and Duster 2002). Yet the desire to have a "healthy" child is pervasive, and even if one opts to continue a pregnancy known to have a genetic abnormality, the blatantly inadequate support of disabled individuals and their families makes it extremely difficult to opt to have a disabled child (Saxton 1984; Rapp 1999).

Some disability activists have protested the assumption that their lives are not worth living (Shakespeare 1999). What is unique about abortion as a result of diagnosis through prenatal testing is that the action is taken to prevent the birth of a human being who will have undesired characteristics, as opposed to other types of disability prevention and medical treatment (Asch 2002). Some doctors express concern over women terminating pregnancies for things they themselves do not believe are worthy of abortion (Harmon 2004; Karlberg 2004).

The issues are never easy, and the pregnant woman bears the brunt of the decision. She is the representative of the action taken, her body bears the scars, and she deals with the emotional ramifications of the decisions.

And I know we were lucky to be able to lose Ezra the way we did, even though that entailed making the hardest decision of our lives. My husband, Jake, says that the decision to terminate a pregnancy that had gone seriously awry just past the legal limits of abortion in our state makes him feel like there is a hole in his soul. For me, it is a more specific hole. I remember sitting in the clinic in Wichita, Kansas—one of the two places in the western hemisphere and Europe where a woman can get an abortion after twenty-four weeks, regardless of the condition of the fetus—feeling Ezra kick, and thinking that he wanted to be with us. For weeks afterwards, I think about that kicking. Small muscle twinges, even elsewhere in my body, remind me of that small but insistent presence, and I fall into the huge hole of this loss, Ezra's absence. (Bell 2003)

References

Asch, Adrienne. 2002. "Prenatal Diagnosis and Selective Abortion." In *The Double-Edged Helix: Social Implications of Genetics in a Diverse Society,* edited by J. S. Alper, C. Ard, A. Asch, J. Beckwith, P. Conrad, and L. N. Geller. Baltimore, MD: Johns Hopkins University Press.

Beck Black, Rita. 1994. "Reproductive Genetic Testing and Pregnancy Loss: The Experience of Women." In *Women and Prenatal Testing: Facing the Challenges of Genetic Technology,* edited by K. H. Rothenberg and E. J. Thomson. Columbus: Ohio State University Press.

Beeson, Diane. 1984. "Technological Rhythms in Pregnancy: The Case of Prenatal Diagnosis by Amniocentesis." In *Cultural Perspectives on Biological Knowledge,* edited by T. Duster and K. Garrett. Stamford, CT: Ablex.

Beeson, Diane, and Troy Duster. 2002. "African American Perspectives on Genetic Testing." In *The Double-Edged Helix: Social Implications of Genetics in a Diverse Society,* edited by J. S. Alper et al. Baltimore, MD: Johns Hopkins University Press.

Bell, Ida. 2003. "Fireflies: Another Kind of Lucky." *Brain, Child,* Spring 2003, 54–56.

Carmichael, Mary. 2004. "No Girls, Please." *Newsweek,* 26 January, 50.

Cleaver, Hannah. 2002. "German Court Award for Disabled Child Creates Controversy." *www.medscape.com/viewarticle/436943*

Glenn, David. 2004. "A Dangerous Surplus of Sons?" *Chronicle of Higher Education* 50 (34), April 30, A14.

Green, Josephine, and Helen Statham. 1996. "Psychosocial Aspects of Prenatal Screening and Diagnosis." In *The Troubled Helix: Social and Psychological Implications of the New Genetics,* edited by T. Marteau and M. Richards. Cambridge, UK: Cambridge University Press.

Harmon, Amy. 2004. "In New Tests for Fetal Defects, Agonizing Choices." *New York Times,* 20 June, 1, 22.

Karlberg, Kristen. 2004. "Genetic Bodies and Genetic Families: Social and Material Constructions of Prenatal Genetic Testing." Ph.D. Dissertation, University of California, San Francisco.

Katz Rothman, Barbara. 1986. *The Tentative Pregnancy: Prenatal Diagnosis and the Future of Motherhood.* New York: W. W. Norton.

Lippman, Abby. 1991. "Prenatal Genetic Testing and Screening: Constructing Needs and Reinforcing Inequities." *American Journal of Law and Medicine* 18 (1–2), 15–50.

Marteau, Theresa, and Elizabeth Anionwu. 1996. "Evaluating Carrier Testing: Objectives and Outcomes." In *The Troubled Helix: Social and Psychological Implications of the New Genetics,* edited by T. Marteau and M. Richards. Cambridge, UK: Cambridge University Press.

Rapp, Rayna. 1999. *Testing Women, Testing the Fetus: The Social Impact of Amniocentesis in America.* New York: Routledge.

Saxton, Marcia. 1984. "Born and Unborn: The Implications of Reproductive Technologies for People With Disabilities." In *Test-Tube Women,* edited by R. Arditti, R. Deulli-Klein, and S. Minden. Boston: Routledge and Kegan Paul.

Shakespeare, Tom. 1999. "Losing the Plot? Medical and Activist Discourses of Contemporary Genetics and Disability." In *Sociological Perspectives on the New Genetics,* edited by P. Conrad and J. Gabe. Oxford, UK: Blackwell.

Stein, Rob. 2004. "A Boy for You, A Girl for Me: Technology Allows Choice." *Washington Post,* 14 December, A1.

Wilson, R. D. 2002. "Fetal Therapy: Current Status and Future Prospects." Invited Session, 52nd Annual Meeting of the American Society for Human Genetics, Baltimore, MD.

Original article commissioned for this book.

New Technologies: Boon or Bane?

When bodies do not procreate the way they should, both men and women confront a social stigma for infertility. In childless couples, both masculinity and femininity may be questioned; men are ridiculed for "shooting blanks," and women are labeled "barren." Regardless of the cause, much of the treatment for infertility takes place inside women's bodies. Even if a woman is fertile, but her male partner is subfertile, she is the one to undergo physical traumas. If she refuses to undergo fertility treatments, she denies her infertile male partner the opportunity to have a biological child, and he may find a willing surrogate or another partner. Infertile women with male partners who are unwilling to participate in fertility treatments are less likely to seek a new partner. The new technologies do not alter old gender dynamics.

The variety of options for technologically assisted human procreation sever genetic, gestational, and parental links. Donor insemination (DI) involves the use of semen from a man who is not the woman's partner. It is usually resorted to in cases of male factor infertility. DI also enables lesbians and single women to reproduce without a male partner. Men with genetic predispositions to diseases, or men exposed to chemotherapy or other toxins that kill or damage semen, can become the social fathers of the children their partners bear after donor insemination. A newer technique for male factor infertility is Intracytoplasmic Sperm Injection (ICSI), which enables subfertile men to participate in genetic procreation: A single sperm cell is injected into an ovum with a microscopic needle.

In cases where either the woman or the man is subfertile but the woman has an intact womb, in vitro fertilization (IVF) joins their egg and sperm in a petri dish or test tube in a laboratory; if an embryo grows, it is placed inside the uterus. The woman must take hormones to induce production of multiple ova and to help sustain the pregnancy. Over 45,000 children have been born using this procedure in the United States. The average cost of IVF is $10,000 to $20,000 per cycle. Many women undergo multiple cycles of IVF, as the success rate is still roughly 30 percent. IVF is also used with egg, sperm, and embryo donation. Where a woman does not have a viable uterus, her male partner's sperm can be used to impregnate a surrogate, who gestates the fetus for the commissioning couple.

There are two types of gestational surrogacy. Partial surrogacy involves the surrogate mother as the genetic mother of the child, where conception usually occurs by insemination using the commissioning father's sperm. Full surrogacy involves the commissioning couple as the genetic parents of the child. Conception takes place at a clinic through IVF, and the embryo is gestated in the surrogate's womb. One research study of 34 surrogate mothers found no psychological problems as a result of the surrogacy arrangement (Jadva et al. 2003). However, some scholars and activists claim that gestational surrogacy is a form of prostitution or slavery, exploitation of the poor and needy by those who are better off (Ber 2000). Surrogacy can also be seen as a way poor women can earn substantial amounts of money. In the United States, surrogacy provides business opportunities for lower-middle-class White women. Websites contain multiple listings from potential surrogates, giving detailed fee schedules for intended parents, and whether the surrogate has medical insurance to cover part of the cost.[2] Potential surrogates also describe their pregnancy rates and live births for their own family and for commissioning couples. Many of these ads also provide photographs of the surrogate and assure the "buyers" of her healthy lifestyle.

The costs of surrogacy, IVF, and other reproductive technologies are high, frequently mounting from $20,000 to $30,000 per attempted pregnancy. Those with medical insurance or economic resources are able to consider procreation if they are infertile or unmarried, and as they age, they may delay procreation until they are in their 40s and sometimes even in their 50s or 60s.

Through the practices of sperm, oocyte, embryo donation, and surrogacy, the taken-for-granted assumption that procreation of human bodies occurs in genetically coherent lineages is disrupted. While women may experience giving birth and men support their partners through full-term pregnancies, their genetic connection to offspring may be nonexistent. Biological "clocks" and the notion of "women of procreative age" are no longer relevant: High-status women with premature ovarian failure as well as postmenopausal women may become pregnant and give birth through egg donations and IVF. The continued research on uterine transplants may soon make it possible for women to become pregnant with a donated uterus, egg, and sperm, further diminishing the strength of the genetic connection.

Through these new technologies and contractual relationships with donors, it is possible for a baby to have five different individuals involved in its creation—an egg donor (genetic mother), a sperm donor (genetic father), a gestational mother (carrier through pregnancy), and a commissioning mother and father. The legal and social issues of who is the "real parent" often reflect patriarchal bargaining, with men often holding more social power to claim a child in disputed cases (Katz Rothman 2000, 15–26).

Pregnancy and Childbirth: Responsibility and Powerlessness

Pregnancy and childbirth are so wrapped up with being "a natural woman" that we don't see the extent to which governments and Western medical systems control both. Becoming pregnant, maintaining a pregnancy, and vaginally birthing a full-term baby are rites of passage into normative femininity. In these images and representations of normal motherhood, conceiving, pregnancy, and childbirth should come naturally to female bodies, since that is what it is believed women are born to do—they are made to be mommies. But not all mommies are rewarded for achieving this cultural rite of passage: Unmarried mothers, teen mothers, mothers with disabilities, lesbian mothers, and poor mothers are often labeled burdens to society and criticized for having children. Clearly, these women should have prevented the pregnancy through abstinence or contraception or given the child to a prosperous heterosexual couple.

Most women in Western societies do not experience pregnancy or childbirth as a natural phenomenon. Rather, they must negotiate relationships with partners and kin, interact with midwives, nurses, physicians, and other professionals, and abide by government rules and regulations. In becoming pregnant for the first time, many women are confronted with new vocabularies, products, and procedures—ovulation predictor kits, genetic screening, sonograms, amniocentesis, alpha-fetal protein screening, gestational diabetes, episiotomies, epidurals, fetal monitors, forceps, caesarean sections, saving cord blood, neonatal intensive care units, lactation consultants. They are expected to become mothering experts, even as they are assumed to have an inborn "maternal instinct."

Women's bodies are always and everywhere viewed and treated as potentially pregnant. Walk into a local bar, and you will see multiple postings that state: WARNING, DRINKING ALCOHOL DURING PREGNANCY HAS BEEN LINKED TO BIRTH DEFECTS AND IS THE LEADING KNOWN PREVENTABLE CAUSE OF MENTAL RETARDATION. In at least two states, South Carolina and Wyoming, women have been arrested for drinking while pregnant (Roth 2000). When taken to an emergency room, women are routinely asked if they are pregnant to limit their exposure to harmful x-ray transmissions.

During March 2001, the U.S. Supreme Court heard arguments in a case considering the constitutionality of a governmental policy of surreptitiously drug testing pregnant women in a South Carolina hospital and then reporting positive cocaine results to law enforcement officers. In this case, the Supreme Court ruled that this policy violated the Fourth Amendment restriction against unlawful searches. Despite rulings to protect them, pregnant women, particularly women of color, are continuously watched and punished for supposedly harming their fetuses. While drug use during pregnancy is known to lead to negative outcomes for mother and fetus, testing pregnant women punishes them and their families. When pregnant women fear they will be prosecuted for drug use, they do not seek prenatal care and may end up delivering at home. They do not have access to drug treatment programs for themselves or their babies (Roberts 1997). Additionally, testing pregnant women is a racist practice. In a 1990 study, researchers found that 15.4 percent of White women and 14.1 percent of African American women used drugs during pregnancy. African American women, however, were ten times more likely than White women to be reported to authorities (Chasnoff, Landress, and Barrett 1990).

Women's bodies are valued for their procreative possibilities, but at the same time, women are deemed untrustworthy and dangerous to the potential life they carry. Recent social policies have emerged to "protect" women's bodies from harmful environments, but at the same time, they control women. Increasingly, women's rights are seen as subordinate to the fetal rights of the unborn or not-even-conceived entity (Casper 1998). The potential for pregnancy has justified discriminatory practices in employment against women, even though male fertility is equally vulnerable to toxic environments.

The U.S. Pregnancy Discrimination Act of 1978 was passed to provide security for working women under federal laws similar to laws for people with disabilities. However, the law has not been successful at curbing discrimination against pregnant women. Pregnancy discrimination complaints filed with the federal Equal Employment Opportunity Commission (EEOC) rose 39 percent from fiscal year 1992 to 2003, outpacing the increase in sexual harassment and sex discrimination claims, according to the Washington-based National Partnership for Women and Families.[3] In this way, pregnancy holds women hostage to the demands of the community, but many communities make it very difficult for a woman to easily prevent a pregnancy or to abort a fetus.

The Medicalization of 'Natural Childbirth'

In childbirth, too, women in industrialized Western countries are not in charge of their own bodies. Birth in every society is attended and ritualistic. In most societies, the attendants are women, usually those who have themselves experienced childbirth, and the rituals are performed to ease the birthing woman's pain. With the professionalization of medicine, male obstetricians replaced women midwives in many Western countries. Childbirth was medicalized, transforming pregnancy into an illness and delivery into a traumatic, surgical event.

Barbara Katz Rothman, a sociologist who studies birth in America, defines two models of pregnancy and birth management, the patriarchial biomedical model and the women-centered midwifery model (2000, 15–26). One outcome of the medicalization of childbirth has been the increasing rates of caesarean sections in many Western hospitals. Another common procedure is episiotomy, cutting the skin between the anus and the vagina. In the United States, episiotomies have been routine since the 1930s, as they have been believed to be better for post-birth repair, but according to a recent review of outcomes over the past 50 years, they may cause more pain and physical trauma. The conclusion of the report recently published in the *Journal of the American Medical Association* stated, "Evidence does not support maternal benefits traditionally ascribed to routine episiotomy. In fact, outcomes with episiotomy can be considered worse since some proportion of women who would have had lesser injury instead had a surgical incision" (Hartmann et al. 2005, 2148).

In contrast, midwives work with the birthing woman throughout labor, helping her respond to her body's signals instead of deadening them with drugs. Rather than forceps and episiotomies, midwives rely on their hands to turn the fetus into a good birthing position and to help the mother deliver. Midwives are best able to manage childbirth with their woman-centered, empathic model in birthing centers or in home births. In hospital settings, they tend to get co-opted into more technologically dominated deliveries.

The "natural childbirth" movement grew in resistance to the medicalization of childbirth. It has been most popular with women who wanted to experience birth "awake and aware." The theory of natural childbirth proponents is that lessons in breathing during contractions and the help of a supportive and knowledgeable coach would enable a woman to give birth without so much pain that she would need to be medicated. In actuality, as Carine Mardorossian's article shows, the process has been co-opted to the needs of the medical system, subverting its intent at empowering women and their partners.

Laboring Women, Coaching Men

Carine M. Mardorossian
State University of New York at Buffalo

In early spring 2000, several months before my due date, my husband and I enrolled in the childbirth class sponsored by the hospital in which I was slated to deliver. . . . My husband and I were extremely pleased that the partners of pregnant women were not only welcome but in fact encouraged and expected to attend and participate in the course and in childbirth. We would not have had it any other way, and it was a relief to know that we would not have to seek another source of "live" support and information when it came to preparing for childbirth together. Like most pregnant women, I could visualize sharing the experience of my child's birth with no one but my partner. Neither he nor I believed that a female presence would or could provide better labor support by virtue of her gender or personal experience of motherhood. Years of activism in the feminist movement had disabused me of the belief that gender identity alone could provide the grounds for the kind of bonding and solidarity identity politics proclaimed. The only kind of closeness I now valued was based on choice and actions, not on biological or social destinies people happened to share by virtue of their gender. The kind of women-only ritual that childbirth education and childbirth itself had been in the context of the second wave represented the separatist feminism I had long disavowed, so I was all the more willing and eager to embrace the husband-as-coach method. . . .

Needless to say, the very choice of "husband" rather than "partner" illustrates the heterosexism that has traditionally characterized the institution of motherhood and that continues to define hospitals' cooptation of alternative childbirth education.[1] In addition, the term "coach" to name the activity of the partner also reveals a lot about what kind of gender roles the parents are expected to play in the delivery room. Tellingly, when the supporting cast is someone other than the husband, they are designated as doula or assistant rather than as coach (Sears and Sears 1993: 23–24). In other words, when the support person is more likely to be female, her role is described as more passive and subordinate. By contrast, the role of coach is reserved to the male partner who is perceived not as taking orders but as giving instruction, training, and directing. The association of the term coach with sports is yet another way in which the husband-as-coach model tries to ensure that the man's conventional role as the site of authority is not threatened by his presence in the unknown and feminine space of labor. By indirectly framing labor as a sporting event, the language of coaching represents the woman's sweaty and straining body as one whose activity and level of pain can and should be directed by her partner. It ultimately turns the alienating experience of labor into a familiar site where a masculinized form of power seeks to reassert itself through the figure of the husband. As a feminist involved with a feminist, I knew that my husband and I would not be perpetuating such conventional norms of masculinity and femininity. This was a script we knew not to follow. What we were not aware of, however, is the extent to which we remained mere pawns in a play even though the hierarchical gender structure underlying the husband-assisted method did come undone (and only marginally through conditions of our own making).

Indeed, what often unravels in the labor and delivery room is anything but the successful coaching scenario for which childbirth classes prepare expectant couples. The reality is in fact radically different from the scenarios depicted in childbirth education (whose worst cases, in retrospect, do not look bad at all). When our much awaited day finally arrived, for instance, my husband was extremely intimidated by the role of "expert" he was supposed to play and not surprisingly, he could only perform it as an amateur, that is, with a complete lack of self-confidence. He was as far from fulfilling the part of a directing coach as one could imagine. His desperate attempts to help were just the pathetic gestures of a person who felt completely out of his depth in the face of so much pain. I knew him too well not to read through the facade, through the periodic smile or nod with which he sought to appease me. Neither he nor I could focus or relax, nor could we go on automatic pilot and do the breathing exercises effectively when they were most needed. My pain was so upsetting to him that he would have done anything to put a stop to it. When I asked for an epidural, he immediately acquiesced even though his job was to guide me through natural childbirth. And when I was not given the epidural, his despair at finding out that it was too late clearly equaled mine. Despite the weekly classes we had attended and the copious readings we had done, neither of us were prepared for the amount of pain delivery entailed.[2] It did not help that it had all been scripted ahead, classified, described, and explained, and that millions had experienced this before. It did not help that the nurses and medical staff around us had an all-knowing face. They were too busy attending to their duties and assumed an understandingly blasé attitude. The nurses have neither the time nor the energy to attend to and manage the expectant mother's fluctuating emotions and needs. And after all, isn't that the husband's function anyway?

While the model of husband as coach is supposedly put into place to provide the laboring woman with continued support, it typically fails to provide the kind of expert guidance she needs to achieve relaxation and calm. One can then only wonder why health care continues to sponsor a model of normative masculinity (the husband as coach, the man in charge) that flounders again and again and fails to provide the kind of guiding and benevolent patriarchal direction it is supposed to represent. What function, then, can an ineffectual coach possibly play in labor? Why is there such institutional commitment to staging a gender performance that almost always results in gender trouble? . . .

Ironically, the repetitive staging of heterosexual structures of gender and power in the husband-as-coach model of childbirth can also be seen as an instance of subversion guaranteed by the systemic level, since over and over again, the coach is unable to live up to the norms of controlling masculinity reinscribed by the system. While drag highlights the unexpected identifications and sexual practices that reveal the arbitrariness of conventional gender distinctions, the model of "natural" childbirth sponsored by hospitals today exposes the constructedness of gender even as it stages it in conventional and heterosexist terms.[3] Through childbirth education, men and women are taught a script on how to perform their proper masculine and feminine roles within the heterosexual matrix of the labor room. That roles which would not have to be taught were they indeed "natural" have to be assigned and learned reveals how unnatural "natural" childbirth actually is. When the couple then fails to convincingly act out the script of "natural" childbirth, the performativity of gender is further exposed. The coach is feminized as his inexperience and incompetence render him passive, while the laboring woman's anger defeminizes her. Far from working to subvert institutional practices, however, this denaturalizing of gender categories through the feminizing of the coach does in fact function as a ruse of power. The performativity of gender thus highlighted is not a byproduct of a system otherwise invested in maintaining the sex binary so much as a crucial aspect of the system's own deployment of the gender script. The couple's inability to carry out the assigned script in the labor room, in other words, ultimately serves the ends of the birthing industry even as it threatens the naturalness of gender. . . .

By incorporating alternative models of childbirth into their delivery practices, hospitals ensure that the responsibility for the failure of "natural" childbirth gets shifted onto the couple's shoulders. Childbirth education trains the laboring partners to think of the coach as the source of comfort and support, so much so that they then automatically attribute her disempowerment and inability to relax during labor to the coach's poor skills. When the responsibility for making labor woman-centered is thus shifted, it is the man and the woman's relationship that is at stake rather than the clients' relationship to the hospital. By foregrounding the traditional structure of masculinity and femininity that governs the domestic sphere, the sponsored husband-assisted method thus privatizes what is primarily an institutional relationship. The expectant couple who, through childbirth education, was given the illusion of autonomy in decision-making simply internalize their incompetence as personal failure. It must be their fault if labor becomes so overwhelming that they cannot take charge of it. They should have paid closer attention in childbirth class, meditated more, or they should have honed the relaxation techniques by longer practice. Never mind that nothing in the high-tech and high-traffic delivery room is conducive to relaxation. Never mind that neither the laboring woman nor her coach could possibly feel like participants in the context of the aggressive labor and birth management style that continues to characterize hospitals today.[4] Never mind that "[i]n the United States, . . . it has become increasingly clear that what parents learn in childbirth classes does not prepare them adequately to deal with the highly medicalized environment and crisis atmosphere in the hospital" (Kitzinger 1995, 88).

Childbirth classes teach the laboring woman "to see her proper role in childbirth as providing a prompt, docile response to a series of medical interventions and instructions, and guided her husband or partner to comply as well" (Wolf 2001, 94). In fact, the coach's inexperience turns the hospital's way of delivering babies into a most welcome and reassuring intervention, while inversely, the hospital's high-tech methods highlight the neophyte's incompetence. The interpersonal conflicts that ensue between the partners as a result of unfulfilled and unrealistic expectations raised in childbirth class further contribute to giving the hospital an aura of neutrality and competent mastery. Despite its alienating effects, the institution is left off the hook because it becomes the backdrop against which the male/female dynamic is acted out. It simply assumes the role of a neutral arbitrating force ready to intervene when, for instance, the husband fails to perform his role. That this scenario perpetuates itself no matter how many couples find the model flawed has a lot to do, I suspect, with the participants' unwillingness to draw attention to what might be perceived as the coaching partner's incompetence.

Thus, what is ironic about health care's apparent reliance on a patriarchal form of power is that whether the model of hegemonic masculinity it propounds lives up to its norms (which it mostly fails to do) or not, is insignificant to the success of corporate profit-making. That hegemonic masculinity may be destabilized in the unfamiliar realm of labor does not ultimately hamper the effectivity of its ideological function for capitalist gain. Economic interests in this context are dependent not on the maintenance of a gendered hierarchy but on the deployment of masculinity tout court. As long as the focus remains on the performance of the partner (where it indeed cannot help but remain), hospital procedures assume an aura of neutrality, and the capitalistic venture of the birth industry in the United States can continue, veiled and unhindered. . . .

Notes

1. Bradley, a product of the conservative fifties, was very heterosexist in his conception of the birthing team, and the institutional appropriation of the Bradley rhetoric perpetuates this heterosexism. In the alternative birthing scene, however, Bradley has changed with the times: there is no assumption, for instance, that the coach will be one's husband or partner. The course is a ten- to twelve-week marathon where the couple spends more time lying on blankets side by side working on pain exercises than listening to lectures. The exercises involve touching, massaging. The coach is taught to be entirely focused on the needs of the laboring woman, and the assumption is that s/he will be as exhausted as the mother by the end of the birth. This new and improved Bradley method is still a very fringe movement that most health insurances do not cover (personal communication).
2. As Wolf points out, one of the things childbirth class does not explain effectively is "the pain of childbirth and what to do about it other than breathe helplessly in its grips and take major drugs simply to cut off sensation" (2001, 91). She also draws attention to the fact that the educational birth videos shown in childbirth classes represent passive and emotionally detached births where no one yells, grunts, or pants and where no one is stroked or kissed during labor.
3. The quotation marks I have used throughout the paper to qualify "natural" are meant to emphasize the fact that hospitals appropriate the term but do not adhere to the drug-free, vaginal delivery it implies. The myth of a "natural" child-

birth in the hospital setting is then maintained, I argue, through the yoking of the practice with a gendered division of labor (pun intended). Because the supposedly "natural" model of childbirth hospitals have endorsed is based on traditional gender roles, the understanding of gender as a resistant variety of natural difference constructs the illusion of naturalness even as delivery is medicalized.

4. See Deana Midmer's article "Does family-centered maternity care empower women?" (1992) for a description of this management style and its effects.

References

Kitzinger, Sheila. 1995. *Ourselves as mothers: The universal experience of motherhood.* New York: Addison-Wesley.

Midmer, Deana. 1992. Does family-centered maternity care empower women? The development of the woman-centered childbirth model. *Family Medicine* 24 (3): 216–221.

Sears, William, and Martha Sears. 1993. *The baby book: Everything you need to know about your baby—from birth to age two.* New York: Little, Brown and Company.

Wolf, Naomi. 2001. *(Mis)conceptions: Truth, lies, and the unexpected on the journey to motherhood.* New York: Doubleday.

The Male Pill

The involvement of men today in most of the social processes of procreation in Western societies seems to show an increasing progression toward sharing and gender equality. The progress, however, is not so straightforward. The development of pharmaceuticals for erectile dysfunction was lightning fast compared with the thirty-year effort to find a safe and effective male contraceptive that would not have the physical disadvantages of condoms or the permanence of vasectomies. In fact, scientists are still looking:

A Norwegian company seeking to develop a male birth control pill has signed a licensing agreement with the University of Massachusetts Medical School covering research that could lead to a drug to block sperm's ability to swim and fertilize an egg. The method that led to the long-term deal could expand the decades-long search for a male pill by targeting a protein found only in sperm cells. Researchers at the University of Massachusetts in Worcester and elsewhere say that approach carries far less risk of side effects than manipulating a man's hormones, the avenue that has attracted the most research aimed at finding alternatives to condoms and vasectomies. (Jewell 2005)

The effort needed far more than drug research and development. It took the creation of a new research and development network, men's clinics and other infrastructure, persuasion of men to participate in clinical trials, and the trust of their partners. Sustaining the male-pill project necessitated a cultural shift about men's sexuality and acceptance by women of the idea of men's responsibility for contraception (Oudshoorn 2003).

The initial impetus for a male contraceptive came in the 1960s from political leaders in China and India who had the goal of population control. The World Health Organization expanded the effort on behalf of developing countries and was important in developing a "demonstration network" when the Western pharmaceutical industry refused to spend money on male contraceptive research. In the 1970s, alarmed at the side effects of hormonal contraceptives for women, feminists argued that Western societies needed the male pill, too, so that the responsibility and risks of contraception could be shared. Oddly, "the need to develop male contraceptives was never articulated by the potential users of any new technology: men" (Oudshoorn 2003, 23). A major shift in discourse about men's sexuality and fertility was needed to make the idea of a male pill culturally acceptable.

At the U.N. International Conference on Population and Development in Cairo in 1994, an alliance of family planning activists and feminist women's health advocates hammered out a shift in discourse. In family planning, men were perceived as wanting more children than their partners. Non-White men in particular were stereotyped as conflating masculinity with fertility. Encouraging these men to take part in family planning was seen as a daunting task. However, devising a strategy for including men ran into opposition from feminists. To them, increasing men's involvement ignored the extent to which men already dominated procreation policies and controlled access to services. Programs for men were a threat to the resources available for women's services. Feminists wanted to be sure that women's procreative rights, autonomy, and empowerment were protected. The solution was the concept of "men as partners" in a couple's sharing responsibility for each other's health and fertility (Oudshoorn 2003, 113–139).

But are women and men equal partners in procreation? We know that women's bodies are sites of pregnancy and childbirth, yet they are not in control of the social parameters, as we have seen. Ironically, it is sperm that are valorized, because they are representations of masculinity and men are dominant in Western society. The supposedly normal and natural processes of pregnancy and childbirth assume a heterosexual couple, and in most such couples, men tend to have the upper hand in procreative decisions, including those involved in contraception. So it is not surprising that the male pill is still not a reality.

Sperm and Insemination: Representations of Masculinity

Just as human bodies are not solely biologically created, so ova, sperm, embryos, and fetuses are not simply biological entities. Rather, through processes of discovering, understanding, and learning about the basics of human procreation, we attribute gendered characteristics to them, as if they were boys and girls, or men and women, instead of parts of procreation. Thus, we are taught "truths" about how gendered bodies behave through the most rudimentary exploration of the behavior of human cells.

Human procreation narratives follow traditionally gendered scripts, in which the married mother and father, who love each other, consciously decide to procreate through penis-vagina heterosexual intercourse. Nine months later, the baby is birthed from the mother's body, and infant and mother quickly settle into a natural relationship of sustenance, nurturing, and protection. This script is an idealization that omits single motherhood, lesbian and gay parenting, adoption, use of procreative technologies to conceive, surrogate mothers, and other variations on the Western heterosexual nuclear family.

The reason for the idealized "how babies are made" script is *heteronormativity.* Western cultural expectations of sexuality and procreation are predicated on the supremacy of heterosexuality as natural and superior to any other sexual expression. These normative cultural expectations create a social environment that regulates sexuality and family structure. Heteronormativity creates the processes by which heterosexual relations are represented as the only natural way to have sex and make babies: Biological boys who become men pair up with biological girls who become women.

One of the ways that heteronormativity is constructed and reinforced is through children's books. Children learning "how babies are made" are also learning how to be "normally" masculine and feminine. The procreative narratives in children's books are not descriptions of biological facts; rather, they are prescriptions of properly gendered sexuality. The following article shows how depictions of sperm in children's books show proper and unacceptable characteristics of "masculinity."

Sperm, the Lovable Character in Facts of Life Books

Lisa Jean Moore
State University of New York at Purchase

Many of our intimate dealings with semen are shrouded in secrecy or confidentiality, such as books read with our mothers, secrets shared in a coatroom, wet dreams hidden in our beds, or procreative services pursued in the fertility industry. Ironically, these private and secret experiences are the products of *social production*—for example, children's books are mass-produced and marketed.

Books about human procreation produced for English-speaking children both construct and perpetuate gendered processes of social procreation. This social procreation takes place within the context of capitalist, patriarchal, and heteronormative sociocultural norms. Information about human procreation is "processed" and "distilled" for the young—it is made sterile and idealized. The stylized and sterilized representations are then narrated to children in order to teach them about *"where they have come from."* Similar to how research scientists and health-care providers sanitize and sterilize medical instruments for their work, knowledge about human procreation must be scrubbed, washed, massaged, and homogenized for consumption by the young. The production of the "perfect child" is both the purpose of contemporary human procreation and the purpose of the social procreation these books represent. As these biological actions are illustrated for the young audience, so too are heteronormative values imparted to produce social hierarchies. Humans, then, are both biologically and materially produced by the circulation of sperm while simultaneously socially produced by images and narratives about the circulation of sperm.

Children's culture is both a fantastic and a dangerous space to explore sperm's discursive and representational constructions. "When we want to prove that something is so basic to human nature that it cannot be changed, we point to its presence in our children" (Jenkins 1998, 15). Both children and sperm are constructed as some form of presocialized creatures that exist as biological and thus remain unmediated, animalistic, primitive, and naïve. The truth of human nature is embodied in children and sperm cells. And we often lament that social forces corrupt children as they get older.

Even though it is an interactive event that requires seemingly endless social negotiation and power transfer, human procreation is assumed to be some innate biological drive that furthers progressive human evolution. The surrounding social interaction is erased when we point to the presence of heterosexual and procreative urges and desires within our children. The naïve child's body, similar to the imagined sperm cell, is shown as naturally heterosexual, monogamous, procreative, gendered. Reading children's facts-of-life books, we are bombarded with fabrications of "universal truths."

Traditional fairy tales are moral fables teaching children proper ways to live. Many contemporary Western stories about human procreation emerge from a scientific context but are similar to fairy tales with their hidden moral discourse. These books rely on procreative biology and anatomy. When labeling and narrating procreative processes, authors and illustrators use scientific terminology, such as "sperm," "egg," "ovum," and "conception." Furthermore, the images, whether rendered through photography, cartooning, or painting, are based on scientific technologies, such as electron microscopes, dissection, and x-rays. This scientific context is important to acknowledge because it is the children's books' reliance on science that bolsters the claim that their contents are objective and truthful. But just because there is a claim of scientific relevance and objectivity does not mean that these stories are not also fantastic and rooted in prevailing moral and social imperatives. Indeed, what is remarkable about these books—published over a 40-year span—is the homogeneity of social messages reiterated through a child-appropriate scientific lens.

'We Was Robbed': Spermatic Hierarchy

In children's books, not all sperm are created equal. Embedded in sperm imagery from cartoon books are smiling, competitive, or befuddled sperm talking to one another and presumably the audience. These sperm evaluate themselves and others based on their ability to follow directions, swim quickly, navigate the difficult terrain, and eventually merge with the egg. In children's books, the measure of the better sperm is loosely based on motility (speed), not morphology (shape). From secular books that anthropomorphize sperm, we learn that sperm have desire, are in a race, and are competitive. There will be one and only one winner, so there is a sense of entitlement and empowerment, but also unfairness.

Sperm are depicted with racing stripes and numbers on them, and state "Gotcha" and "We was robbed" as they are racing to the egg (Cole 1993, 24). There is also a sense of male bonding in that sperm cheer each other on. "Come on, boys" appears in three of the books as a rallying cry from the masses of sperm in pursuit of the egg (Smith 1997, 5). But there can be only one "winner," and out of the millions and millions of sperm that exist in a male body, the one that aggressively "swims" to join with the egg is exceptional. This distinction of being the sperm that gets to inseminate the egg is noted almost universally (Andry and Schepp 1968). Hierarchies among men are thus naturalized: As with sperm, competitions based on physical strength, endurance, and speed are the natural—and adaptive—way to figure out hierarchies among boys and men.

Moral Lessons

Children's books about human procreation attempt to explain biological processes to a young audience. However, they are also socially producing normative guidelines for gender display, sexual orientation, and citizenship. Adults who write, publish, read, control, or criticize these books are part of the interactive process to train potential parents. Through the creation of the sperm and egg as characters, many children's books anthropomorphize these entities, presenting personalities for easy identification. It is open to empirical analysis how successful these books are at naturalizing gender, sexuality, relations of production, and divine intervention for children.

By relegating the entire "natural order" to God, Christian children's books are able to code prescriptive social norms as God's will when describing human procreation. Remarkably, secular children's books, even those that strive to be feminist, rely on the sperm and egg in eerily stereotypic ways to transmit normative socialization for gender, sex, and sexuality development, showing the bonding of an aggressive sperm and a passive egg.

Children's books are only one enterprise that produces representations and meanings of human sperm. Sperm is almost universally viewed as the bringer of life within children's books. These books neglect to mention that sperm can also be the bringer of sexually transmitted diseases and death.

There is traffic between the notions of semen and the categorization of men. Again and again, children's books, semen bank enterprises, sex workers, DNA forensics, scientists, and pornographers socially produce semen and sperm in stylized ways that draw on existing tropes of masculinity while simultaneously constructing new ones. Sperm enterprises, whether religious, scientific, sexual, or popular, create partial representations of sperm that rely on existing beliefs about power, hierarchies, and dualisms.

For example, lively semen and men are depicted in children's books as loving, heterosexual, monogamous, intentional, God-fearing, fertile fathers who are never violent or abusive. Deadly semen and men are depicted in the semen industry and forensic practice as homosexuals, bisexuals, men who have sex with men, often men of color, unfaithful men, sexual predators.

Unfortunately, many of these representations are taken as a version of a singular truth about biology and destiny. We must remember that these are not arbitrarily produced representations, and we must work to reinsert social analyses of the belief systems that these images and practices re-create and perpetuate.

References

Andry, Andrew, and Schepp, Steven (1968). *How Babies Are Made*. Boston: Little, Brown.

Cole, Babette (1993). *Mommy Laid an Egg: Or, Where Do Babies Come From?* San Francisco: Chronicle Books.

Jenkins, Henry (1998). "Introduction" in Henry Jenkins (ed.), *The Children's Culture Reader*. New York: New York University Press.

Mayle, Peter (1977). *Where Did I Come From? The Facts of Life Without Any Nonsense and With Illustrations.* Secaucus, NJ: Carroll Publishing Group.
Smith, Alistair (1997). *How Are Babies Made?* London: Usborne.

Adapted for this book from Lisa Jean Moore, 2003, "Billy, the Sad Sperm With No Tail: Representations of Sperm in Children's Books." *Sexualities* 6 (3–4), 279–305.

Critical Summary

Human procreation has the potential to be a joyous experience. However, for a vast majority of the world's people, individual men and male-dominated institutions have control over who has babies, when they have them, and who claims ownership of those babies. Women's procreative bodies are kept under strict control through social norms, laws, and biomedicine. For example, today most women live in cultures where they are considered the property of their fathers (they are given their father's last name) until they are married off to husbands (they usually take their husband's last name). From early ages we teach children to see male superiority and heterosexuality as naturally ingrained in sperm. We instruct children to be mommies and daddies in gender-specific ways and then reward them for the "correct" performance. But as children age, we do not provide their bodies with adequate tools to protect themselves from pregnancy and disease. If they procreate in ways that are not mandated, they are stigmatized and punished. When their bodies do not procreate, individuals are stigmatized, and if they have the resources, they pursue expensive and complicated technologies to achieve pregnancies and produce particular types of babies. Gendered power dynamics even infiltrate the labor and delivery experience.

In addition to the greater social power of men in procreation and normative beliefs about gender and sexuality, processes of medicalization have dominated our procreative knowledge and practices. Medicalization establishes biomedical and technological meanings and interpretations of procreation as the most legitimate. Through medicalization, the nexus of pharmaceutical, biotechnological, economic, and professional interests dominate prevention of pregnancy, fertility, pregnancy itself, and childbirth. As a result, the costs of procreation have escalated in Western industrialized countries, while women in poor countries, like those in Africa, lack medical help in difficult pregnancies or births. For example, in pregnancies in preteen women whose bodies are not fully developed, the baby may get stuck because the birth canal is too narrow. These births often cause tears of the bowel and urinary tract, medically referred to as fistulas. Even though there are simple surgeries that can repair fistulas, many women face a lifetime of leaking urine and feces and accompanying social stigma (Miller et al. 2005; Wall et al. 2005). In Western countries, long and difficult labors can produce similar problems, but their incidence is much smaller. While we fully encourage continued investigation into cultural, biomedical, and holistic knowledge and practices of human procreation aimed at retaining the life-affirming values of the experiences of parenthood, we must also acknowledge the gross inequities in access to medical and surgical options where they are most needed.

Notes

1. We prefer to say *procreation* rather than *reproduction* because human beings don't reproduce or replicate like copying machines. What we are talking about is the whole process of egg and sperm joining, gestation through pregnancy, and childbirth. That process is "procreation."
2. See, for example, *www.surromomsonline.com*
3. *www.nationalpartnership.org/portals/p3/library/WorkplaceDiscrimination/Pregnancy25th AnnivFacts.pdf*

References and Recommended Readings

Agigian, Amy. 2004. *Baby Steps: How Lesbian Alternative Insemination Is Changing the World.* Middletown, CT: Wesleyan University Press.

Apple, Rima. 1990. *Women, Health, and Medicine: A Historical Handbook.* New Brunswick, NJ: Rutgers University Press.

Becker, Gay. 2000. *The Elusive Embryo: How Women and Men Approach New Reproductive Technologies.* Berkeley: University of California Press.

Beckett, Katherine. 2005. "Choosing Cesarean: Feminism and the Politics of Childbirth in the United States." *Feminist Theory* 6, 251–275.

Ber, R. 2000. "Ethical Issues in Gestational Surrogacy." *Theories of Medical Bioethics* 21, 153–169.

Casper, Monica. 1998. *The Making of the Unborn Patient: A Social Anatomy of Fetal Surgery.* New Brunswick, NJ: Rutgers University Press.

Chasnoff, I., H. Landress, and M. Barrett. 1990. "Prevalence of Illicit Drug or Alcohol Use During Pregnancy and Discrepancies in Mandatory Reporting in Pinellas County, Florida." *New England Journal of Medicine* 322 (17), 1202–1206.

Chatterjee, Nilanjana, and Nancy E. Riley. 2001. "Planning an Indian Modernity: The Gendered Politics of Fertility Control." *Signs* 26, 811–845.

Clarke, Adele. 1998. *Disciplining Reproduction: Modernity, American Life Sciences, and the "Problem of Sex."* Berkeley: University of California Press.

Cooper, Susan, and Ellen Glazer. 1998. *Choosing Assisted Reproduction: Social, Emotional, and Ethical Considerations.* Indianapolis: Perspectives Press.

Davis-Floyd, Robbie E. 1992. *Birth as an American Rite of Passage.* Berkeley: University of California Press.

Ettore, Elizabeth. 2002. *Reproductive Genetics, Gender, and the Body.* New York: Routledge.

Fogg-Davis, Hawley. 2001. "Navigating Race in the Market for Human Gametes." *Hastings Center Report* 5 (31): 13–21.

Ginsburg, Faye, and Rayna Rapp (eds.). 1995. *Conceiving the New World Order: The Global Politics of Reproduction.* Berkeley: University of California Press.

Greenhalgh, Susan. 2001. "Fresh Winds in Beijing: Chinese Feminists Speak Out on the One-Child Policy and Women's Lives." *Signs* 26, 847–886.

Hänsch, Anna. 1997. "The Body of the Woman Artist: Paula Modersohn-Becker and Rainer Maria Rilke on Giving Birth and Art." *European Journal of Women's Studies* 4, 435–449.

Hartmann, Katherine, Meera Viswanathan, Rachel Palmieri, Gerald Gartlehner, John Thorp, Jr., and Kathleen N. Lohr. 2005. "Outcomes of Routine Episiotomy: A Systematic Review." *Journal of the American Medical Association* 293, 2141–2148.

Jadva, Vasanti, Clare Murray, Emma Lycett, Fiona MacCallum, and Susan Golombok. 2003. "Surrogacy: The Experiences of Surrogate Mothers." *Human Reproduction* 18 (10), 2196–2204.

Jewell, Mark. 2005. "Deal Could Lead to Male Birth Control Pill." *Kansas City Star,* 1 February. *www.kansascity.com*

Karsjens, Kari L. 2002. "Boutique Egg Donations: A New Form of Racism and Patriarchy." *DePaul Journal of Health Care Law* 5, 57–89.

Katz Rothman, Barbara. 1991. *In Labor: Women and Power in the Birthplace* (reprint edition). New York: W. W. Norton.

———. 2000. *Recreating Motherhood: Ideology and Technology in a Patriarchal Society* (second edition). New Brunswick, NJ: Rutgers University Press.

Lorber, Judith, and Lakshmi Bandlamudi. 1993. "Dynamics of Marital Bargaining in Male Infertility." *Gender & Society* 7, 32–49.

Marantz Henig, Robin. 2004. *Pandora's Baby: How the First Test Tube Babies Sparked the Reproduction Revolution.* New York: Houghton Mifflin.

Martin, Emily. 1991. "The Egg and the Sperm: How Science Has Constructed a Romance Based on Stereotypical Male-Female Roles." *Signs* 16, 485–501.

———. 1992. *The Woman in the Body: A Cultural Analysis of Reproduction.* Boston: Beacon Press.

Mies, Maria. 1994. "New Reproductive Technologies: Sexist and Racist Implications." *Quilt* 9 (1), 41–47.

Miller, S., F. Lester, M. Webster, and B. Cowan. 2005. "Obstetric Fistula: A Preventable Tragedy." *Journal of Midwifery and Women's Health* 50, 286–294.

Moore, Lisa Jean. (Forthcoming). *Sperm: Understanding Man's Most Precious Fluid.* New York: New York University Press.

O'Brien, Mary. 1981. *The Politics of Reproduction.* New York: Routledge.

Oudshoorn, Nelly. 2003. *The Male Pill: A Biography of Technology in the Making.* Durham, NC: Duke University Press.

Plotz, David. 2005. *The Genius Factory: The Curious History of the Nobel Prize Sperm Bank.* New York: Random House.

Reed, Richard K. 2005. *Birthing Fathers: The Transformation of Men in the American Rites of Birth.* New Brunswick, NJ: Rutgers University Press.

Rich, Adrienne. 1976. *Of Woman Born: Motherhood as Experience and Institution.* New York: Bantam Books.

Roberts, Dorothy. 1997. *Killing the Black Body.* New York: Pantheon Books.

Roth, Rachel. 2000. *Making Women Pay: The Hidden Costs of Fetal Rights.* Ithaca, NY: Cornell University Press.

Rothschild, Joan. 2005. *The Dream of the Perfect Child.* Bloomington: Indiana University Press.

Schoen, Johanna. 2005. *Choice and Coercion: Birth Control, Sterilization, and Abortion in Public Health and Welfare.* Chapel Hill: University of North Carolina Press.

Spar, Debora L. 2006. *The Baby Business: How Money, Science, and Politics Drive the Commerce of Conception.* Cambridge, MA: Harvard Business School Press.

Thompson, Charis. 2005. *Making Parent: The Ontological Choreography of Reproductive Technologies.* Cambridge, MA: MIT Press.

Wall, L. L., S. D. Arrowsmith, N. D. Briggs, A. Browning, and A. Lassey. 2005. "The Obstetric Vesicovaginal Fistula in the Developing World." *Obstetrical and Gynecological Survey* 60 (7 Suppl. 1), S3–S51.

Wertz, Richard W., and Dorothy C. Wertz. 1989. *Lying-in: A History of Childbirth in America* (expanded edition). New Haven, CT: Yale University Press.

Internet Sources

Alan Guttmacher Institute
  www.agi-usa.org
Centers for Disease Control and Prevention
  www.guttmacher.org
Global Reproductive Health Forum
  www.hsph.harvard.edu/grhf
National Libraries of Medicine
  www.nlm.nih.gov/medlineplus/reproductivehealth.html
Population Council
  www.popcouncil.org
Reproductive Health Technologies Project
  www.rhtp.org
Reproductive Technologies Web
  www.hsph.harvard.edu/rt21
United Nations Population Fund (UNFPA)
  www.unfpa.org
Women of Color Web
  www.hsph.harvard.edu/grhf/WoC
World Health Organization
  www.who.int/reproductive-health ✦

Chapter 3

Barbie and G.I. Joe

Making Bodies Masculine and Feminine

Key concepts: body morphology and body practices, gendering through sports, sports and violence, sports as empowering women, use of steroids in sports

As infants, little boys have "strong grips," "hearty howls," and "sturdy, powerful legs." Little girls have "dainty fingers," "gentle cries," and "shapely calves." As toddlers, boys are active little sluggers, and girls are sweet little mommies. But children are not born this way; their parents and the other adults around them see them that way. Just as children are biologically reproduced as humans, they are socially reproduced as properly feminine girls and properly masculine boys.

A common way that parents socially produce gendered children is through the toys they buy. These toys encourage children to play in gender-appropriate ways—girls with dolls, boys with "action figures." Not only are toys marketed and bought in gender-specific parts of stores; parents and caregivers encourage their use in gendered ways—action figures should fight, not be hugged; dolls should be hugged, not fight. Our expectations of children's gender-appropriate play is so profound that it is impossible to tell if the way children prefer to play is natural or learned. We may not even see gender-inappropriate behavior when it is in front of our eyes, as when girls bash their Barbie dolls against the wall.

The patterns of gendered behavior not only become part of a child's identity as a boy or a girl; they become embodied. The embodiment, or the physical manifestation and enactment of cultural and social norms, especially those that make bodies and body practices feminine and masculine, is a global phenomenon. A French anthropologist, Pierre Bourdieu, viewed the body as a site where culture, social power, and social structure are produced and manifested. In his ethnographic fieldwork, he interpreted the way women and men were taught to eat and walk in one African tribe. He observed masculine and feminine embodiment of gender norms, where men ate with their "whole mouth, wholeheartedly, and not, like women, just with the lips, that is halfheartedly, with reservation and restraint" (Bourdieu [1980] 1990, 70). The way they were supposed to walk indicated the dominance of the men and the subordination of the women:

> The manly man . . . stands up straight into the face of the person he approaches, or wishes to welcome. Ever on the alert, because ever threatened, he misses nothing of what happens around him. . . . Conversely, a well brought-up woman . . . is expected to walk with a slight stoop, avoiding every misplaced movement of her body, her head or her arms, looking down, keeping her eyes on the spot where she will next put her foot, especially if she happens to have to walk past the men's assembly. (p. 70)

Across time and cultures, societies differ in the norms of gendered embodiment. In some societies, girls and boys, women and men are allowed only a fairly rigid range of appropriate body dimensions and physical expressions of their bodies. These societies limit gender blurring and may punish girls who physically emulate boys and vice versa. Other societies have roles for men who dress and behave as women and allow some women to act as men. Western societies tend to be somewhere in the middle range—freer on physical gendering than some societies, but actively discouraging physical appearance that does not allow easy identification of the child as a girl or boy, or an adult as a woman or a man.

The Shape of the Ideal Body

Morphology, the study of shapes, and studies of body communication by walk, gesture, and placement provide insight into the way masculinity and femininity are embodied. The ideals are culturally represented in the mass media and subliminally taught to children in the way their dolls and other body-based toys look. Take Barbie, for example. Introduced in the United States in 1959, Barbie makes up about one-third of Mattel's revenues (Palmeri 2000). Despite Mattel's efforts to make Barbie more contemporary by creating professional identities for her (Dr. Barbie, Veterinarian Barbie), her physical dimensions, if applied to an adult female, would be the impossible 36-18-38. For Barbie, thin is always in, but with big breasts and shapely hips.

In contrast, G.I. Joe, the popular male action figure, has had body changes. Like Barbie dolls for girls, G.I. Joe action figures have also had a long run as a favorite toy for boys, but the figures have undergone changes to keep up with the newer ideal of a more muscled male body. Originally introduced in 1964, the current G.I. Joe

> has been putting in a little time at the gym. His biceps have grown to the equivalent of 15 inches—already 2 or 3 inches bigger than the biceps of the average untrained man. And Joe has been doing sit ups, too. His abdominal muscles, hardly visible in his predecessor, are now nicely defined. [With a new Joe] introduced in 1991, his waist has shrunk to only 29 inches, and his biceps are 16½ inches—approaching the limits of what a lean man might be able to attain without steroids. Not only that, but Joe now has a six-pack of abdominals that would be the envy of even many bodybuilders. And he even has visible serratus muscles—the comblike muscles that run along the ribs on the sides of his body. (Pope, Phillips, and Olivardia 2000, 42)

Barbies and G.I. Joes have also been transported to big and small screens—movies and the video/digital world—more places for depicting ideal bodies. Through Playstation games, Game Boy, internet sites such as Barbie.com, and the hugely successful Barbie films, girls and boys see impossibly beautiful or strong gendered bodies. As they grow up, children and teenagers compare themselves with these muscular men and busty women. Some end up with *body dysmorphia,* "an excessive preoccupation with perceived flaws in appearance" (Pope, Phillips, and Olivardia 2000, xiii).

The groundwork for gendered body perfection that is laid by early toys is expanded for many children in sports competitions that separate boys and girls. They often play different games, but even if they play the same games, there are strict gender norms for how they should play them. Boys from disadvantaged communities are particularly encouraged to excel in popular sports as a way to go to college on scholarship and to make a lot of money as professional athletes. Their dreams are fueled by the male-dominated sports industry, which bombards children and adolescents (not to mention adults) with nonstop media coverage. Only in the last twenty years have girls' school teams flourished in the United States, thanks to antidiscriminatory legislation, such as Title IX. Women's basketball and soccer teams have drawn large audiences, but the amount of money and media time for women's sports is minuscule compared with men's sports.

Given the evidence of rampant childhood obesity, no one would deny the potential benefits to children of participation in sports, but each sport encourages an idealized, gendered body shape. The downside is steroid drug use to build up muscle mass, eating disorders to stay slim and wiry, and violence in the players of men's games and often in their audiences as well. In these myriad ways, sports is a prime site for illustrating the social construction of gendered bodies.

Children's Games: The First Playing Grounds of Gender

Children's body gendering starts very early. Children's play is organized in gendered ways, especially when it takes place in groups. Boys and girls are first separated by gender; then these groups are gender-marked and expected to behave in gendered ways. In his book about sports, *Taking the Field*, Michael Messner describes the ways that gendered sports in turn gender their players. In this excerpt, he describes his community's opening ceremony of the American Youth Soccer Organization season, where a soccer team of 4- to 5-year-old girls and one of boys the same age get their first taste of gendered sports behavior.

Barbie Girls Versus Sea Monsters

Michael A. Messner
University of Southern California, Los Angeles

The Sea Monsters is a team of four- and five-year-old boys. Later this day, they will play their first ever soccer game. A few of the boys already know each other from preschool, but most are still getting acquainted. They are wearing their new uniforms for the first time. Like other teams, they were assigned team colors—in this case, green and blue—and asked to choose their team name at their first team meeting, which occurred a week ago. Though they preferred Blue Sharks, they found that the name was already taken by another team, so they settled on Sea Monsters. A grandmother of one of the boys created the spiffy team banner, which was awarded a prize this morning. While they wait for the ceremony to begin, the boys inspect and then proudly pose for pictures in front of their new, award-winning team banner. The parents stand a few feet away, some taking pictures, some just watching. The parents are also getting to know each other, and the common currency of topics is just how darned cute our kids look, and will they start these ceremonies soon before another boy has to be escorted to the bathroom?

Queued up one group away from the Sea Monsters is a team of four- and five-year-old girls in green and white uniforms. They too will play their first game later today, but for now, they are awaiting the beginning of the opening ceremony. They have chosen the name Barbie Girls, and they too have a new team banner. But the girls are pretty much ignoring their banner, for they have created another, more powerful symbol around which to rally. In fact, they are the only team among the 156 marching today with a team float—a red Radio Flyer wagon base, on which sits a Sony boom box playing music, and a three-foot-plus tall Barbie doll on a rotating pedestal. Barbie is dressed in the team colors; indeed, she sports a custom-made green and white cheerleader-style outfit, with the Barbie Girls' names written on the skirt. Her normally all-blond hair has been streaked with Barbie Girl green and features a green bow with white polka dots. Several of the girls on the team have supplemented their uniforms with green bows in their hair as well.

The volume on the boom box nudges up, and four or five girls begin to sing a Barbie song. Barbie is now slowly rotating on her pedestal, and as the girls sing more gleefully and more loudly, some of them begin to hold hands and walk around the float, in synch with Barbie's rotation. Other same-aged girls from other teams are drawn to the celebration and, eventually, perhaps a dozen girls are singing the Barbie song. The girls are intensely focused on Barbie, on the music, and on their mutual pleasure.

While the Sea Monsters mill around their banner, some of them begin to notice and then begin to watch and listen when the Barbie Girls rally around their float. At first, the boys are watching as individuals, seemingly unaware of each other's shared interest. Some of them stand with arms at their sides, slack jawed, as though passively watching a television show. I notice slight smiles on a couple of their faces, as though they are drawn to the Barbie Girls' celebratory fun. Then with side glances, some of the boys begin to notice each other's attention on the Barbie Girls. Their faces begin to show signs of distaste. One of them yells out, "NO BARBIE!" Suddenly, they all begin to move, jumping up and down, nudging, and bumping one other, and join in a group chant: "NO BARBIE! NO BARBIE! NO BARBIE!" They now appear to be every bit as gleeful as the girls as they laugh, yell, and chant against the Barbie Girls.

The parents watch the whole scene with rapt attention. Smiles light up the faces of the adults while our glances sweep back and forth, from the sweetly celebrating Barbie Girls to the aggressively protesting Sea Monsters. "They are so different!" exclaims one smiling mother approvingly. A male coach offers a more in-depth analysis: "When I was in college," he says, "I took these classes from professors who showed us research that showed that boys and girls are the same. I believed it, until I had my own kids and saw how different they are." "Yeah," another dad responds. "Just look at them! They are so different!"

The girls, meanwhile, show no evidence that they hear, see, or are even aware of the presence of the boys, who are now so loudly proclaiming their opposition to the Barbie Girls' songs and totem. The girls continue to sing, dance, laugh, and rally around the Barbie for a few more minutes, before they are called to reassemble in their groups for the beginning of the parade.

After the parade, the teams reassemble on the infield of the track, but now in a less organized manner. The Sea Monsters once again find themselves in the general vicinity of the Barbie Girls and take up the "NO BARBIE!" chant. Perhaps put out by the lack of response to their chant, they begin to dash, in twos and threes, invading the girls' space and yelling menacingly. With this, the Barbie Girls have little choice but to recognize the presence of the boys; some look puzzled and shrink back, some engage the boys and chase them off. The chasing seems only to incite more excitement among the boys. Finally, parents intervene and defuse the situation, leading their children off to their cars, homes, and eventually to their soccer games.

The Performance of Gender

In the past decade, especially since the publication of Judith Butler's highly influential book *Gender Trouble*,[1] it has become increasingly fashionable among academic feminists to think of gender not as some "thing" that one "has" (or not), but rather as situationally constructed through the performances of active agents. The idea of gender-as-performance analytically foregrounds the agency of people in the construction of gender, thus highlighting the situational fluidity of gender: here, conservative and reproductive, there, transgressive and disruptive. Surely, the Barbie Girls vs. Sea Monsters scene that I witnessed can be fruitfully analyzed as a moment of group-based, cross-cutting, and mutually constitutive gender performances: The girls, at least at first glance, appear to be performing (for each other?) a conventional version of femininity for four- and five-year-olds. At least on the surface, there appears to be nothing terribly transgressive here. They are just "being girls" together. The boys initially are unwittingly constituted as an audience for the girls' performance but quickly begin to perform (for each other? for the girls, too?) a masculinity that constructs itself in opposition to Barbie, and to the girls, as not feminine. They aggressively confront—first through loud verbal chanting, eventually through bodily invasions—the girls' ritual space, apparently with the intention of disrupting its upsetting influence. The adults are simultaneously constituted as an adoring audience for their children's performances and as parents who perform for each other by sharing and mutually affirming their experience-based narratives concerning the natural differences between boys and girls.

In this scene, we see children performing gender in ways that constitute them as two separate, opposed groups (boys vs. girls), and we see parents performing gender in ways that give the stamp of adult approval to the children's performances of difference while constructing their own ideological narrative that naturalizes this categorical difference. In other words, the parents do not seem to read the children's performances of gender as social constructions of gender. Instead, they interpret them as the inevitable unfolding of natural, internal differences between the sexes. That this moment occurred when it did and where it did is explicable, but not entirely with a theory of performativity. . . .

The parents' response to the Barbie Girls vs. Sea Monsters performance suggests one of the main limits and dangers of theories of performativity. Lacking an analysis of structural and cultural context, performances of gender can all too easily be interpreted as free agents' acting out the inevitable surface manifestations of a natural inner essence of sex difference.[2] An examination of structural and cultural contexts, though, reveals that there was nothing inevitable about the girls' choice of Barbie as their totem or in the boys' response to it.

The Structure of Gender

In the entire subsequent season of weekly games and practices, I never once saw adults point to a moment in which boy and girl soccer players were doing the *same* thing and exclaim to each other, "Look at them! They are *so similar!*" The actual similarity of the boys and the girls, evidenced by nearly all of the kids' routine actions throughout a soccer season—playing the game, crying over a skinned knee, scrambling enthusiastically for their snacks after the games, spacing out on a bird or a flower instead of listening to the coach at practice—is a key to understanding the salience of the Barbie Girls vs. Sea Monsters moment for gender relations. In the face of a multitude of moments that speak to similarity, it was this anomalous Barbie Girls vs. Sea Monsters moment, where the boundaries of gender were so clearly enacted, that the adults seized to affirm their commitment to difference. It is the kind of moment, to use Judith Lorber's phrase, where "believing is seeing,"[3] where we selectively "see" aspects of social reality that tell us a truth that we prefer to believe, such as the belief in categorical sex difference. No matter that our eyes do not see evidence of this truth most of the rest of the time.

In fact, it was not so easy for adults actually to "see" the empirical reality of sex similarity in everyday observations of soccer throughout the season. That difficulty is due to one overdetermining factor: an institutional context that is characterized by informally structured sex segregation among the parent coaches and team managers and by formally structured sex segregation among the children. Organizations, even while appearing gender neutral, tend to reflect, re-create, and naturalize a hierarchical ordering of gender.[4]

Notes

1. Butler, *Gender Trouble.*
2. Or, conversely, theories of performativity can easily fall into a celebration of apparently free-floating "transgressions" of gender norms and boundaries. In ignoring the constraining nature of social contexts, theories of performativity can fall into a simplistic voluntarism.
3. Lorber, *Paradoxes of Gender,* 37.
4. Acker, "Hierarchies, Jobs, Bodies."

References

Acker, Joan. 1990. "Hierarchies, jobs, and bodies: A theory of gendered organizations." *Gender & Society* 4: 139–58.
Butler, Judith. 1990. *Gender Trouble.* New York and London: Routledge.
Lorber, Judith. 1994. *Paradoxes of Gender.* New Haven, CT: Yale.

As Messner's work demonstrates, preschool boys and girls construct masculinity and femininity for their bodies and personalities by using symbolic descriptive language and colors. In the process, they test out the "appropriate," socially sanctioned ways boys and girls are supposed to play. As children get older, gender socialization progresses from informal play and pickup teams to more and more formally organized sports, where gendered norms determine which sports girls and boys can participate in.

For children, sports are important sites of developing self-esteem. They also offer talented athletes from poor families the possibility of upward mobility through college scholarships. Until recently, boys were encouraged to join sports teams as sites for the development of competitive masculinity; girls were trained through physical education to maintain their femininity. Over the past thirty years, through the strides of feminism and its advocacy of gender equity, girls and women have formed their own sports teams.

Title IX and Gender Equity in Sports

In 1972, in an effort to create gender equity in the distribution of federal educational resources, the U.S. Congress included Title IX as an amendment to the Civil Rights Act of 1964. Title IX states: "No person in the United States shall, on the basis of sex, be excluded from participation in, be denied the benefits of, or be subjected to discrimination under any education program or activity receiving federal financial assistance." Title IX created regulatory policies to foster gender parity of high school and college athletes in recruitment, facilities, scholarships, teams, and coaching. When Title IX is enforced, it creates positive change for girls' athletic opportunities. The change in the United States was described by the National Coalition for Women and Girls in Education:

> In 1971 fewer than 295,000 girls participated in high school varsity athletics, accounting for just 7 percent of all high school varsity athletes. . . . Before Title IX, female college athletes received only 2 percent of overall athletic budgets, and athletic scholarships for women were virtually nonexistent. . . . By 2001 nearly 2.8 million girls participated in athletics, representing 41.5 percent of varsity athletes in U.S. high schools—an increase of more than 847 percent from 1971. (2002, 14)

However, Title IX is not universally enforced and over the past thirty years has not completely eradicated the male bias in athletic resources. According to the National Coalition, "For every new dollar going into athletics at the Division I and II levels, male sports receive 65 cents while female sports receive 35 cents" (2002, 4). Despite being shortchanged in resources, there is significant evidence that girls' participation in organized athletics has the potential to increase academic achievement (Hanson and Kraus 1998), improve body image (Robinson and Ferraro 2004), and reduce sexual risk taking (Miller et al. 2002).

Gendering in sports extends to the way athletes are depicted on television and described in newspapers. One research study comparing the coverage of the men's and women's NCAA and U.S. Open events found that women basketball and tennis players were always gender-marked, as "women," while men athletes were just athletes (Messner, Carlisle Duncan, and Jensen 1993). The researchers concluded:

> Men appeared to succeed through talent, enterprise, hard work and risk taking. Women also appeared to succeed through talent, enterprise, hard work and intelligence. But commonly cited along with these attributes were emotion, luck, togetherness and family. Women were also more likely to be

framed as failures due to some combination of nervousness, lack of confidence, lack of being "comfortable," lack of aggression, and lack of stamina. Men were far less often framed as failures—men appeared to miss shots and lose matches not so much because of their own individual shortcomings but because of the power, strength and intelligence of their (male) opponents. . . . Men were framed as active agents in control of their destinies, women as reactive objects. (p. 130)

A retrospective study of televised reports of women's sports in the Los Angeles area from 1989 to 2004 found that women were less frequently trivialized or humorously sexualized than in the past, but the extent of coverage had declined (Carlisle Duncan, Messner, and Willms 2005). In 2004, women's sports received only 6.3 percent of the air time; in 1999, they had received 8.7 percent.

Most recently, women athletes have become increasingly recognized for their contributions to sport. As role models, they have transformed the cultural milieu about girls and women as legitimate and competitive athletes. Mia Hamm's longtime NCAA soccer coach, Anson Dorrance, noted, "She laid to rest the insult, 'You play like a girl'" (Longman 2004).

The increasing popularity and visibility of women's sports in their own countries has led women athletes from the United States, Canada, Europe, and Australia to form global organizations to encourage the participation in sports of girls from all over the world (Hargreaves 1999). A parallel development has been the establishment of professional women's sports associations, such as the Women's Tennis Association, the Women's National Basketball Association, and the Ladies' Professional Golf Association. These organizations encourage women student and professional athletes to excel in the gender-segregated world of sports.

Women who have challenged men at their own game have done so to show that women are as good athletes as men are, but they have not usually challenged sports' gender segregation. A young woman golfer, Michelle Wie, did so in 2005. She played successfully against men, and in the process, upset both women and men professional golfers, men because she invaded their space and women because she implied that the women's competitions are not good enough for her:

"In simple terms, people say, 'Michelle just wants to play against men,'" said Jeff O'Brien, an expert on gender issues in sports at Northeastern University.

"It's far more complicated than that." On one level, her enamored view of the P.G.A. plays into cultural biases in sports. "She is basically following the norm of culture," Mr. O'Brien said. "By the TV deals and the endorsement money, dunk highlights on ESPN and the salaries male athletes are paid, society is inherently saying what we value: men's sports." (Roberts 2005)

Steroids and Sports

One of the dangers of the involvement of girls and boys in sports is extreme body modification, in particular, steroid use to build muscle mass in emulation of professional athletes, who are increasingly using these drugs.

As the sports entertainment industry has grown into a multi-billion dollar enterprise, there is unremitting pressure on athletes to win. Whether it is in the college stadium or the large commercial sports arena, winning translates into high salaries or large scholarships, corporate profits, player endorsement deals, and celebrity status. As a result of the competitive pressure to win these prizes, athletes enhance their physical performance with extreme exercise, ultra-specific dieting, and ingenious body-enhancing drugs. At the same time, athletes, coaches, and sports spectators continue to pretend that superhuman physical feats are being performed by natural bodies, just a little better trained. But even the training is high-pressured. Increasingly, men and women athletes must cross-train year-round, not just during the sports season. They also undergo multiple bio-technical measurements of their physiological capacities (blood volume, heart rate, oxygenation). Adding drugs and foods known as "nutraceuticals" does not seem like a major step, but just another part of the training routine.

Being "juiced up" typically refers to the use of anabolic steroids to promote tissue-building and muscle bulk. Testosterone was isolated in 1935. Since then, synthetic versions with various brand names have flooded the legal and underground markets. Anabolic steroids can cause liver damage, testicular atrophy, and infertility, and may lead to depression and suicide. Despite the risks of steroid use, American professional sports as well as Olympic competitions are tainted by men and women who must relinquish their awards and accolades after testing positive for steroid use. However, some sports, like professional baseball, have been ambivalent about drug use. In the following excerpt, Michael Sokolove, a sports writer for the *New York Times,* discusses the prevalence and consequences of the use of steroids and other drugs in many sports.

In Pursuit of Excellence

Michael Sokolove
New York Times

There is a murky, "Casablanca"-like quality to sport at the moment. We are in a time of flux. No one is entirely clean. No one is entirely dirty. The rules are ambiguous. Everyone, and everything, is a little suspect. Months before the great slugger Barry Bonds was summoned before a grand jury in December to answer questions about his association with the Bay Area Laboratory Co-Operative, known as Balco, which has been at the center of a spreading drug scandal after the discovery of a new "designer steroid," tetrahydrogestrinone (THG), a veteran American sprinter named Kelli White ran the track meet of her dreams at the World Championships in Paris. She captured the gold medal in the 100-meter and 200-meter races, the first American woman ever to win those sprints in tandem at an outdoor world championship. In both events, the 5-foot-4, 135-pound White, a tightly coiled ball of power and speed, exploded to career-best times.

On a celebratory shopping trip on the Champs-Elysées, White, 26, glimpsed her name in a newspaper headline and asked a Parisian to translate. She learned that she had flunked a postrace drug test and that her medals and $120,000 in prize money were in jeopardy. Later, she acknowledged that she had taken the stimulant modafinil, claiming that she needed it to treat narcolepsy but had failed to list it on a disclosure form. What she added after that was revealing, perhaps more so than she intended. "After a competition," she told reporters in Europe, "it's kind of hard to remember everything that you take during the day."

The THG scandal and the attention focused on Balco, which has advised dozens of top athletes (including Kelli White) on the use of dietary supplements, has opened the curtain on a seamy side of sport and on the fascinating cat-and-mouse game played between rogue chemists and the laboratory sleuths who try to police them.

But White's statement exposed another, deeper truth: elite athletes in many different sports routinely consume cocktails of vitamins, extracts and supplements, dozens of pills a day—the only people who routinely ingest more pills are AIDS patients—in the hope that their mixes of accepted drugs will replicate the effects of the banned substances taken by the cheaters. The cheaters and the noncheaters alike are science projects. They are the sum total of their innate athletic abilities and their dedication—and all the compounds and powders they ingest and inject.

A narrow tunnel leads to success at the very top levels of sport. This is especially so in Olympic nonteam events. An athlete who has devoted his life to sprinting, for example, must qualify for one of a handful of slots on his Olympic team. And to become widely known and make real money, he probably has to win one of the gold medals that is available every four years.

The temptation to cheat is human. In the realm of elite international sport, it can be irresistible.

After Kelli White failed her drug test, the United States Olympic Committee revealed that five other American athletes in track and field had tested positive this summer for modafinil. Did they all suffer from narcolepsy? That would be hard to believe. More likely, word of modafinil and its supposed performance-enhancing qualities (perhaps along with the erroneous information that it was not detectable) went out on the circuit. It became the substance du jour.

For athletes, performance-enhancing drugs and techniques raise issues of health, fair play and, in some cases, legality. For sports audiences, the fans, the issues are largely philosophical and aesthetic.

On the most basic level, what are we watching, and why? If we equate achievement with determination and character, and that, after all, has always been part of our attachment to sport—to celebrate the physical expression of the human spirit—how do we recalibrate our thinking about sport when laboratories are partners in athletic success?

Major League Baseball, which came late to drug testing and then instituted a lenient program, seems to have decided that the power generated by bulked-up players is good for the game in the entertainment marketplace. The record-breaking sluggers Mark McGwire and Sammy Sosa have been virtual folk heroes and huge draws at the gate. Their runs at the record books became the dominant narratives of individual seasons. (Barry Bonds has been less popular only because of a sour public persona.) But the sport is much changed. Muscle Baseball is the near opposite of what I and many other fans over 30 were raised on, a game that involved strategy, bunting, stolen bases, the hit-and-run play—what is called Little Ball.

Professional basketball is not generally suspected of being drenched in steroids and other performance enhancers. But anyone who has seen even a few minutes of old games on the ESPN Classic network from, say, 20 years ago, is immediately struck by the evolution of players' physiques. Regardless of how it happened, today's N.B.A. players are heavier and markedly more muscled, and the game is tailored to their strengths. It is played according to a steroid aesthetic. What was once a sport of grace and geometry—athletes moving to open spaces on the floor, thinking in terms of passing angles—is now one primarily of power and aggression: players gravitate to the same space and try to go over or through one another.

But it is sports that have fixed standards and cherished records that present fans with the greatest conundrum. If what's exciting is to see someone pole vault to a new, unimaginable height—or become the "world's fastest human" or the first big-leaguer since Ted Williams to hit .400—how do we respond when our historical frame of reference is knocked askew by the suspicion, or known fact, that an athlete is powered by a banned substance?

Reprinted from Michael Sokolove, "The Lab Animal: In Pursuit of Doped Excellence." *New York Times Magazine,* 18 January 2004, 30. Copyright © 2004 *New York Times.* Reprinted by permission.

In an effort to keep athletics pure and "safe," the World Anti-Doping Agency (WADA), created in 1999, works with governments and designated national organizations, including the United States Anti-Doping Agency, to regulate athletes' adherence to antidoping regulations. WADA also attempts to detect "masking agents" commonly used to trick regulators. But as WADA's Medical Advisory Committee races to update its list of banned substances and refine its science of detection, laboratories are inventing new drugs and techniques for concealing drug use. Furthermore, there is a culture of lying about using steroids that proliferates even when testifying before the U.S. Congress. In March 2005, Rafael Palmeiro, an Orioles first baseman, pointed his finger at the Government Reform Committee and stated, "I have never used steroids. Period. I don't know how to say it any more clearly than that. Never." In August of that same year, Palmeiro tested positive for steroid use (Rhoden 2005). As the testing becomes more sophisticated, athletes might resort to modified genes injected into their bloodstreams to impede detection.

One of the most dangerous consequences of the enhanced performance of juiced athletes is how it has trickled into amateur and junior high and high school athletics. The American College of Sports Medicine reported that "lifetime prevalence rates for steroid use among male adolescents generally range between 4 and 12 percent, and between .5 and 2 percent for female adolescents" (1999, 1). Another study found significant risk factors for anabolic steroid use among student athletes, in particular football players, wrestlers, weightlifters, and body builders (Bahrke et al. 2000).

Simply because boys' rates are greater than girls' does not mean that girls are immune from steroid abuse. Over the past twenty years, researchers at Penn State and the University of Michigan have been conducting longitudinal studies to explore girls' use of steroids. As reported on CNN (2005), "Overall, up to about 5 percent of high school girls and 7 percent of middle-school girls admit trying anabolic steroids at least once, with use rising steadily since 1991, various government and university studies have shown." During interviews, young girls report that they use steroids to increase their competitive edge in sports and also to achieve the "toned and sculpted" look of movie stars and models. Clearly, the gender-specific desire to achieve the ideal body morphology of a star athlete or a supermodel has led children to be vulnerable to extremes of body modification.

Sports and Violence

It is interesting to consider how many war or battle metaphors there are in sports. First, there is the internal battle to conquer physical limits and fight through pain. Part of the masculine embodiment in sports is to suffer pain as a rite of passage to legitimate manhood. Often the pain is flaunted as a physical distinction of male bodies as different from and inherently superior to female bodies. To motivate their male teams, coaches will use female descriptors to humiliate or degrade, yelling at a soccer team during a dribbling drill, "You look like a bunch of girls," and to a boxer in the ring, "You hit like a lady." Alternatively, pejorative homosexual references are made about opponents—"Look at those fags." These degradations are an attempt to motivate boys and men to use their bodies more aggressively.

Second, competition becomes an external battle, where individuals and teams are exhorted to "kill" their opponents. Third, sporting events often inspire violence among spectators in the form of hooliganism and riots. In the United States after major football and basketball victories, there is a rise in looting, arson, and assault. In Britain, a study of racist, xenophobic, and drunk British football fans showed the connection between sports fanaticism and mob violence (Buford 1993).

Vicarious participation in sports as fans is a way that men who have limited access to resources in educational and corporate institutions can express their masculinity. Another way is to engage in a one-on-one sport where training can be found locally. Boxing, a relatively inexpensive sport, has traditionally induced participation by men from minority ethnic backgrounds (Woodward 2004). Through this training, a young man enters a ritual-filled world and a community of men whose masculinity rides on being able to control and use violence to knock out a competitor.

As part of an ethnographic study of an economically depressed African American neighborhood in Chicago, Loïc Wacquant, a White graduate student at the University of Chicago, signed up for boxing training at a gym a few blocks from his apartment. He stayed on for three-and-a-half years and turned his experience of the education of a boxer into a book, *Body and Soul,* from which the following excerpt is taken. Influenced by Bourdieu's work on the body, Wacquant argued that not only the body is trained but also the mind and emotions.

Controlled Violence: The Manly Sport

Loïc Wacquant
University of California, Berkeley

. . . Sparring is not only a physical exercise; it is also the means and support of a particularly intense form of "emotion work."[1] Because "few lapses of self-control are punished as immediately and severely as loss of temper during a boxing bout,"[2] it is vital that one dominate at all times the impulses of one's affect. In the squared circle, one must be capable of managing one's emotions and know, according to the circumstances, how to contain or repress them or, on the contrary, how to stir and swell them; how to muzzle certain feelings (of anger, restiveness, frustration) so as to resist the blows, provocation, and verbal abuse dished out by one's opponent, as well as the "rough tactics" he may resort to (hitting below the belt or with his elbows, head-butting, rubbing his gloves into your eyes or over a facial cut in order to open it further, etc.); and how to call forth and amplify others (of aggressiveness or "controlled fury," for instance) at will while not letting them get out of hand.[3] In gloving up at the gym, boxers learn to become "businesslike" in the ring, to channel their mental and affective energies toward "getting the job done" in the most effective and least painful manner.

A boxer must exercise not only a constant inner surveillance over his feelings but also continual "expressive control" over their external "signaling"[4] so as not to let his opponent know if and when punches hurt him, and which one. Legendary trainer-manager Cus D'Amato, the "discoverer" of Mike Tyson, sums up the matter thus: "The fighter has mastered his emotions to the extent that he can conceal and control them. Fear is an asset to a fighter. It makes him move faster, be quicker and more alert. Heroes and cowards feel exactly the same fear. Heroes react to it differently."[5] This difference has nothing innate about it; it is an acquired ability, collectively produced by prolonged submission of the body to the discipline of sparring. Butch explains:

> BUTCH: *You have to stay in control, because yer emotions will burn up all yer oxygen, so you have to stay calm and relaxed though you know this guy's tryin' to knock yer head off. You have to stay calm and relaxed. So you have to deal with the situation.*
>
> LOUIE: *Was it hard learning to control emotions, like to not get mad or frustrated if a guy is slippery and you can't hit him with clean shots?*
>
> BUTCH: *It was hard for me. It took me years-an'-years-an'-years to git that and juuus' when I was gittin' it under control real goo', then thin's, hum, started movin' for me. It works, well, I guess when it was time, it worked itself into place.*
>
> LOUIE: *Is that something that DeeDee taught you?*
>
> BUTCH: *He kept tellin' me to stay calm, relax. Jus' breathe, take it easy—but [his pace picks up] I foun' it har' to stay calm and relax when this guy's tryin' to kill ya over in the next corner, but eventually it sunk in and I understood what he was sayin'.*

. . . Finally, the strictly physical aspect of sparring should not be neglected on account of being self-evident: one must not forget that "[b]oxing is more about getting hit than it is about hitting"; it is "primarily about being, and not giving, hurt."[6] The idiolect of boxing is replete with terms referring to the ability to take a punch and glorifying the capacity to endure pain. Now, beyond one's congenital endowment such as an "iron chin" or the mysterious and revered quality called "heart" (which also holds a central place in the masculine street culture of the ghetto), there is only one way to harden yourself to pain and to get your body used to taking blows, and that is to get hit regularly. For, contrary to a widespread popular notion, boxers have no personal predilection for pain and hardly enjoy getting pummeled. A young Italian-American welterweight from the Windy City Gym who recently turned pro gets indignant when I mention the lay stereotype of the "sadomasochistic" fighter.[7] "*Nah, we're human man! We're human,* you know, we're jus' like anybody else, our feelings are jus' as much as your feelin's, we—you can't put us outside, you know, (vehemently) *we're no different than you:* we're in the same world, we're the same world, the same flesh, same blood, same everything." What boxers have done is to elevate their threshold of tolerance for pain by submitting to it in graduated and regular fashion. . . .

To learn how to box is to imperceptibly modify one's bodily schema, one's relation to one's body and to the uses one usually puts it to, so as to internalize a set of dispositions that are inseparably mental and physical and that, in the long run, turn the body into a virtual punching machine, but *an intelligent and creative machine capable of self-regulation* while innovating within a fixed and relatively restricted panoply of moves as an instantaneous function of the actions of the opponent in time. The mutual imbrication of corporeal dispositions and mental dispositions reaches such a degree that even will power, morale, determination, concentration, and the control of one's emotions change into so many reflexes inscribed within the organism. In the accomplished boxer, the mental becomes part of the physical and vice versa; body and mind function in total symbiosis. This is what is expressed in the scornful comments that DeeDee makes to boxers who argue that they are not "mentally ready" for a fight. After Curtis's loss in his first nationally televised fight in Atlantic City, the old trainer is fuming: "He don't lose 'cos he's not 'mentally ready.' That don' mean nuthin', mentally ready. If you're a fighter, you're ready. I was just tellin' Butch mentally ready, tha's bullshit! If you're a fighter, you get up in d'ring an' [hissing for emphasis] you *fight* there's no bein' mentally ready or not ready. It's not mental, ain't nuthin' mental bout it. If you're not a fighter, you don't get up in there, you don't fight. If you're a fighter, you're ready and you fight—tha's all. All d'rest is just *bullshit for the birds.*" [Fieldnotes, 17 April 1989]

Notes

1. On the notion of "emotion work," see Arlie Hochschild, "Emotion Work, Feeling Rules, and Social Structure," *American Journal of Sociology* 85, 3 (November 1979): 551–575.
2. Konrad Lorenz, *On Aggression* (New York: Harcourt, Brace and World, 1966), 281.
3. One could show that this "sentimental education" is not limited to the sole pugilist: it encompasses all the specialized agents of the pugilistic field (trainers, managers, referees, judges, promoters, etc.) and even extends to spectators.
4. Erving Goffman, *Presentation of Self in Everyday Life*, 59–60.
5. Cited by Stephen Brunt, *Mean Business*, 55. (Markham, Can: Penguin Books, 1987).
6. Joyce Carol Oates, *On Boxing*, 25 and 60. (Garden City, N.Y.: Doubleday, 1987).
7. This stereotype can be found in numerous scholarly works, such as Allen Gutman's historical thesis on the evolution of sports, *From Ritual to Record: The Nature of Modem Sports* (New York: Columbia University Press, 1989: see 160), as well as non-scholarly works, such as the encyclopedia of academic and journalistic cliches about prizefighting compiled from newspaper and sports magazine articles by André Rauch, *Boxe violence du XXe siècle* (Paris: Aubier, 1992). I detail other problems with Rauch's tome in the French edition of this book, *Corps et âme* (Marseilles: Agone, 2d expanded ed. 2002), pp. 276–277.

A tough, take-charge, don't-feel image of masculinity frequently dominates male athletic socialization, especially among boys and young men who want to enhance their social status. Hypermasculinity, the extreme embodied expression of masculinity, is both demanded of and expressed by many Black male athletes as a means to receive social rewards. Renford Reese (2004), a political scientist, conducted interviews with 756 African American males aged 13 to 19 in Los Angeles and Atlanta. These young men overwhelmingly rated Allen Iverson, the multi-tattooed, temperamental basketball player as a "real man" over Tiger Woods, a mild-mannered golfer, who was considered "too

White." If athlete heroes are hypermasculine rebels who excel at their sport, boys are likely to mimic these behaviors as a means to gain social acceptance.

Athletics, although thought of as a way for disenfranchised men to participate in upward social mobility, actually relies on existing social inequities to exploit them. The ownership of professional sports teams and the coaching of athletes, very lucrative and powerful enterprises, are usually in the hands of those of higher economic status than the players. These disparities allow the owners and the trainers who work for them to ignore the costs to the athletes—permanent injuries, poor health, minimal academic achievement, and low life expectancy. There is much less participation in violent sports for upward mobility by disadvantaged girls, a form of gender inequity that should not be deplored (Hager Cohen 2005).

Critical Summary

There are two interrelated social processes that run through this chapter. These social processes are mutually reinforcing and, when not critically examined, create an illusion that embodiment is the result of natural physiologic programming. The first process occurs through gendered social practices shaping children's and adults' bodies, making them feminine or masculine. The ways the resulting gendered bodies are used—in sports, in particular—feed the gendering back into the culture. The second process is the proliferation of the belief that female and male bodies are naturally different. This belief masks the extent to which they are *made* different, particularly through sports.

In an article that challenged the gendered division of bodies in sports, Mary Jo Kane (1995) argues that we are prevented from seeing sports as a continuum. Through several interrelated practices, we become blinded to the extent of overlap between women's and men's sport performances. The most obvious is that women and men don't play on the same teams and also don't compete against each other. The argument is that if a women's team played against a men's team, the women would invariably lose. But who is being protected from failure? Kane said,

Although we should never underestimate the importance of male bonding as an exclusionary practice or of men's extreme desire to differentiate themselves from women, we have tended to ignore another reason why men resist integration so fiercely: They are deeply afraid that many women can outperform them, even in those sports and physical skills/attributes that they have claimed as their own. What better way to deflect such fears than to create segregationist ideologies and practices that will ensure that these possibilities rarely (if ever) come to pass. (p. 206)

Exactly how women and men are segregated in sports is easy to list: Many sports are sex-typed—few women play football, and few men are synchronized swimmers. There are many instances where women play rugby or ice hockey on all-women teams, but they are not popularized because they are all-women. Where women and men play the same popular sports, such as tennis and gymnastics, the rules or events are different. The women front-runners in marathons, who have beaten the times of a couple of hundred men, are compared only with the men front-runners, who run faster, although women are fast catching up to them.

What if boys and girls were grouped into teams by size or ability and learned to use their bodies together? What if there were some professional gender-integrated sports playing on television? What variety of physical capabilities would we see if gender was not constantly inscribed on bodies? As a spillover, gender-segregated sports as a social activity would have much less of a rationale, and we might also see less glorification of violence as intrinsic to sports. Of course, if sports were not equated with masculinity, professional teams might lose their glamour and their audiences, and poor boys would have one less avenue to what they now dream of as a better life.

References and Recommended Readings

American College of Sports Medicine. 1999. "Anabolic Steroids." *Current Comment*, April, 1. Washington, DC.

Anderson, Eric. 2005. *In the Game: Gay Athletes and the Cult of Masculinity*. Albany: State University of New York Press.

Bahrke, Michael, Charles Yesalis, Andrea Kopstein, and Jason Stephens. 2000. "Risk Factors Associated With Anabolic-Androgenic Steroid Use Among Adolescents." *Sports Medicine* 29, 397–405.

Black, David R. (ed.). 1991. *Eating Disorders Among Athletes*. Reston, VA: American Alliance for Health, Physical Education, Recreation, and Dance.

Bourdieu, Pierre. [1980] 1990. *The Logic of Practice*. Stanford, CA: Stanford University Press.

Cahn, Susan K. 1994. *Coming On Strong: Gender and Sexuality in Twentieth-Century Women's Sport*. New York: Free Press.

Carlisle Duncan, Margaret, and Michael Messner, with Nicole Willms. 2005. "Gender in Televised Sports: News and Highlights Shows, 1989–2004." Amateur Athletic Foundation of Los Angeles (AAF). *www.aafla.org/9arr/ResearchReports/tv2004.pdf*

CNN. 2005. "Girls Are Abusing Steroids, Too." 25 April. *www.cnn.com/2005/HEALTH/04/25/girls.steroids.ap/index.html*

Dowling, Collette. 2000. *The Frailty Myth: Redefining the Physical Potential of Women and Girls*. New York: Random House.

Grasmuck, Sherri. 2005. *Protecting Home: Class, Race, and Masculinity in Boys' Baseball*. New Brunswick, NJ: Rutgers University Press.

Griffin, Pat. 1998. *Strong Women, Deep Closets*. Champaign, IL: Human Kinetics.

Hager Cohen, Leah. 2005. *Without Apology: Girls, Women, and the Desire to Fight*. New York: Random House.

Hanson, Sandra L., and Rebecca S. Kraus. 1998. "Women, Sports, and Science: Do Female Athletes Have an Advantage?" *Sociology of Education* 71, 93–110.

Hargreaves, Jennifer. 1994. *Sporting Females: Critical Issues in the History and Sociology of Women's Sports*. New York: Routledge.

———. 1999. "The 'Women's International Sports Movement': Local-Global Strategies and Empowerment." *Women's Studies International Forum* 22, 461–471.

Heywood, Leslie. 1998. *Bodymakers: A Cultural Anatomy of Women's Bodybuilding*. New Brunswick, NJ: Rutgers University Press.

Heywood, Leslie, and Shari Dworkin. 2003. *Built to Win: The Female Athlete as Cultural Icon*. Minneapolis: University of Minnesota.

Jacobs Brumberg, Joan. 1997. *The Body Project: An Intimate History of American Girls*. New York: Vintage.

Buford, Bill. 1993. *Among the Thugs*. New York: Vintage.

Kane, Mary Jo. 1995. "Resistance/Transformation of the Oppositional Binary: Exposing Sport as a Continuum." *Journal of Sport and Social Issues* 19, 191–218.

Klein, Alan M. 1993. *Little Big Men: Bodybuilding Subculture and Gender Construction*. Albany: State University of New York Press.

Lindemann, Gesa. 1996. "The Body of Gender Difference." *European Journal of Women's Studies* 3, 341–361.

Longman, Jere. 2004. "Mia Hamm, Soccer Star, to Retire Tonight." *New York Times*, 8 December. *www.nytimes.com/2004/12/08/sports/soccer/08hamm.html*

Martin, Karin A. 1998. "Becoming a Gendered Body: Practices of Preschools." *American Sociological Review* 63, 494–511.

McCaughey, Martha. 1997. *Real Knockouts: The Physical Feminism of Women's Self Defense.* New York: New York University Press.

Messner, Michael A. 1992. *Power at Play: Sports and the Problem of Masculinity.* Boston: Beacon Press.

———. 2002. *Taking the Field: Women, Men, and Sports.* Minneapolis: University of Minnesota Press.

Messner, Michael A., Margaret Carlisle Duncan, and Kerry Jensen. 1993. "Separating the Men From the Girls: The Gendered Language of Televised Sports." *Gender & Society* 7, 121–137.

Messner, Michael A., and Donald F. Sabo (eds.). 1994. *Sex, Violence, and Power in Sports: Rethinking Masculinity.* Freedom, CA: Crossing Press.

Miller, Kathleen, Grace Barnes, Merrill Melnick, Donald Sabo, and Michael Farrell. 2002. "Gender and Racial/Ethnic Differences in Predicting Adolescent Sexual Risk: Athletic Participation Versus Exercise." *Journal of Health and Social Behavior* 43, 436–450.

National Coalition for Women and Girls in Education. 2002. *Title IX at Thirty: Report Card on Gender Equity.* Washington, DC.

Palmeri, Christopher. 2000. "Barbie, You Look Bodacious." *Business Week,* 24 July. *BW Online.*

Pope, Harrison, Katharine Phillips, and Roberto Olivardia. 2000. *The Adonis Complex: The Secret Crisis of Male Body Obsession.* New York: Free Press.

Reese, Renford. 2004. *American Paradox: Young Black Men.* Durham, NC: Carolina Academic Press.

Rhoden, William C. 2005. "Baseball Should Investigate the Orioles." *New York Times,* 28 September, D1.

Roberts, Selena. 2005. "Where the Boys Are. There She Is." *New York Times Week in Review,* 17 July, 14.

Robinson, Kirsten, and Richard F. Ferraro. 2004. "The Relationship Between Types of Female Athletic Participation and Female Body Type." *Journal of Psychology* 138, 115–129.

Sokolove, Michael. 2004. "The Lab Animal: In Pursuit of Doped Excellence." *New York Times Magazine* 18 January, 28–33, 48, 54, 58.

Stinson, Kandi M. 2001. *Women and Dieting Culture.* New Brunswick, NJ: Rutgers.

Theberge, Nancy. 2000. *Higher Goals: Women's Ice Hockey and the Politics of Gender.* Albany: State University of New York Press.

Thorne, Barrie. 1993. *Gender Play: Girls and Boys at School.* New Brunswick, NJ: Rutgers University Press.

Verbrugge, Martha H. 1997. "Recreating the Body: Women's Physical Education and the Science of Sex Differences in America, 1900–1940." *Bulletin of the History of Medicine* 71, 273–304.

Wacquant, Loïc. 2004. *Body and Soul: Notebooks of an Apprentice Boxer.* New York: Oxford University Press.

Woodward, Kath. 2004. "Rumbles in the Jungle: Boxing, Racialization, and the Performance of Masculinity." *Leisure Studies* 23 (1), 517.

Internet Sources

Homophobia in Sports Project
www.homophobiainsports.com/

Ladies' Professional Golf Association
www.lpga.com/

North American Society for the Sociology of Sport
www.nasss.org

Save Title IX
www.savetitleix.com/

Tucker Center for Research on Girls and Women in Sport
education.umn.edu/tuckercenter/

UNICEF Gender Parity and Primary Education
www.unicef.org/

U.S. Department of Education Title IX Archives
www.ed.gov/pubs/TitleIX/index.html

U.S. Department of Justice, Title IX
www.usdoj.gov/crt/cor/coord/titleixstat.htm

U.S. Department of Labor, Title IX Amendment
www.dol.gov/oasam/regs/statutes/titleix.htm

Women's National Basketball Association (WNBA)
www.wnba.com/

Women's Professional Football League
www.womensprofootball.com/

Women's Sports Foundation
www.womenssportsfoundation.org/cgi-bin/iowa/index.html

Women's Tennis Association
www.wtatour.com/

World Anti-Doping Agency
www.wada-ama.org/en/ ✦

Chapter 4

Eve, Venus, and 'Real Women'

Constructing Women's Bodies

Key concepts: clitoris and female sexuality, cosmetic surgeries, eating disorders, menstrual activism, ritual genital cutting

In the summer of 2005, Dove, a company that markets body lotions and other products for women, ran a series of advertisements that featured what it called "real women." They were a bit plump—some even more than a bit—ethnically and racially diverse, and they flaunted their bodies joyfully, even sexually. From a feminist perspective, this departure from a fantasy world of young, thin, airbrushed, cosmetically enhanced female models was somewhat progressive. However, the models were in their 20s, not older, and none was differently abled, so the depiction of "realness" was rather narrow. Perhaps most significant was their attire. The reality of womanhood was still being defined by underwear-clad, young bodies.

What version of women is "real"? There are even two versions of Adam and Eve. In one, Eve and Adam are both created from earth, equally. In the other, more familiar story, Eve is created from Adam's rib, to be a helpmate. Because women are culturally defined by their biology or their bodies, it is crucial that they have some power to do the defining. As we have seen, in pregnancy and childbirth, women have all the responsibility for good outcomes, but little power over the surrounding social, political, physical, or medical environments.

In this chapter, we look at menstrual activism, female sexuality, ritual genital cutting, mastectomy and body image, eating disorders, and elective cosmetic surgeries, and examine the extent to which women can take control over the social definition of their bodies. In some instances, women choose to go along with fairly conventional norms and expectations of femininity, but see it as their choice, not as succumbing to oppressive norms. Other women go beyond the norms by flaunting their sexuality or menstrual status. Other women use the norms as a means of control over their own bodies, dieting to the point of illness. Still other women defy or resist the pressure of the norms, refusing to have breast reconstruction after a mastectomy or a face-lift when wrinkles appear.

Menstrual Activism

Menstruation, in biological terms, is the end result of hormonal preparation of the uterus for pregnancy after ovulation. If a fertilized ovum is not implanted in the uterus, the lining sloughs off—and that is menstruation. When a woman's ovaries stop maturing and releasing eggs, the cycle ceases—and that is menopause. These cycles are imbued with cultural and social significance in many societies. Menstruation, as a mark of becoming a woman, is often celebrated. In modern Western societies, a girl's first period (menarche) is not ritualized. Rather, it begins a monthly worry about showing blood and the danger of getting pregnant. Worse, the "condition" has become somewhat shameful and stigmatizing—something to be hidden.

In a famous political fantasy in *Ms. Magazine,* Gloria Steinem (1978) asked:

> What would happen . . . if suddenly, magically, men could menstruate and women could not? The answer is clear—menstruation would become an enviable, boast-worthy, masculine event. Men would brag about how long and how much. Boys would mark the onset of menses, that longed-for proof of manhood, with religious ritual and stag parties. . . . Military men, right-wing politicians, and religious fundamentalists would cite menstruation ["*men*-struation"] as proof that only men could serve in the Army ["you have to give blood to take blood"], occupy political office ["can women be aggressive without that steadfast cycle governed by the planet Mars?"], be

priests and ministers ["how could a woman give her blood for our sins?"]. . . .
In short, if men could menstruate, the power justifications could probably go
on forever. If we let them. (p. 110)

The equation of menstruation with high or low status, Steinem said,
depends on the status of women. Whether women have high or low status
in a society determines whether menstruation is celebrated publically or
hidden in menstrual huts, whether it confers a sacred aura or one of pollu-
tion that needs to be "sanitized," and whether it is medicalized as a pathological condition or handled as a proud part of daily life.

In the following excerpt, Chris Bobel, professor of women's studies,
describes the menstrual activism of third-wave feminists, young women
who define their bodies and their sexuality as forms of power.

Resistance With a Wink: Young Women, Feminism and the (Radical) Menstruating Body

Chris Bobel
University of Massachusetts, Boston

Menstrual activism—a persistent but little known presence in the
women's health movement since the early 1970s, and more recently,
the environmental movement, the "punk scene," and anarchist communities,
began with a scathing critique of the dominant Western cultural narrative of
menstruation, resisting the framing of menstruation as dirty, shameful, and
something best hidden. Its goal is to make menstruation, in the words of documentary filmmaker Giovanna Chesler, "audible and visible." The coun-
ter-narrative of menstrual activism explicitly politicizes and demystifies the
personal experience of menses, aiming to give women back the power over
their bodies.

A large part of menstrual activism is resistance to the "femcare" industry,
seen as the producers of polluting, underregulated (and thus unsafe), and
ultimately unnecessary products that exploit the taboos surrounding menstruation. Many menstrual activists are primarily concerned about the content of conventional products—tampons and pads. Toxic residues left behind
by pesticide-laden and bleached cotton (a main ingredient) and the potentially irritating effects of rayon (another main ingredient) lead activists to
promote reusable products, such as washable cloth pads and internally worn
devices that collect rather than absorb blood.

Though menstrual activism is practiced by mostly White, college-educated women, many of whom identify as queer, it is diverse in the ways it
manifests itself—spanning the terrain from the sacred to the ribald and the
practical to the abstract. It can be a mother-daughter ceremony in prepara-

tion for a young woman's first menses in suburban San Francisco, a "Tampon Send-Back" campaign at a prestigious college, a small group of women hand-sewing their own reusable cloth menstrual pads (called a "Stitch 'N' Bitch"), and the "Red Brigade" contingent of the Michigan Womyn's Music Festival annual parade—a boisterous cadre of women, some naked and most decorated with red paint and red accessories, carrying cardboard signs emblazoned with slogans such as "Love Your Blood!" and "Corporations Out of My Cunt!"

Menstrual Activism History

In the late 1970s and throughout the 1980s, members of the Boston Women's Health Book Collective (authors of the "bible of women's health": *Our Bodies, Ourselves*) and the Society for Menstrual Cycle Research (founded in 1979) led a series of courageous efforts to improve the safety profile of conventional menstrual products, especially tampons (Rome and Wolhandler 1992). One brand of tampons was implicated in a wave of Toxic Shock Syndrome (TSS), a bacterial infection that killed 38 women in the early 1980s and caused the serious illness of 813 more (FDA 1999). By 1983, more than 2,200 menstrual-related TSS cases had been reported to the Centers for Disease Control (Tierno 2001).

In 1989, a small group of British feminist environmental activists called the Women's Environmental Network (WEN) organized a national media blitz designed to publicize the dangerous by-products of the chlorine bleaching process used to produce tampons and sanitary napkins (Costello, Vallely, and Young 1989). There was some positive response from manufacturers, but not enough, stimulating the founding of several alternative product companies.

In the 1990s, two influential books were published that challenged readers to rethink the ways they manage their monthly bleeding—*The Curse: Confronting the Last Unmentionable Taboo* (Houppert 1999) and *Cunt: A Declaration of Independence* (Muscio 1998). The Student Environmental Action Coalition (SEAC 2003), a national grassroots organization, started its "Dioxin Out of Tampons" campaign (later renamed "Tampaction") in 1999. In 2000, the first antitampon conference was held at James Madison University in Virginia. Also in 2000, poet Geneva Kachman and filmmaker Molly Strange established "Menstrual Monday," a "holiday" designed to challenge menstrual taboos, secrecy, and negativity (see *www.moltx.org*). It is in this context that contemporary menstrual activists, including a small group of urban punk feminists, founded "The Bloodsisters"; their call to arms is "Ax Tampax!"

What explains the upsurge in activity and the shift in focus that took place in the menstrual activism movement in the mid-1990s and continues today? The simple answer is that feminism changed. While today's actions were set in motion by activists who confronted the femcare industry by working *within* the system, the current movement is shaped by different, though related, cultural and ideological developments, namely, the emergence of third-wave feminism infused with the sprit of punk (Henry 2004). Choosing to work *outside* the system, the newest phase of menstrual activism centered on what's commonly called "radical menstruation," or as one activist puts it, "breaking the tampon addiction."

From Talking Cunts to Grrrls With Pom Poms: Menstrual Activist Strategies

A central theme in the discourse of menstrual activism centers on identity. In particular, the activists seem compelled to enunciate very clearly who they are *not*. They are *not*, as the website *Whirling Cervix* (n.d.) stated, "the type to enthuse about becoming one with the chalice and the Goddess"; "cramps still suck, but it's nice to be a little more in touch with 'that time of the month'" (p. 7). This view intentionally dissociates from the cultural feminist celebration of the body and the Goddess, rooted in a vision of menstruation as a source of women's power. Across the movement—in self-published zines, on websites, in spoken discourse—is this theme of distancing from the feminist "I Bleed, Therefore I Am" perspective. The menstrual activists' break with this tradition is even more clearly articulated in their linguistic choices. At a cloth-pad-making workshop organized by the environmental group E* Funk at Macalester College in St. Paul, Minnesota, the leaders stated very clearly:

> We say "menstruator" instead of woman when we refer to those who menstruate. We do this because not ALL women menstruate and not ONLY women menstruate. (Bobel 2005)

Yonah EtShalom, menstrual activist and former coordinator of SEAC's national Tampaction campaign, was among the first in the movement to push for gender-neutral language. Calling attention to nonmenstruating women, such as those who suppress their periods with diet, exercise, or contraceptives, postmenopausal women, and ill women, and to some intersexual and transgendered people, some of whom identify as men, who *do* menstruate, EtShalom (n.d.) stands for a truly inclusive movement. The menstrual activist opposition to the rigid gender binary—a paradigm which equates menstruation with womanhood—is a clear reflection of third-wave feminist ideals of defying gender and sexual categorization and alternatively blurring body boundaries.

Given the strength of the menstrual taboo, menstrual activists must deploy a number of creative strategies to grab and sustain attention. One strategy commonly used is humor. The zines produced by menstrual activists, with titles such as *Red Scare* (Fawn n.d.), *Pull the Plug on the Feminine Hygiene Industry,* and *It's Your Fucking Body* (Abbondanza n.d.) are unashamedly outrageous. For example, in the zine *Femmenstruation Rites Rag* (Chantal and Brackin n.d.), "Cunt Woman," a hand-drawn image of a vulva with arms and (hairy) legs, speaks in "thought" bubbles about key topics like menarche, sex during menstruation, PMS, and tampon alternatives. The use of humor draws in readers who might otherwise find this historically silenced and shamed topic too gross or personal to engage.

Often the humor takes the form of reappropriation, that is, taking practices and representations typically used to debase women and using them to resist. In the widely circulated Bloodsisters' zine *Red Alert #2*, the authors offer "thanks for the (respectfully) stolen images" (n.d., p. 3) that pepper their pages. Notable images from the zine include a skipping, pinafored-and-black-patent-leather-shoes-clad little girl; models posing in a circa 1950s sewing pattern publication; cowgirls with the copy "why ride the ol' cotton pony? GET UNPLUGGED. Choose reusables"; and a circa 1950s model sporting a high-style bathing suit and cat's eye sunglasses, with the superimposed text, "our revolution has style." Sometimes the images are used as exposé (i.e., pretty silly how those women are posing, isn't it?) or reclamation (i.e., let's celebrate the innocence of little girls rather than exploit it, and/or she may look innocent but don't underestimate her!).

Another reappropriative tactic is the increasingly popular "radical cheerleading." Gaining a (sneakered) foothold in anarchist and punk communities and fast becoming a fixture at antiwar and antiglobalization protests, radical cheerleading reclaims a practice typically associated with the worst of patriarchy and reinvents it to mean something wholly different (Zobl 2004). Sparkle Motion, a Colorado-based radical cheer group defines radical cheerleading as

> . . . activism with pom poms and middle fingers extended. It's screaming FUCK CAPITALISM while doing a split. . . . You don't have to be a dancer, coordinated, or even female-identified. . . . We're all about kicking corporate ass, taking on the social justice and women's issues of the day, and having a fucking blast doing it. (radcheer.uproot.info)

One menstrual activist wrote a "Blood Cheer" set to a Beastie Boy tune that exhorts women to "let it go, let your blood flow" and "smear it on your face and rub it on your body, it's time to start a menstrual party" (Chantal and Brackin n.d, 19). The author performed at a Halloween party while dressed as a bloody tampon.

Still another common strategy used by the menstrual activists involves reproducing advertisements of the femcare industry and altering them as a means of parody. Reminiscent of graffiti seen on billboards, this strategy directly confronts what the activists regard as the industry's dishonest and empty promises and rewrites the ads to reflect a more authentic story, for example, that tampons are linked to toxic shock syndrome. The use of Raggedy Ann in *Red Alert #2* (Bloodsisters n.d.) is illustrative. Here, the familiar icon of innocent girlhood is seated alone in the corner of an otherwise blank page looking very angry. Her eyebrows are redrawn, arched at a severe angle, and her mouth is down-turned. She sits opposite the page that features a manipulated box of Always® maxi pads, which is altered to read "Go Away." The message to the manufacturer is: "We don't want you or your dangerous product." This form of activism is called "culture jamming," a term coined by the San Francisco-based band Negativeland in 1984, and defined as "the practice of parodying advertisements and hijacking billboards in order to drastically alter their messages" (Klein 1999, 280). Culture jammers, according to Klein, boldly reject the passive absorption of advertising and challenge what is intended as the one-way flow of communication from advertiser to hapless, uncritical consumer, to a "talk back" where the consumer reveals the truth in advertising, the story beneath the ad.

Taken together, the uses of humor, reappropriation, and culture jamming subvert the feminine protection industry's control over women's bodies. Menstrual activists laughingly redefine the symbols of femininity and challenge the gender binary at its core. With a wry smile and a wink, menstrual activists claim a stylized space where bleeding is normal and every menstruator exercises agency and autonomy over "that time of the month."

Sources

Abbondanza, M. (n.d.). *It's your fucking body #2.* Self-published zine.

Armstrong, L. and Scott, A. (1992). *Whitewash: Exposing the health and environmental dangers of women's sanitary products and disposable diapers—and what you can do about it!* New York: Harper Perennial.

Bloodsisters. (n.d.). *Red alert #2.* Self-published zine.

Bobel, C. (2003). "When did tampons become a health hazard? Mapping a contemporary history of menstrual activism in *Our Bodies, Ourselves,* 1969–2005." Paper presented at the National Women's Studies Association Annual Meetings, Milwaukee, WI.

——. (2005). "Menstrual discourse, gender identity, and the essentialist knot: Toward a new feminist view of menstruation?" Paper presented at the Society for Menstrual Cycle Research Biennial Meetings, Boulder, CO.

Chantal and Brackin [sic] (n.d.). *Femmenstruation rites rag: Stories of wimmin's blood rites of passage.* Self-published zine.

Costello, A., B. Vallely, and J. Young. (1989). *The sanitary protection scandal.* London: Women's Environmental Network.

EtShalom, Y. (n.d.) "Below the belt." *www.deadletters.biz/belowthebelt/bhealth.html#who*

Fawn P. (n.d.). *Red scare #2.* Self-published zine.

FDA (Food and Drug Administration). (1999). "Tampons and asbestos, dioxin and toxic shock syndrome." *www.fda.gov/cdrh/consumer/tamponsabs.html*

Henry, A. (2004). *Not my mother's sister: Generational conflict and third-wave feminism.* Bloomington: Indiana University Press.

Houppert, K. (1999). *The curse: Confronting the last unmentionable taboo.* New York: Farrar, Strauss, & Giroux.

Kissling, E. (in press). *Capitalizing on the curse: The business of menstruation.* Boulder, CO: Lynne Reiner.

Klein, N. (1999). *No logo: Taking aim at the brand bullies.* New York: Picador.

Muscio, I. (1998). *Cunt: A declaration of independence.* New York: Seal Press.

Rome, E., and J. Wolhandler. (1992). "Can tampon safety be regulated?" In A. Dan and L. Lewis (eds.). *Menstrual health in women's lives.* Champaign: University of Illinois Press.

Student Environmental Action Coalition. (2003). "Tampaction." *www.seac.org/tampons/*

Tierno, P. (2001). *The secret life of germs: What they are, why we need them and how we can protect ourselves against them.* New York: Atria Books.

Whirling Cervix. (n.d.). *http://nofuncharlie.com/whirlingcervix.* Accessed 24 January 2003.

Wilkins, E. (2000). *Pull the plug on the feminine hygiene industry.* Self-published zine.

Zobl, E. (2004). "Revolution grrrl and lady style, now!" *Peace Review* 16 (4), 445–452.

Adapted for this book from Chris Bobel. 2006. "Our Revolution Has Style: Menstrual Activists 'Doing Feminism' in the 'Third Wave,'" *Sex Roles* (in press).

Women's Sexuality: Discovering the Clitoris

Menstruation may conventionally be a mark of womanhood, but until the eighteenth century, Western philosophers and scientists believed that there was one sex and that women's internal genitals were the inverse of men's external genitalia (Laqueur 1990). To them, the womb and vagina were the penis and scrotum turned inside out. The clitoris, if it was mentioned at all, was described as a small penis. It couldn't have been totally ignored, because it was also believed that a woman could not conceive unless she had an orgasm, so some men must have known where to find the clitoris and stimulate it.

This knowledge about the location and purpose of the clitoris, though, keeps getting lost. Judging from questions to a sex-information hotline, the clitoris is hard to find, and its purpose is mysterious. If we look at some of the Western "experts" who have produced meanings about female bodies and sexualities, it is clear that the clitoris is a very elusive, dangerous, and complicated organ.

Anatomists, psychoanalysts, sexologists, and pornographers have all established their professional reputations by claiming expertise about the clitoris. Different male anatomical explorers dispute the "scientific" discovery of the clitoris. In 1559, Realdo Colombo wrote of his discovery of the clitoris, "the seat of women's delight"; he called it "so pretty and useful a thing" in his *De Re Anatomica*.

In the biomedical textbooks of the 1900s through the 1950s, the clitoris was depicted and described as homologous to the penis, that is, as formed from the same anatomical tissue. In 1905, Sigmund Freud, the father of psychoanalysis, published essays that argued for a differentiation of clitoral/vaginal orgasms. To Freud, clitoral orgasms were immature; as women became properly socialized into their mature sexual orientation of heterosexuality, he believed, they should experience orgasm in their vaginas. Sexologists of the 1930s and 1940s read female genital physiology as evidence of their sexual experiences, often citing an enlarged clitoris as proof of prostitution or lesbianism. To them, the clitoris revealed a woman's transgression against patriarchal sexual norms.

In 1953, Kinsey's *Sexual Behavior in the Human Female* used interviews with 5,940 women as its database. Kinsey and his colleagues interpreted this data to define the clitoris as the locus of female sexual sensation and orgasm. Despite this scientific evidence culled from women's descriptions of their sexual experiences, the clitoris virtually disappeared from anatomical textbooks from the 1950s to the1970s. A survey of lay and medical dictionaries found that definitions of the clitoris referred to the male body as a template or norm from which the female body is somehow derived (Braun and Kitzinger 2001). This definition often implied that the clitoris was inferior to the penis. Basing one's knowledge on historical anatomical rendering and dictionary definitions of the time would have led one to believe that the clitoris was a small, purposeless organ.

During the 1970s, consciousness-raising groups of women equipped with plastic vaginal speculums, mirrors, and flashlights taught one another how to explore their sexual and procreative organs. These groups of women created fertile ground for feminist reformation of anatomical texts. The self-examinations and group meetings revolutionized existing descriptions and renderings of the clitoris (Federation of Women's Health Centers 1981). A study that also challenged the conventional denigration of the clitoris, the *Hite Report* on female sexuality, published in 1976, was based on data from 1,844 anonymous questionnaires distributed to American women between 14 and 78 years old. Although many questioned the methodological rigor of this study, the project amassed significant and compelling data about the importance of clitoral stimulation for female orgasm.

These feminist insurgencies were met with great resistance from mainstream medicine. Throughout the 1980s and 1990s, the backlash to feminism reasserted that women's sexual response was linked exclusively to procreation. Certain anatomical texts of this time seemed to purposefully render the clitoris as useless or unnecessary (Moore and Clarke 2001). More recently, videos, CD-ROMs, and websites have joined medical texts and pornography as modes of viewing genital anatomy. But the new ways of accessing images and descriptions of the clitoris did not necessarily change the definition of the clitoris: "Continuities with previous textual anatomies abound in new visual and cyber forms, such as the heterosexual requirement, the female body as reproductive not sexual, and the biomedical expert as the proper and dominant mediator between humans and their own bodies" (Moore and Clarke 2001, 87).

Pornography, another place where individuals get information about human genitalia, contributes to knowledge as well as confusion and mystique about the clitoris. In *Men's Health* magazine, an article called "Sex Tricks From Skin Flicks" provides advice for readers from 40 X-rated films, such as: "You know her clitoris needs attention, especially as she nears climax. But it's hard to find such a tiny target when both your bodies are moving. Use the flat of your palm to make broad, quick circular motions around the front of her vaginal opening. That way, you're sure to hit the spot" (2000, 54).

Feminist research on women's genital anatomy, such as that of Rebecca Chalker (2002), a pioneer of the self-help health movement, has established that the clitoris is made up of eighteen distinct and interrelated structures. Biometric analysis of a diverse sample of female genitals has "proven that there is a great range of variation in women's genital dimensions, including clitoral size, labial length and color" (Lloyd et al. 2005). However, mapping, representing, and defining the clitoris is not just a matter of genital anatomy; it is a political act.

The clitoris has many competing and contradictory narratives that vary depending upon personal, cultural, political, and historical circumstances. Based on who is defining the clitoris, it can be classified as an inverted and diminutive penis, a small erectile female sex organ, a love button, an unhygienic appendage to be removed, a site of immature female sexual expression, a key piece of evidence of sexual perversion, a vibrant subject of pornographic mediations, or an important part of female sexual experience.

Ritual Genital Cutting

The relationship between genital anatomy and sexuality has led Western women to use elective genital surgery to make the vaginal labia look "pretty" and to enhance clitoral sensitivity, yet they condemn ritual genital cutting in Africa. African feminists have claimed that "Western eyes" only see cultural oppression and subordination of women in these practices, calling it mutilation, whereas they themselves are not so condemnatory. In the following excerpt, Wairimũ Ngaruiya Njambi, a women's studies and sociology professor, described the Kenyan ritual of *irua ria atumia*, a circumcision coming-of-age ceremony for girls, from an African perspective.

Telling My Story

Wairimũ Ngaruiya Njambi
Florida Atlantic University, Jupiter

M y intent in this section is not to provide yet another universal account of how female circumcision should be viewed, or even a comprehensive or "authentic" view of Gĩkuyũ practices, but rather to demonstrate the situatedness of bodies in relation to such practices, all the while recalling Haraway's point that "Location is also partial in the sense of being *for* some worlds and not others" (1997: 37, emphasis in original). Additionally, I see myself as a post-colonial product; a hybrid; raised as a Catholic in a rural peasant family in central Kenya, now living and teaching in the US—with all ambivalences about cultural practices that such a mixture can produce. Such a story matters to me first of all because it is rendered invisible and unimportant by anti-FGM discourse.

In Gĩkuyũ context, culture and bodies are not held separately, and they are historically tied very closely to circumcision, for both women and men. The oral history I encountered while growing up presented *irua ria atumia* (female circumcision) as a ritual that was appropriated by the Gĩkuyũ women, from a neighbouring ethnic group, as a way of introducing a celebration of "womanhood" to a culture that only celebrated "manhood." Yet this empowering image was reconfigured within Christianity. As Edgerton notes, "for reasons that remain obscure, the church did not object to the [Gĩkuyũ] practices of circumcising teen-aged boys, but it regarded the circumcision of adolescent girls as barbaric" (Edgerton, 1989: 40). To me this reflects a common Judeo-Christian assumption that circumcised male bodies are normal and acceptable, and even that painful passage to manhood is desirable. On the other hand, the same tradition upholds a presumption that female bodies are innately passive and should be protected from such pain. Contrary to missionary concern, for Gĩkuyũ women, as for men, enduring pain bravely is also integral to the passage of womanhood, as Kratz (1994) observed. Additionally, given the dominant view that men transcend nature while women remain nature-associated, it is possible to suggest that *irua* offers a clear case in which women disrupt such a paternalistic dualism as a way of marking their entry into culture.

While the cultural significance of female circumcision has been waning in the past few decades, due mainly to church pressures, its cultural importance was still strong enough during my youth that I saw it as a necessity. It may seem ironic, given the tales of "flight from torture" told in the media, but my parents refused to allow me to be circumcised, as it was against Catholic teachings. I had to threaten to run away from home and drop out of school before my parents relented and allowed me to be circumcised. The procedure was performed with a medical scalpel in a local clinic run by a woman who was a trained nurse in the western sense, and also a relative of an important Gĩkuyũ female medical healer and powerful leader of the early 20th century, Wairimũ Wa Kĩnene. During the operation, the hood of the clitoris was cut through its apex which caused the hood to split open and the clitoris to become more completely exposed. Such exposure has been associated with sexual enhancement. However, any generalization here might be unwise as it is likely that women's experience of *irua* varies, perhaps significantly.

Performed in a time of many social transformations in the 1970s, my circumcision was not the communal experience it would have been in earlier decades, an event that would have tied me forever to other women and men of my "age-set" *(riika).* However, despite shifting cultural forms, circumcision still continued to be fundamentally important in that those who were circumcised were inscribed with the status and privilege of "womanhood." Usually performed on girls aged 14–16, Gĩkuyũ female circumcision, like many other forms, does not involve holding young women down so that they cannot escape their "torture" from "mutilating villains." Rather, it is a chance for teenage girls to demonstrate their bravery by unflinchingly accepting their moment of pain, as mentioned in some Gĩkuyũ songs.

Prior to my circumcision, my circumcised age-mates still considered me (16, at the time) a child. With their newly acquired "womanhood," they wore a new "no nonsense" attitude that demanded the attention of most adults around. I was not allowed to join the more serious conversations about topics such as menstrual cycles, pregnancy, and sexual fantasies. I could not talk to other adults without having to worry about the words I chose to employ, without having to worry about interrupting someone. I was required, with all the other little kids (!), to cover my ears with my hands whenever grown-ups made sexual jokes with one another that children were not allowed to hear. All the uncircumcised girls (Irĩgũ) and boys (Ihĩĩ), seen as childish and immature, were required to respect and to give up their seats when requested. In fact, the most profoundly humiliating insult that one can level at a Gĩkuyũ adult is to accuse them of acting like an "uncircumcised" boy or girl. Today, however, as the importance of female circumcision declines, this insult has less power over women than it does over men, for whom circumcision remains a must.

By completing my *irua,* I became a Gĩkuyũ woman. And even though the concept of "age-set" had been disrupted by the time of my circumcision, I entered a category whose pleasures and benefits were previously denied to me. As a 16-year-old girl, I just wanted to become a woman like many other Gĩkuyũ girls, problematically or unproblematically. . . .

Far from maliciously torturing women, circumcision not only gave Gĩkuyũ women some access to social, political and economic power in an undeniably patriarchial society, but it also allowed them to be keepers of Gĩkuyũ history, a valuable responsibility. Furthermore, apart from their obvious gendered differences in relation to the surgical operation and cultural expectations associated with each, there was little difference in the ceremonial aspects of female and male circumcision. Both women and men were circumcised on the same day, they wore the same ceremonial clothing, they both were secluded in the forest (for educational instructions) for the same time period.

For the Gĩkuyũ, the circumcision initiation did not stand by itself, but was integrated with other social activities, such as *ngwĩko*, a communal sexual practice for newly circumcised women and men after the healing period. According to my grandmother (Njoki), *ngwĩko* itself was accompanied by a series of long dances that took place throughout the day after which, as the night approached, groups of women and men were paired and moved together into a *kĩrĩrĩ* (women's hut), or a *thingira* (men's hut). During this time, both women and men were expected to engage in sexual activity where both would take multiple sexual partners in a one-night session. . . .

A Reflexive Look at *Irua Ria Atumia*

My intention here is not to suggest that *irua* for the Gĩkuyũ is better or any less problematic than other cultural practices that mark women's bodies in one way or another. And probably no amount of critical reflexivity will protect me here from those who, when criticized for imperialist and arrogant representations of "Others," are quick to dismiss such criticism as nothing more than a mindless defence of tradition. However, far from blindly celebrating the Gĩkuyũ *irua ria atumia* and my experience of it, I am perfectly aware that it is never possible for any cultural practice, no matter how small, powerful, acceptable or desirable, to be non-problematic. For values and interests only exist in competition with other values and interests. Consider that, to some extent, the deployment of circumcision rituals is part of an attempt to galvanize an essential "Gĩkuyũ identity" in relation to neighbouring ethnicities and later to colonial intrusions. In 2003 a contemporary Gĩkuyũ social movement called *Mũngiki* is engaged in what one would call a dangerous form of revivalism, even fundamentalism, of "Gĩkuyũ culture" in the face of social change. Embracing female circumcision as an important component of this revival, some *Mũngiki* members are reported in the Kenyan media to have resorted to violence against some Gĩkuyũ women who resist this reinscription. As Edward Said makes clear in *Culture and Imperialism,* one danger here lies in the assumption that there is such a thing as one uncontaminated (Gĩkuyũ) "identity" or "culture" that exists "out there" in the first place—and into which some would automatically (or forcibly) be included while others are excluded.

At the same time, to re-emphasize a question I raised earlier, in the presence of so many religious and other cultural disputes over practices of female circumcision, is it possible to say that the decision to refrain from such practices is not equally a product of specific values and interests? For example, should we say that those in my village who refrained from practices of female circumcision but who chose Christianity instead (like those who assert "science" as on their side) cleverly and safely managed to escape the markings of culture? Are their bodies any less culturally marked than those whose bodies underwent practices of female circumcision? To answer "yes" to these ques-

tions allies one with common fixations (feminist or otherwise) on dichoto-
mies of bodily oppression (via circumcision) versus freedom (via eradication).
I instead would like to move the dialogue to rethink this idea that bodies
exist outside of cultural performativity, and to look at multiple and heterogeneous ways in which not only cultures, bodies, and sexualities emerge in
contextualized entanglements, but also the kinds of negotiations and ambi-
guities that are involved in such processes. For instance, while circumcised
women are at times invited to describe its impact on their sexuality or their
ability to achieve orgasm, there is no interrogation of the constructions of
"sexuality" and "orgasm" upon which the discussion is based.

Also, it is important to point out that all genital operations (like all other
physical operations) come with the risk of infections and bleeding, and *irua* is
not an exception to such problems. This is especially the case in places where
the healing practices that once accompanied *irua* have been discontinued
and the new healing procedures are expensive, or have not been adopted
due to fear of prosecution in places where circumcision is outlawed. My question is how do we situate the potential for infections associated with female
circumcision in the context of similar risks with the multitude of other body
modifications practised by people worldwide?

Besides those of female circumcision, consider similarities with abortion
practices, which, when driven underground, routinely result in serious health
problems and even death for women and girls. Yet our consistent call is for
"safe and legal" abortions, rather than their eradication, on the basis that
women should control their own bodies. Also consider the host of legal and
fashionable body modifications (in the US especially) such as tattooing, pierc-
ing, penis/clitoris slicing, tongue slicing, and cosmetic procedures (including
Botox injections, liposuction, breast implants, and female genital trimming)
that escape the "mutilation" label. How is it determined which of these practices leads to a risk that warrants the emergence of a global eradication
movement? How do we discuss these issues without creating an imperialistic
impression that only those with some social, political, and economic power
and who live in the west have rights to take risks with their bodies?

References

Edgerton, R. B. (1989) *Mau Mau: An African Crucible*. New York: The Free Press.
Haraway, D. J. (1997) *Modest_Witness@Second_Millennium.FemaleMan©_Meets_OncoMouseTM;
Feminism and Technoscience*. New York: Routledge.
Kratz, C. A. (1994) *Affecting Performance: Meaning, Movement and Experience in Okiek
Women's Initiation*. Washington and London: Smithsonian Institution Press.
Said, Edward (1994) *Culture and Imperialism*. London: Vintage.

Western feminists commenting on Njambi's article noted that culture itself is socially constructed, shaped by power relations, changeable over time, and not universally accepted in a society. Western femi-

nists, therefore, can ally with African feminists opposed to ritual genital cutting and support their efforts at education and development of rituals that do not involve body modification.

The Unattainable Venus: Cosmetic Surgeries

Elective cosmetic surgery—breast implants or reshaping, face-lifts, liposuction to remove fat deposits, Botox injections to smooth out wrinkles, and collagen injections to enlarge lips—are extremely popular in Western societies. From a feminist perspective, there is, on the one hand, a sense that people who have elective procedures to alter their faces and bodies are hapless conformists to culturally imposed ideals of youth and beauty, and on the other, there is recognition of choice and autonomy in women's decisions to have cosmetic surgery. Of course, the choices are considerably narrowed by the cost of these procedures. There are also medical issues; the surgeries may be cosmetic, but they are still surgeries. In the following excerpt, Victoria Pitts, a sociologist, explores the issue of how medicalization affects social pressures and women's agency in the use of cosmetic surgeries.

The Surface and the Depth: Medicalization, Beauty, and Body Image in Cosmetic Surgery

Victoria Pitts
Queens College and the Graduate Center, City University of New York

One of the reasons why feminists have been so opposed to cosmetic surgery is that the practice medicalizes norms of appearance, making it seem as if only beautiful people are healthy. What is a social issue—idealization of certain looks and their economic and social rewards—is turned into a supposedly objective medical issue. Any deviation from a standardized ideal then becomes a curable illness. The too-long nose can be shortened, the too-short chin can be lengthened, protruding ears can be flattened, and bags under the eyes can be removed. The wrinkles and laugh lines of age can be erased, and fat deposits can be liposuctioned away. Breasts can be made larger or smaller, vaginas can be tightened, and penises can be lengthened.

The standards by which these features are measured are certainly racialized, classed, and gendered—in other words, they are expressions of primary power relationships in society. In fact, much of the history of cosmetic surgery can be seen as the history of "passing," where devalued ethnic groups and recent immigrants came to plastic surgeons for remedies for their physical signs of "otherness," in the hope that economic and social success would follow (Gilman 1999). Male and female American Jews, African Americans, and Irish immigrants were targeted candidates for cosmetic surgery in the nineteenth and early twentieth century.

In the twentieth century, cosmetic surgery became even more gendered, particularly with the advent of breast implants in the 1960s. Eventually, cosmetic surgeons began to promote a female body that was not so much normalized as technologized, with body proportions unlikely to be found outside of the surgeon's office. For instance, in addition to the enormous popularity of breast implants, we have seen the advent of rib removals to create a tiny waistline and foot reshaping to allow fitting into narrow, pointy-toed shoes. Procedures like these allow the creation of female bodies that seem to transcend the ordinary aging process, that adhere to current standards of beauty, and sometimes, that fulfill the most spectacular heteronormative imaginaries of enormous breasts, tiny waists, and seemingly ageless skin.

The medicalization of beauty masks social norms with the scientific language of objectivity, making less visible the political implications of the dominance of Anglo-Saxon ideal faces and thin, busty bodies. Even so, cosmetic surgery has always been controversial among doctors and the larger public, partly because it is highly commercialized, and partly because it operates on (and thus puts in some risk) healthy bodies. To buttress their medical legitimacy, cosmetic surgeons have relied on psychological theories like Alfred Adler's "inferiority complex" to establish a medical basis for the gains of cosmetic surgery. The inferiority-complex argument suggested that patients would improve their self-esteem, unburden themselves from the stigma of abnormalcy, and alleviate their long-term feelings of inferiority by undergoing cosmetic surgery. Thus, if scientific medicalization of the body's surface was not enough to convince people of cosmetic surgery's medical worth, then the medicalization of the body's depth—its psyche—might accomplish it.

In recent years, however, with the unprecedented explosion of popular interest in cosmetic surgery, surgeons have become less defensive about their practices. Now surgeons are much more willing to operate on people who have normal features, to perform multiple operations on a single patient, and to design body transformations that were unthinkable only one or two decades ago. There is a much greater market for cosmetic surgery than ever before, and cosmetic surgery has responded by embracing its new role with enthusiasm and market savvy. Surgeons have begun to use more aggressive direct-to-consumer advertising, and they have endorsed television reality shows on cosmetic surgery, such as *Extreme Makeover*. (The American Society of Plastic Surgery approved its doctor members' participation on the show.) Some surgeons now even advertise their own "extreme makeovers"—packages of multiple surgeries performed at once—for prospective patients.

In a number of ways, cosmetic surgeons mix medical with aesthetic indications, blurring the line between them to be able to do more than one lucrative procedure at a time and to negotiate medical insurance payments. For instance, patients seeking help for drooping eyelids that are interfering with eyesight may be persuaded to also have bags under their eyes removed, surgery that medical insurance will not pay for alone. Patients who want to improve the appearance of their noses have been diagnosed with deviated septums, which they might not otherwise have had corrected, so that they can get insurance coverage for rhinoplasty. In the United Kingdom and the Netherlands, even cosmetic surgeries like breast reductions and implants have been paid for by national health programs when the patients' bodies have met certain guidelines that allowed the procedures to be deemed medically necessary.

In addition, some surgeries are touted as good for physical health. Until recently, when published studies began to show otherwise, liposuction (removing fat deposits) was touted as a quick and easy surgical response to the health problems caused by obesity. Studies now suggest that losing weight through liposuction offers none of the health benefits of losing weight through exercise and diet (Klein et al. 2004). Genital cosmetic surgeries for women are being advertised as reconstructions for sexual health: vagina-tightening surgery to restore women to their pre-childbirth naturally "healthy" state.

The pathologization of the effects of aging and childbirth and any deviations from narrow norms of beauty are deeply worrying to feminists. Virginia Blum (2003) argued that women will "become surgical": After their first cosmetic surgery they will begin to see their bodies as cosmetic surgeons do, as infinitely repairable. Kathryn Pauly Morgan (1991) described a "technological imperative" that coerces women into seeing themselves from the perspective of "fix-up" technologies. Other feminists argue that cosmetic surgery defines women's looks by the "male gaze" that objectifies and sexualizes them. In this sense, cosmetic surgeons, most of whom are men, are replicating and reinforcing the way male-dominated Western culture views women. If women are dissatisfied with their bodies, they are viewing themselves through men's eyes. Kathy Davis argued that women are using cosmetic surgery to alleviate the psychological suffering that attends women's concern with appearance (2003, 41).

The medicalized, high-tech male gaze is not only heteronormative; it also makes women's bodies into objects that need constant maintenance and improvement. The female body is measured against the airbrushed images presented in celebrity culture, advertising, and pornography, and an increasing range of women's body parts are subject to surgical "improvement" modeled after idealized images. One recent addition to the offerings by cosmetic surgeons is labiaplasty, in which women's vaginal lips are cut and reshaped to look prettier and more erotically appealing. The surgical "beautification" of female genitalia, as transparently heteronormative and gendered as the project may be, proceeds like all cosmetic surgeries under the auspices of medical authority and legitimacy. In addition to beautification, women are promised better self-esteem, better sexual relations with their partners, and enhanced sexual sensation through removal of skin that may cover the clitoris.

Body Image 'Disorder'

Ironically, the use of cosmetic surgery itself is being turned into a medical disorder—body dysmorphic disorder (BDD), or distortion of body image. While psychological theories have long been used in cosmetic surgery discourse to promote its benefits, the vast rise in the number of cosmetic surgery patients in the past twenty years has been accompanied by a psychiatric assessment of "appropriate" criteria for its use. Cosmetic surgery patients are now being sorted as "good" and "bad" through tests of their body-self attitudes. These are formal and informal screenings for BDD, a relatively new psychiatric diagnosis formally recognized by the *Diagnostic and Statistical Manual of Mental Disorders* in 1997 (Arthur and Monnell 2005). It is now being applied to some cosmetic surgery patients who appear obsessed with their bodies.

In the mass media, BDD is discussed as a new social problem. It is accompanied by efforts from some psychiatrists—specialists in BDD—to publicize the disorder through the proliferation of books, websites, and television shows to educate the public on appropriate expectations for cosmetic surgery. There is even a cosmetic surgery self-help culture that teaches prospective patients which reasons for it are legitimate and which are illegitimate, and which kinds of patients are normal and which might be pathological. For example, "flags" for psychological problems "in dealing with your body image" include having surgery in the same area more than several times; being under treatment for anxiety, depression, or sleep disorder; having a drug or alcohol problem; being in the "middle of a life crisis"; and having "concerns regarding gender/sexual identity issues" (Ganny and Collini 2000, 41).

Taming the Cosmetic Surgery 'Frankenstein'

The diagnoses of BDD and surgery addiction, the development of screening practices for surgeons, and the framing of body-image dissatisfaction and too much cosmetic surgery as social problems are ways the medical profession is trying to socially manage the virtual explosion of cosmetic surgery in the United States. Now that it is more affordable and socially acceptable, doctors and the lay public are attempting to establish new normative boundaries for cosmetic surgery. What kinds of surgeries, and which kinds of patients, will we culturally, medically, and legally accept? What are the acceptable and unacceptable reasons for cosmetic surgery? Who are the acceptable and unacceptable patients? Who will have the power to determine the answers to these questions will set new norms for surgical body modification and healthy body images.

References

Arthur, Gary K., and Kim Monnell. 2005. "Body Dysmorphic Disorder." *Emedicine*, 29 June. *www.emedicine.com/med/topic3124.htm*

Blum, Virginia. 2003. *Flesh Wounds: The Culture of Cosmetic Surgery.* Berkeley: University of California Press.

Davis, Kathy. 2003. *Dubious Equalities and Embodied Differences: Cultural Studies on Cosmetic Surgery.* New York: Rowman and Littlefield.

Ganny, Charlee, and Susan J. Collini. 2000. *Two Girlfriends Get Real About Cosmetic Surgery.* Los Angeles: Renaissance Books.
Gilman, Sander L. 1999. *Making the Body Beautiful: A Cultural History of Aesthetic Surgery.* Princeton, NJ: Princeton University Press.
Klein, Samuel, Luigi Fontana, V. Leroy Young et al. 2004. "Absence of an Effect of Liposuction on Insulin Action and Risk Factors for Coronary Heart Disease." *New England Journal of Medicine* 350, 2549–2557.
Pauly Morgan, Kathryn. 1991. "Women and the Knife: Cosmetic Surgery and the Colonization of Women's Bodies." *Hypatia* 6 (3), 25–53.

Original article commissioned for this book.

Breasts and Body Image

Given the social importance of breasts in modern Western gendered societies, the incidence of both breast augmentation and breast reduction have skyrocketed with the increasing popularity of cosmetic surgeries in the last twenty years. During the same period, mammograms and self-examinations have led to a rise in the number of women who find they have breast cancer. So, on the one hand, we have elective cosmetic surgery on breasts to enhance sexual attractiveness to men, and on the other, we have women faced with losing a breast in a society that equates breasts with femininity.

A compilation of statistics shows that breast cancer is the leading cancer among White and African American women in the United States, but African American women are more likely to die from this disease. In 2005, it was estimated that about 212,000 new cases of invasive breast cancer would be diagnosed, along with 58,000 new cases of noninvasive breast cancer, with 40,000 women expected to die from it (Breastcancer.org 2005).

Treatment choices today are combinations of chemotherapy, radiation, hormonal therapies, breast-conserving surgery (removal of the cancerous lump), and mastectomy (removal of the entire breast). The course of treatment is supposedly governed by type and stage of the cancer, risk and benefit statistics, and prognosis, but as with so much about the body, social, cultural, and power issues enter into the choices. Less invasive surgery (lump removal) conserves the breast but entails undergoing radiation. Complete breast removal is usually followed by a course of chemotherapy.

For women with breast cancer, the choice of type of treatment (lump removal versus removal of the entire breast and reconstruction) are heavily influenced by their body image. Many doctors advocate less invasive surgery, but studies have shown that patients make their decision based on body image as well as assessment of risks and their medical and financial resources (Figueiredo et al. 2004). Their feelings about their bodies also influence whether they will undergo the additional surgery for breast reconstruction (Kasper 1995). In general, breast-conserving surgery is chosen more often by younger, richer, urban women treated in larger teaching hospitals, with lower use by African Americans (Katz et al. 2005; Nattinger 2005). The researchers conclude that women of all ages should be given a range of treatment choices and that their feelings about their body image should be taken seriously by their doctors. As one woman said,

> The physical reconstruction and the emotional well-being are two separate things. I don't see it just because now I have a reconstructed breast, I'm whole again. It's something I have to work out for myself, cognitively, emotionally, instead of just looking in the mirror and seeing another breast there. (Kasper 1995, 212)

Eating Disorders: Controlling the Body

Dieting to control weight is so common among women that it seems to be a perennial topic of dinner-table conversation, at least among older women. Younger women are more likely to resort to extreme dieting and to hide their not eating or eating and throwing up from their family and friends, going online for support. *Anorexia* (self-starvation) and *bulimia* (binge eating and induced vomiting) are extreme ways to lose weight in order to meet Western cultural standards of beauty and to maintain control over one's body (Bordo [1993] 2005; Gremillion 2002; Jacobs Brumberg 1988, 1998). Medical measurements of "obesity" are based on idealized averages for height, weight, and gender, but body imagery as "fat" or "thin" or "perfect" emerges from cultural influences. Racial ethnic and social class eating patterns and views of healthy weight combine with available food and ideals of feminine beauty to make a group prone to obesity and to developing eating disorders (Markey 2004).

Young, White, heterosexual, middle-class college women who are dissatisfied with their body image are particularly vulnerable to eating disorders (Cooley and Toray 2001). Heterosexual women are subject to pressure from the media and the significant men in their lives to stay thin to be sexually attractive. Lesbians, whose views of beauty are not influenced by men's opinions, are heavier than comparable heterosexual women, more satisfied with their bodies, and less likely to have eating disorders (Herzog et al. 1992).

A different rationale for eating problems was found in intensive interviews with women who were heterogeneous on racial group, class, and sexual orientation (Thompson 1994). For these African American, Latina, and White women, binge eating and purging were ways of coping with the traumas of their lives—sexual abuse, poverty, racism, and prejudice against lesbians. Eating offered the same comfort as drinking but was cheaper and more controllable. Rather than a response to the culture of thinness, for these women, anorexia and bulimia were responses to injustice.

More personalized factors have emerged in cult-like positive views of anorexia and bulimia as demonstrations of the power to control one's body and even to have a transcendental "out-of-body" experience (Lintott 2003). Not eating or getting rid of what one has eaten becomes a way of life, a crusade for self-control (Hornbacher 1998). Eating disorders, in this view, are a triumph of mind over body:

> Eating disorders involve the view of one's body as "other," as something that can be dominated. In order to view the body and its needs as a natural force that can be overcome, there must be something responsible for the overcoming. . . . The eating-disordered individual locates herself in that part of her that is able to contemplate objects immense in size and to resist forces that threaten to destroy her: her hunger and desire for food. . . . (Lintott 2003, 75)

In this sense, eating disorders are seen not as giving in to oppressive norms of beauty or thinness but as going beyond the body entirely.

Critical Summary

In the social construction of women's bodies, a good touchstone is, "Don't take anything for granted." First, there's no such thing as a "real woman." All women's bodies are made in conformity or resistance or inventive adaptation to social norms and expectations. Second, the lines between agency and submission to social pressures are not so clear. A woman who conforms to heteronormative standards of beauty by undergoing cosmetic surgery may feel liberated and empowered by her choice. A woman with breast cancer has to come to terms with a new body image and a realization that no surgery will return her to "normal." A woman with an eating disorder may see herself as triumphantly transcending her body, just as a woman who has had a face-lift may see herself as conquering age.

Feminists are divided on many of these body issues. Third-wave feminist menstrual activists are reclaiming their bodies from medicalization and industrialization and freeing themselves from taboos and shame. They reject the biologically centered goddess imagery of radical feminism, but they end up making menstruation a major part of their lives, in a way that many second-wave feminists long put behind them. The politics of the anti-genital cutting movement produces friction between African and Western feminists.

From one point of view, elective cosmetic surgery to enhance one's looks and sexuality is autonomous, but from another, it is a choice within a cultural atmosphere of the importance of men's admiration. Undergoing surgery to look young, thin, and sexy conforms to the prevailing heteronormativity—appeal to the opposite sex. Ironically, when men have face-lifts to look younger, they are often seeking to maintain their economic positions and social status, not to enhance their physical appeal to women.

Eating disorders and obesity are a particularly problematic issue. Feminists may claim that women should be able to do whatever they want with their bodies, whether it is conforming or rebellious. But obesity is not just a matter of eating too much—there are racial, ethnic, social class, and environmental public health issues implicated in "fat as feminist issue" (Yancey, Leslie, and Abel 2006). Extreme dieting can be seen as a reaction to the stigmatization of fatness or an autonomous choice. But, like pride in a fat body, cosmetic surgery, and other body manipulations, extreme dieting is a way to literally take one's life into one's own hands, since they all increase the chances of ill health.

References and Recommended Readings

Braun, Virginia, and Celia Kitzinger. 2001. "Telling It Straight? Dictionary Definitions of Women's Genitals." *Journal of Sociolinguistics* 5, 214–233.

Buckley, Thomas, and Alma Gottlieb (eds.). 1988. *Blood Magic: The Anthropology of Menstruation.* Berkeley: University of California Press.

Carpenter, Laura M. 2005. *Virginity Lost: An Intimate Portrait of First Sexual Experiences.* New York: New York University Press.

Chalker, Rebecca. 2002. *The Clitoral Truth: The Secret World at Your Fingertips.* New York: Seven Stories Press.

Chrisler, Joan C., and Ingrid Johnston-Robledo (eds.). 2002. Special Issue: Behavioral Science Research on Menstruation and Menopause. *Sex Roles* 46 (1/2), 1–59.

Colombo, Realdo. 1559. *De Re Anatomica.* Venice: N. Bevilaqua.

Davis, Kathy. 1995. *Reshaping the Female Body: The Dilemma of Cosmetic Surgery.* New York: Routledge.

Federation of Feminist Women's Health Centers. 1981. *A New View of the Woman's Body.* New York: Simon & Schuster.

Figueiredo, M. I. et al. 2004. "Body Image Important for Older Women in Choosing Surgery." *Journal of Clinical Oncology,* 1 October. *www.breastcancer.org/research_surgery_113004.html*

Freud, Sigmund. [1905] 1962. *Three Essays on the Theory of Sexuality* (trans. James Strachey). New York: Basic Books.

Gimlin, Debra L. 2002. *Body Work: Beauty and Self-Image in American Culture.* Berkeley: University of California Press.

Haiken, Elizabeth. 1999. *Venus Envy: A History of Cosmetic Surgery.* Baltimore: Johns Hopkins.

Hite, Shere. 1976. *The Hite Report: A Nationwide Study on Female Sexuality.* New York: Macmillan.

Hobson, Janell. 2005. *Venus in the Dark: Blackness and Beauty in Popular Culture.* New York: Routledge.

Kinsey, Alfred C. et al. 1953. *Sexual Behavior in the Human Female.* Philadelphia: W. B. Saunders.

Knight, Chris. 1991. *Blood Relations: Menstruation and the Origins of Culture.* New Haven, CT: Yale University Press.

Laqueur, Thomas. 1990. *Making Sex: Body and Gender From the Greeks to Freud.* Cambridge, MA: Harvard University Press.

Laws, Sophie. 1990. *Issues of Blood: The Politics of Menstruation.* London: Macmillan.

Lloyd, Elisabeth A. 2005. *The Case of the Female Orgasm: Bias in the Science of Evolution.* Cambridge, MA: Harvard University Press.

Lloyd, Jillian, Naomi Crouch, Catherine Minto, Lih-Mei Liao, and Sarah Creighton. 2005. "Female Genital Appearance: 'Normality' Unfolds." *British Journal of Obstetrics and Gynaecology* 112 (5), 643.

Moore, Lisa Jean, and Adele E. Clarke. 1995. "Clitoral Conventions and Transgressions: Graphic Representations of Female Genital Anatomy, c1900–1991." *Feminist Studies* 21, 255–301.

———. 2001. "The Traffic in Cyberanatomies: Sex/Gender/Sexualities in Local and Global Formations." *Body and Society* 7, 57–96.

Murphy, Michelle. 2004. "Immodest Witnessing: The Epistemology of the Vaginal Self-Examination in the U.S. Feminist Self-Help Movement." *Feminist Studies* 30, 115–147.

Roach Anleu, Sharyn. 2006. "Gendered Bodies: Between Conformity and Autonomy." In *Handbook of Gender and Women's Studies,* edited by Kathy Davis, Mary Evans, and Judith Lorber. London: Sage.

"Sex Tricks From Skin Flicks." 2000. *Men's Health* 15 (7), 54.

"Special Feature on Body Image." 2004. *Off Our Backs* 34 (11/12), November–December, 13–69.

Steinem, Gloria. 1978. "If Men Could Menstruate—A Political Fantasy." *MS. Magazine* October, 110.

Aging

Cruikshank, Margaret. 2003. *Learning to Be Old: Gender, Culture, and Aging.* Lanham, MD: Rowman and Littlefield.

Kelly, Jennifer. 2005. *Zest for Life: Lesbians Experience Menopause.* Melbourne, Australia: Spinifex Press.

Lock, Margaret, and P. Kaufert. 2001. "Menopause, Local Biologies, and Cultures of Aging." *American Journal of Human Biology* 13, 494–504.

Morganroth Gullette, Margaret. 2004. *Aged by Culture.* Chicago: University of Chicago Press.

"Special Feature on Women and Aging." 2005. *Off Our Backs* 35 (9/10), September–October, 22–50.

Winterich, Julie. 2003. "Sex, Menopause, and Culture: Sexual Orientation and the Meaning of Menopause for Women's Sex Lives." *Gender & Society* 17, 627–642.

Winterich, Julie, and Debra Umberson. 1999. "How Women Experience Menopause: The Importance of Social Context." *Journal of Women and Aging* 11 (4), 57–73.

Breast Cancer

Breastcancer.org. 2005. *www.breastcancer.org/press_cancer_facts.html*

Gagné, Patricia, and Deanna McGaughey. 2002. "Designing Women: Cultural Hegemony and the Exercise of Power Among Women Who Have Undergone Elective Mammoplasty." *Gender & Society* 16, 814–838.

Hartman, Stephanie. 2004. "Reading the Scar in Breast Cancer Poetry." *Feminist Studies* 30, 155–177.

Hobler Kahane, Deborah. 1995. *No Less a Woman: Femininity, Sexuality, and Breast Cancer* (second revised edition). Alameda, CA: Hunter House.

Kasper, Anne S. 1995. "The Social Construction of Breast Loss and Reconstruction." *Women's Health Research on Gender, Behavior, and Policy* 1, 197–219.

Kasper, Anne S., and Susan J. Ferguson (eds.). 2000. *Breast Cancer: Society Shapes an Epidemic.* New York: St. Martin's.

Katz, Steven J., Paula M. Lantz, Nancy K. Janz et al. 2005. "Patient Involvement in Surgery Treatment Decisions for Breast Cancer." *Journal of Clinical Oncology* 23 (24), 5526–5533.

Lorde, Audre. 1980. *The Cancer Journals.* San Francisco: Aunt Lute Books.

Nattinger, Ann B. 2005. "Variation in the Choice of Breast-Conserving Surgery or Mastectomy: Patient or Physician Decision Making?" *Journal of Clinical Oncology* 23 (24), 5429–5431.

Yalom, Marilyn. 1997. *History of the Breast.* New York: Knopf.

Eating Disorders

Bordo, Susan R. [1993] 2005. *Unbearable Weight: Feminism, Western Culture, and the Body.* Berkeley: University of California Press.

——. 1998. *The Body Project: An Intimate History of American Girls.* New York: Vintage.

Cooley, E., and T. Toray. 2001. "Body Image and Personality Predictors of Eating Disorder Symptoms During the College Years." *International Journal of Eating Disorders* 30, 28–36.

Gremillion, H. 2002. "In Fitness and in Health: Crafting Bodies in the Treatment of Anorexia Nervosa." *Signs* 27, 381–414.

Herzog, David B., Kerry L. Newman, C. J. Yeh, and Meredith Warshaw. 1992. "Body Image Satisfaction in Homosexual and Heterosexual Women." *International Journal of Eating Disorders* 11, 391–396.

Hornbacher, Marya. 1998. *Wasted: A Memoir of Anorexia and Bulimia.* New York: HarperCollins.

Jacobs Brumberg, Joan. 1988. *Fasting Girls: The Emergence of Anorexia Nervosa as a Modern Disease.* Cambridge, MA: Harvard University Press.

Lintott, Sheila. 2003. "Sublime Hunger: A Consideration of Eating Disorders Beyond Beauty." *Hypatia* 18, 65–86.

Markey, Charlotte. 2004. "Culture and the Development of Eating Disorders: A Tripartite Model." *Eating Disorders: Journal of Treatment and Prevention* 12, 139–156.

Miller, M. N., and A. J. Pumariega. 2001. "Culture and Eating Disorders: A Historical and Cross-Cultural Review." *Psychiatry* 64, 93–110.

Shaw, Gina. 2005. "Pro-Anorexia Web Sites: The Thin Web Line." *www.webmd.com/content/Article/109/109381.htm*

Thompson, Becky W. 1994. *A Hunger So Wide and So Deep: American Women Speak Out on Eating Problems.* Minneapolis: University of Minnesota Press.

Wann, Marilyn. 1998. *Fat!So? Because You Don't Have to Apologize for Your Size.* Berkeley, CA: Ten Speed Press.

Yancey, Antronette K., Joanne Leslie, and Emily K. Abel. 2006. "Obesity at the Crossroads: Feminist and Public Health Perspectives." *Signs* 31, 425–443.

Genital Cutting

Abusharaf, Rogaia Mustafa. 2001. "Virtuous Cuts: Female Genital Mutilation in an African Ontology." *Differences* 12, 112–140.

Frueh, Joanna. 2003. "Vaginal Aesthetics." *Hypatia* 18, 137–158.

Gruenbaum, Ellen. 2000. *The Female Circumcision Controversy: An Anthropological Perspective.* Philadelphia: University of Pennsylvania Press.

Mahklouf Obermeyer, Carla. 1999. "Female Genital Surgeries: The Known, the Unknown, and the Unknowable." *Medical Anthropology Quarterly* 13, 79–106.

Njambi, Wairimũ Ngaruiya. 2004. "Dualisms and Female Bodies in Representations of African Female Circumcision." *Feminist Theory* 5, 281–303. Responses by Kathy Davis (305–311), Claudia Castañeda (311–317), Millsom Henry-Waring (317–323), and reply (325–328).

Rahman, Anika, and Nahid Toubia. 2000. *Female Genital Mutilation: A Guide to Laws and Policies Worldwide.* London: Zed Books.

Shell-Duncan, Bettina, and Ylva Hernlund (eds.). 2000. *Female "Circumcision" in Africa: Culture, Controversy, and Change.* Boulder, CO: Lynn Reinner.

Walker, Alice. 1992. *Possessing the Secret of Joy.* New York: Harcourt, Brace, Jovanovich.

Webber, Sara. 2003. "Cutting History, Cutting Culture: Female Circumcision in the United States." *American Journal of Bioethics* 3, 65–66.

Internet Sources

American Cancer Society
  www.cancer.org
Ana's Underground Grotto
  ca.dir.yahoo.com/Health/Diseases_and_Conditions/Anorexia_Nervosa/Pro_Anorexia

Below the Belt
www.deadletters.biz/belowthebelt

Breast Implants
www.fda.gov/cdrh/breastimplants

Community Message Board
dmoz.org/Society/Issues/Health/Body_Image/Pro-Anorexia

Female Genital Mutilation Education and Networking Project
www.fgmnetwork.org/html/index.php

Museum of Menstruation and Women's Health
www.mum.org

Museum of the Menovulatory Lifetime
www.moltx.org

National Association to Advance Fat Acceptance (NAAFA)
www.naafa.org

National Cancer Institute
www.nci.nih.gov

National Comprehensive Cancer Network®
www.nccn.org

Old Lesbians Organizing for Change
www.oloc.org

Our Bodies, Ourselves Web Companion
www.ourbodiesourselves/org

Pro-anorexia and Pro-bulimia Information
www.womensissues.about.com/cs/proanorexia

Red Web Foundation
www.theredweb.org

Size Matters Online
www.sizematterstoo.com

Society for Menstrual Cycle Research
http://menstruationresearch.org

The SPOT: Tampon Health
www.spotsite.org

Student Environmental Action Coalition Tampaction Campaign
www.seac.org/tampons ✦

Chapter 5

Adonis, Don Juan, and 'Real Men'

Constructing Men's Bodies

Key concepts: bear bodies, coolness, Don Juan and male sexuality, the male circumcision controversy, masculine identity and prostate cancer, metrosexuals

"**H**e's so hot!" she exclaimed while thumbing through *People* magazine's 50 Most Beautiful People issue (or was it the Sexiest Man Alive issue?). Is this woman's remark based on some personal idiosyncratic preference for a particular male body? It is difficult to decipher her preference for one man over the next when the pictures on page after page seem to show the same male body, slightly modified by hair color, clothing, or gestures. This body is usually tall, muscular, sexy, and the face is handsomely "chiseled" into White or White-looking features—an Adonis. In Greek mythology, Adonis was a handsome young man loved by the goddess Venus. In our own society, an Adonis is a model of male beauty.

The standards for beauty are so narrow that one good-looking man in a magazine looks much like any other. What explains the uncanny similarity all these beautiful men have to one another? Does *People* magazine see and choose only one "look"? Knowing what the preferred look is, do models, actors, and movie stars have some template of a body that they make themselves into, so that they emerge molded into a precise male form? Is this young woman's remark, like so many of our own, part of a process of socially producing and consuming representations of the ideal male body? We praise individuality, but do we admire and valorize the human body in all its shapes, sizes, and capacities, or are we overwhelmingly encouraged to develop preferences for certain bodies over others? And what do these preferences tell us about the social power, status, and virtue we imbue to the individuals inside these bodies?

Adonis: The Ideal Masculine Body

Similar to the ideal female body, the ideal male body is constructed by dominant social institutions and depicted through frequently reproduced images. From art, sculpture, television, films, the internet, newspapers, and magazines, we are always reminded of the ideal male body through a constant parade of virile, young, able-bodied men. But ideal bodies do not emerge from a vacuum. Clearly, ideal images of human bodies must be historically and socially situated to be understood. In Western contemporary cultures, a sampling of popular images would suggest that the ideal male body is over six feet tall, 180 to 200 pounds, muscular, agile, with straight white teeth, a washboard stomach, six-pack abs, long legs, a full head of hair, a large penis (discreetly shown by a bulge), broad shoulders and chest, strong muscular back, clean-shaven, healthy, and slightly tanned if White, or a lightish brown if Black or Hispanic. Asian Adonises are rarely seen. With such imagery all around them, boys and men in Western societies are encouraged to emulate this perfection. Their "audience" of girls, women, and older men judge their bodies—and their characters—by these standards. Even though it is not openly admitted, tall, strong-looking men have the advantage over short, flabby men in business careers and politics, not just in the realm of romance.

Our culture, like most throughout the world, stratifies individuals based on phenotypic variables—color of the skin, size of the body, and the presentation of gender and heterosexuality—and on achieved qualities—economic wealth, political power, and influence or authority over others. Ironically, these are linked: The right physical attributes advantage people in achieving power, prestige, and wealth, and those at the top of the social ladder can use their assets for cosmetic surgery, personal training, and sexual enhancement. More insidiously, the standards of beauty are modeled on what those at the top prefer.

One of the paradoxical effects of patriarchal systems of domination is that even though men have dominance over women, men are not a monolithic group. In addition to being gendered, men are differently raced, differently abled, and differently classed. They can be gay, straight, bisexual, transgendered. In many cultures, these sexual and social differences are used to stratify groups of men into different categories of privilege and power. Each man's ability to wield and benefit from patriarchal power is thus different. The ranking of culturally desirable male bodies mirrors their social standing.

R. W. Connell coined the term *hegemonic masculinity,* meaning "the configuration of gender practice which embodies the currently accepted answer to the problem of the legitimation of patriarchy, which guarantees (or is taken to guarantee) the dominant position of men and subordination of women" (1995, 77). By describing the historical and social processes that put certain men at the top of the patriarchal hierarchy and make others complicit in supporting their position, Connell and other scholars in masculinity studies challenge the assumption that the characteristics of masculinity arise from natural male bodies. In contemporary Western society, the characteristics of hegemonic masculinity are embodied in an "ideal type," exhibiting the potential for physical power and violence but acting with total rationality and control of emotion. It is an artificial image, based on cultural icons, such as successful tycoons, movie actors, and sports figures, and does not reflect the reality of most men's actual behavior. These icons, though, are powerful models, and they influence the behavior of men of many social classes and racial ethnic groups.

Mister Cool

Almost in defiance of their subordinate position in the U.S. stratification system, which disadvantages them in so many ways, young African American men, playing "Mr. Cool," display an exaggerated version of hegemonic masculine characteristics. In *Cool Pose: The Dilemmas of Black Manhood in America,* sociologists Richard Majors and Janet Mancini Billson explore how urban African American young men use their bodies to adopt a cool pose—a stance, a walk, a posture, a speech pattern. A cool pose enables these men to establish a confident masculine identity but may also disable them from full participation in a racist and hegemonically masculine society that sees their swaggering as hostile and dangerous. White boys may adopt this pose just because it is "cool," but to White teachers and bosses, it defies proper middle-class manners. The following excerpt shows this dual meaning of Black "cool"—dominance and defiance.

Walkin' the Cool Walk

Richard Majors
University of Glasgow

Janet Mancini Billson
George Washington University, Bloomery, West Virginia

The conspicuous and expressive nature of the African-American male's walk has become a way to announce his presence, to accentuate his self, and to broadcast his prideful power. Those in the black community who choose not to use this culturally specific behavior may be subject to ridicule or even harm.

Most black walks are improvised. While there is probably one basic walk, regional and city differences create a colorful array of walks in vogue at any given moment. The mainstay of the walk is rhythm and style. In contrast to the white male's robotlike and mechanical walk, the black walk is slower—more like a stroll. The head is slightly elevated and tipped to one side. One arm swings at the side with the hand slightly cupped. The other hand hangs straight to the side or is slipped into the pocket: "The gait is slow, casual . . . almost like a walking dance, with all parts of the body moving in rhythmic harmony."[1] Even macho sixth-grade boys can develop the swaggering, springy walk. The walk can serve as a threatening and confirming means of power in the face of hostile representatives of the mainstream: teachers, police, and store owners.

Like walking, black male stance is one of the most recognized nonverbal behaviors used to impress females during courtship rituals and to establish territory among peers. The lowered shoulder stance is the basic black position to express power and pride. With one shoulder crouched lower, the head tilted toward the shoulder, and chin protruding, the black male may then sport the stance with his hands in his pockets, tucked under the belt, or cupped loosely over the genitals. Cooke uses the term "lowered shoulder kineme" to describe this stance and says that different stances can be detected among black males: player stance, pimp stance, rapper stance, and cat stance. We see them as variations on the same theme.

Another symbolic stance is the "stationary pimp strut," in which the male puts his hands in his pockets and moves in a fluid dance to accentuate talk: "The free arm will swing, point, turn, and gesture, as conversation proceeds. It is as if they are walking in place."[2] Cooke says the "pimp stance" is used to show defiance toward authority figures.

In "peeping," the male crunches his shoulders upward and tilts one slightly higher while his head slants in the opposite direction, and his eyes take on a staring, gazing, or fixed expression. This behavior is used for courtship and calling attention to himself.

Few nonverbal behaviors symbolize the consciousness of black people and the Black Power Movement as dramatically as the black handshake. Although handwork is used to make statements of approval, solidarity, and greeting, it also signifies power, identity, and pride.

"Giving skin" and "getting skin" have many variations: palm-to-palm, agreement, complimentary, greeting, emphatic, superlative, parting, five-on-the-sly, and regular skin. Other handshakes and hand gestures used during the 1960s and 1970s were the black thumb grasp, wrist grasps, placing hands on the shoulders, flexing biceps, and making a fist. The thumb grasp is still in vogue today, but the others are less often seen. High-five—mutual raising of arms high with palms open and touching—is popular today. Low-fives involve downward extension of the arms with palms open and touching. Both are used in sports, while high fives are often seen as everyday greetings.

African-American fraternities, gangs and other organizations have their own secret handshakes and gestures. Some fraternities use a frat shake or hand-body shake—any handwork combined with an embrace. Some call it "givin' up the da-dap." A popular black military handshake is called the "clap-hand-to-hand greeting." Variations and new inventions quickly proliferate.

Similarly, visual behavior—eye contact, gazing, staring, or rolling the eyes—gives cues to underlying feelings and intentions. Rolling the eyes conveys disapproval, anger, or dislike, especially toward authority figures. Cutting the eyes—an exaggerated moving of the eyes toward another person followed by a short stare—also expresses negative feelings. A wide repertoire of eyework is used for courting and communicating feelings and intentions between African-American males and females: Cooke calls this the "silent rap."

Research suggests that blacks look at others while listening less often than do whites.[3] Blacks make more eye contact while speaking, just the opposite of whites. In America, blacks staring at whites has often been associated with racial tension and hostility. Phil explains an encounter with a white authority figure: "Watch him, and look him in the eyes. He can't stand that! Look at him dead in his eyes and talk to him and don't take your eyes off him. You might burn your eyes, but you've psyched him out . . . that's another cool system."

Notes

1. Johnson 1971, 185.
2. Johnson 1971, 186. This section also benefitted from the work of Hannah 1984; Rich 1974; Cooke 1980; Barnes 1988.
3. Smith 1983; Hannah 1984; LaFrance 1974; Shuter 1979.

References

Barnes, 1988, telephone conversation.
Cooke, B. 1980. Nonverbal communication among Afro-Americans: An initial classification. In *Black psychology,* 2nd ed., ed. R. L. Jones. New York: Harper & Row.
Hannah, J. L. 1984. Black/white nonverbal differences, dance and dissonance: Implications for desegregation. In *Nonverbal behavior: Perspectives, applications, intercultural insight,* ed. A. Wolfgang. Lewiston, NY: C.J. Hogrefe.
Johnson, K. R. 1971. Black kinesics: Some nonverbal communication patterns in black culture. *Florida Foreign Language Reporter* 9: 95–122.
LaFrance, M. 1974. Nonverbal cues to conversational turn taking between black speakers. Paper presented at the annual meeting of the American Psychological Association, New Orleans.
Rich, A. L. 1974. *Interracial communication.* New York: Harper & Row.
Shuter, R. 1979. Gaze behavior in interracial and intra-racial interaction. In *Intercultural communication annual,* ed. N. C. Jain. Falls Church, VA: Speech Communication Association.
Smith, A. 1983. Nonverbal communication among black female dyads: An assessment of intimacy, gender and race. *Journal of Social Issues* 39: 55–67.

Metrosexuals and Bears

Just as women and girls have body projects, men in pursuit of hegemonically male bodies are encouraged to modify their bodies to fit the ideal type. As explored in Chapter 3, men deploy their bodies in athletics to create a presentation of self as fit, strong, and potent. Psychological research studies have determined that men's media exposure is significantly associated with rising concern about their own physique, in particular their weight, muscularity, and general fitness. The more films and men's magazines the research subjects consumed, the greater their preoccupation with muscularity, and the more they dieted, exercised, and used beauty products (Hatoum and Belle 2004). Other social psychological research indicates that through the life span, boys' and men's self-concepts of their bodies change. As adolescents, boys are primarily focused on increasing muscle mass; when they become adults, they are increasingly concerned about their weight (McCabe and Ricciardelli 2004).

Some men turn to medications to maintain an "authentic" and virile masculinity. They face the world armed with prescriptions for Rogaine or Propecia for hair growth and Viagra or Cialis for firm and lasting erections, or they buy under-the-counter illegal substances like steroids for muscle mass and amphetamines for nervous energy. But men need not visit the doctor, the gym, or a dealer to participate in the increasingly expensive world of body perfection—body grooming tools are available over the counter or at the local salon. Enter the metrosexual:

> So what makes a metrosexual man? He's been defined as a straight, sensitive, well-educated, urban dweller who is in touch with his feminine side. He may have a standing appointment for a weekly manicure, and he probably has his hair cared for by a stylist rather than a barber. He loves to shop, he may wear jewelry, and his bathroom counter is most likely filled with male-targeted grooming products, including moisturizers (and perhaps even a little makeup). He may work on his physique at a fitness club (not a gym) and his appearance probably gets him lots of attention—and he's delighted by every stare. (Nazario 2003)

Since men are differently situated in the world, different groups have developed different standards of beauty. Peter Hennen did participant observation with a group of men in a gay subculture that valorizes a larger, hirsute body, like his own. In this excerpt from an article on his research, Hennen, a sociologist, describes the Bear culture as physical resistance to the AIDS epidemic, cultural resistance to stereotypical effeminacy, and sexual resistance to a focus on the phallus.

Bear Bodies, Bear Masculinity

Peter Hennen
The Ohio State University at Newark

Just what is a Bear? Responses to this question reveal a variety of answers but almost all reference the Bear body in an attempt either to describe what the typical Bear looks like or to refute the idea that Bears can be defined exclusively by their bodies. As Travis, one of my interview participants, put it, "You know, physical attributes such as stockiness, height, weight, how much facial fur you have, things along those lines. But other people see it as being 90 percent attitude, 10 percent looks." What constitutes Bear attitude? Responses I encountered ranged from "natural, down-to-earth, easy going, likes to have fun" (Larry), "closer to the heterosexual community in their tastes" (Brian), "a sense of independence" (Burt), and finally "an easiness with the body" and "the masculinity thing" (Grant). "The masculinity thing" within Bear culture is complex and inextricably tied to the workings of hegemonic masculinity outside of it. "I think some of what is really appealing to me about the Bear group is that if you saw these guys on the street, they could just as easily be rednecks as gay guys," says Franklin. This suggests that the Bear image not only is conventionally gendered but includes a specifically classed presentation of self.

Bear culture was born of resistance. According to historian and founding figure Les Wright, in the early 1980s men frequenting leather bars in San Francisco and other cities began placing a small teddy bear in their shirt or hip pocket as a way of "refuting the clone colored-hanky code," whereby gay leathermen place different colored hankies in their back pockets to signal their interest in a variety of sex practices. Not willing to be objectified and reduced to an interest in one specific sexual activity, these men sported teddy bears to emphasize their interest in "cuddling" (1997b, 21). According to Wright, this was a way of saying, "I'm a human being. I give and receive affection" (1990, 54).

Bears reject the self-conscious, exaggerated masculinity of the gay leatherman in favor of a more "authentic" masculinity. This look includes (but is not limited to) jeans, baseball caps, T-shirts, flannel shirts, and beards. To the uninitiated, Bears seem above all to be striving for "regular-guy" status. "The Bear look is all-natural, rural, even woodsy," noted Silverstein and Picano; "full beards are common, as are bushy moustaches. . . . They're just regular guys—only they're gay" (1992, 128–30). But are Bears "just regular guys"? Feminist scholars Kelly and Kane (2001, 342) saw subversive potential in this community: "Is there perhaps something radically subversive of orthodox masculinity at work here, despite all the butch trappings? Might not bears represent the sort of 'marginalized men' that Susan Bordo describes as 'bearers of the shadow of the phallus, who have been the alchemical agents disturbing the (deceptively) stable elements' of orthodox masculinity in a newly percolating social psyche?"

With the Bears' emphasis on camaraderie instead of competition, the rejection of "body fascism" (as evidenced by the acceptance of heavier and older men), and by popularizing cuddling and "the Bear hug," one finds ample evidence that this is not the type of masculinity that predominates in other gay cultures. As Wright remarked, "Competition with other gay men for sex partners and the depersonalizing effects of a steady stream of sexually-consumed bodies is balanced by the humanizing effort to . . . establish contact with the person inside of each of those bodies" (1997c, 10). But at the same time, one finds signs of a recuperative current, a rejection of the insights of feminism, even outright hostility. As Lucie-Smith noted, "There is a challenge to aggressive feminism, which not only seeks female equality, but often tries to subject men to the tastes and standards imposed by women. To be a 'Bear' is to assert a homosexual masculinism which rejects this" (1991, 8).

Thus, in staking their claim to gay masculinity, Bears challenge hegemonic assumptions about male sexuality by introducing what feminists have identified as an "ethic of care" (Gilligan 1982) into an objectified sexual culture perceived as alienating. On the other hand, insofar as their rejection of effeminacy signals a broader devaluation of the feminine, Bear masculinity recuperates gendered hierarchies central to the logic of hegemonic masculinity. Furthermore, the pastoral fantasy encoded in Bear semiotics can be linked with earlier movements aimed at revitalizing an "essential" masculinity under assault from the feminizing effects of civilization by retreating to the wilderness, if only symbolically. How then, from a feminist perspective, is one to adjudicate these simultaneously resistant and recuperative features of Bear culture? In this research, I draw on ethnographic and historical evidence as I attempt to make sense of these conflicting currents, with a special emphasis on the way that Bear masculinity is embodied and the effect this has on Bear sexual culture. . . .

In addition to its appeal as a hedge against effeminacy and its eroticization of the heavier body, there are at least two factors contributing to the emergence of the Bear phenomenon during the 1980s. One was, unquestionably, the AIDS pandemic and the effect of AIDS-related wasting syndrome on the erotic imagination of gay men. In an era when thinness could be linked with disease and death, the fleshier body was reinterpreted as an indicator of health, vigor, strength, and virility. The second contributing factor was the Bear movement's ability to co-opt an existing subculture that had been operating on an informal basis for decades prior to the Bears' arrival on the scene. In 1976, a national network of "chubbies" (big men) and "chasers" (men who were sexually attracted to them) emerged as a new national organization called Girth and Mirth. A dozen years later, as the Bears became a recognizable subculture within the gay community, an uneasy relationship developed between the two groups. Interestingly, in many cities, Girth and Mirth chapters went into decline just as Bear organizations were cropping up (Suresha 2002). One reason for the out-migration from Girth and Mirth may be the more appealing imagery employed by the Bears. The iconic figure of the bear was enormously successful in linking the bigger body with nature, the wilderness, and more conventional notions of masculinity. . . .

Do Bears make gender trouble (Butler 1990)? What does it mean when Silverstein and Picano observe of Bears, "They're just regular guys—only they're gay" (1992, 128)? Clearly, there is a move toward normalization here, as well as an identification with heterosexual men, a move that may ironically turn out to be profoundly disruptive of hegemonic masculinity. When Franklin remarks, "Some of what is really appealing to me about the Bear group is that if you saw these guys on the street, they could just as easily be rednecks as gay guys," he speaks for many men who identify as Bears. Herein lies the possibility of subversion, as Bears have been largely successful in divorcing effeminacy from same-sex desire and creating a culture that looks like a bunch of "regular guys." The subversive implications, however, have everything to do with reorganizing sexuality and very little to do with challenging gendered assumptions. Most of these men would like nothing more than to have their masculinity accepted as normative, something that is largely accomplished within the group but remains problematic outside of it.

How is it that Bears come to understand their particular brand of masculinity as natural? It seems clear that this is accomplished quite deliberately, through the appropriation of back-to-nature masculinity narratives that are sustained intersubjectively, as group members reinforce these meanings and associations through their day-to-day interactions. Thus, Bear culture seems currently disposed toward renaturalizing rather than denaturalizing gender relations. It seems far more likely, then, that increasing acceptance of Bear masculinity will encourage greater investment in a heteronormative sexual culture, less experimentation with new pleasures, less dispersal of pleasure across the body, and a renewed appreciation for insertive intercourse as "doing what comes naturally." In this case, the perceived naturalness of the Bear body may be extended to naturalized understandings of sex practices that are increasingly compliant with norms of hegemonic masculinity.

References

Butler, J. 1990. *Gender trouble.* London: Routledge.

Gilligan, C. 1982. *In a different voice.* Cambridge, MA: Harvard University Press.

Kelly, E. A., and K. Kane. 2001. In Goldilocks's footsteps: Exploring the discursive construction of gay masculinity in Bear magazines. In *The Bear book II,* edited by L. K. Wright. New York: Harrington Park Press.

Lucie-Smith, E. 1991. The cult of the Bear. In *The Bear cult.* Swaffam, UK: GMP.

Silverstein, C., and F. Picano. 1992. *The new joy of gay sex.* New York: Harper Perennial.

Suresha, R. J. 2002. *Bears on Bears.* Los Angeles: Alyson Books.

Wright, L. K. 1990. The sociology of the urban Bear. *Drummer* 140: 53–55.

———. 1997b. A concise history of self-identifying Bears. In *The Bear book,* edited by L. K. Wright. New York: Harrington Park Press.

———. 1997c. Introduction: Theoretical Bears. In *The Bear book,* edited by L. K. Wright. New York: Harrington Park Press.

Don Juan: The Importance of Sexual Performance

Casanova was an eighteenth-century man who fathered children in every city he lived in. Don Juan, the hero of Mozart's opera *Don Giovanni,* slept with 3,000 women of every size, shape, hair color, nationality, and rank. They both are much admired icons of male sexuality in Western culture, which is said to be phallocentric, focused on men and their sexual performance. The visual representation of sexual performance is the heroic phallus. *Phallus,* which literally means penis, also refers to imagery and symbolism that celebrates male generative power, often to the exclusion or denigration of female generative power.

The phallus is a model for both ancient and contemporary architectural structures. From the Mayan phallic structures of Chichén Itzá in Mexico, stone phallic symbols recovered at Zimbabwean ruins, the Washington Monument in the District of Columbia, the Eiffel Tower in Paris, and most recently, the Swiss Re Building in London, phallic structures have been erected to celebrate masculine accomplishment and male power. The destruction of the 110-story Twin Towers in New York City on September 11, 2001, was widely considered a castration of American power.

The preoccupation with the phallus is not only manifested in buildings. Linguist Deborah Cameron (1992) conducted a study of American college students to explore words and phrases that refer to the penis. She compiled a list of more than 140 terms, which she divided into categories, such as

- Titles of authority: "Kimosabe, his Excellency, your Majesty, the chief, the commissioner, the mayor, the judge" (p. 370)

- Personal authority: "scepter, rod of lordship, Excalibur, hammer of the gods" (p. 370)

- Tool: "screwdriver, drill, jackhammer, chisel, lawnmower, hedge-trimmer, and fuzzbuster" (p. 371)

- Weapon: "squirt gun, love pistol, passion rifle, lightsaber" (p. 372)

Cameron concluded that the ways the penis is signified through language reinforce the underlying ideology that "the phallus must act, dominate, avenge itself on the female body. It is a symbol of authority to which we all must bow down. Its animal desires are uncontrollable; it has a life of its own" (1992, 373). Any reference to the vulnerable penis is notably absent.

Although men often boast about their penises, the grandiose vernacular and self-congratulatory talk indicates that the confidence men feel in their sexual performances may be somewhat exaggerated. When Lisa Jean Moore was working on a national sex information line throughout the 1990s, the most common question from male callers was, "What is the normal penis size?" Trained to provide anonymous, nonjudgmental, and accurate information to callers, she would respond that most penises when erect were between five and seven inches. The relief in their voices was evident—they were now secure in the validation that they (and their penises) were "okay." Anecdotal and research evidence from physician-patient interactions concurs that men and boys have a lot of questions about how large their penises should be (Lee 1996). The personal and cultural anxiety about penises has been elaborated upon by philosopher Susan Bordo:

> Most of our metaphors for the penis, as you will recall, actually turn it into some species of dildo: stiff torpedoes, wands, and rods that never get soft, always perform. These metaphors, I suggested, may be a defense against fears of being too soft, physically and emotionally. But at the same time as these metaphors "defend" men as they joke with each other in bars—or more hate-fully—act as a misogynist salve for past or imaginary humiliations, they also set men up for failure. For men don't really have torpedoes or rods or heroic avengers between their legs. They have penises. And penises, like the rest of the human body and unlike dildoes, feel things. (1999, 64)

What has socialized men to be so concerned with presenting a certain image of their penis? We argue that this focus on sexual performance as a proof of masculinity is something that is learned by boys and reinforced in men in Western cultures through multiple sources. From pornography to sexology research, the erotic image and the human sexual response cycle are defined as almost exclusively phallocentric. The sexual act is penetration (vaginal, oral, or anal) and the goal is male orgasm and ejaculation. Anything less is tantamount to an embarrassing failure; repeated experiences end up with a diagnosis of "erectile dysfunction"—impotence (Tiefer 1994). Recent innovations in pharmaceuticals, as well as a long history of penis-improvement gadgets, also construct male sexuality in this limited way. (We are bombarded with constant spam e-mail messages selling penile enhancement!) As psychologist Barry Bass observed, we have created a sexual-performance perfection industry where "good sex changes the basic nature of a sexual encounter from one of intimacy and pleasure to one of achievement and performance. In addition, these often unattainable standards of performance are guaranteed to make most of us feel like failures" (2001, 337).

This vulnerability goes a long way to explaining the enormous popularity of Viagra and similar medications and their use by men whose only medical indication is fear of sexual failure (Kirby 2004; Loe 2004; Tuller 2004). To create less shame about the threat to masculinity due to impotence, drug companies select dominant males to be spokesmen for their products, for example, Bob Dole and Mike Ditka. Despite their soft-focus imagery, advertisements for Viagra, Cialis, Levitra, and similar pharmaceuticals are not selling the sensuality and emotions of sexual relationships but a way to achieve otherwise unattainable standards of the perfectly functioning penis and the always successful sexual performance.

Prostate Cancer and Masculine Identity

Given Western culture's preoccupation with the phallus, what happens when men become sick? Research suggests that, in general, men's health-seeking practices are lower than women's, because admission of illness is unmasculine. One report said that "many men suggested that the 'macho' image is adversely affected if illness means that they have to seek help or become dependent on others" (Chapple and Ziebland 2002, 836). It could be hypothesized that if illness were to strike a particularly vulnerable part of a man's body, he might be even less inclined to seek health care. Indeed, there have been numerous campaigns from public health organizations and community-based groups to encourage men (and their partners) to get screened for sexually transmitted diseases.

A similar area of vulnerability is sexual performance, which can be affected by treatment for prostate cancer and testicular cancer. Icons of masculinity such as Joe Torre, coach of the New York Yankees, and Rudy Giuliani, former mayor of New York City, implore men to get screened for prostate cancer. Mass media campaigns invoke "experts" to dispel the prevailing wisdom that prostate cancer is a threat to masculinity (Clarke 1999, 67). Another male cancer, of the testes, is the most common cancer in men aged 15 to 34, and it is on the rise (Gurevich et al. 2004). In a qualitative study of men's most humiliating experiences, the rankings were, from the most to the least, not maintaining an erection during sex, losing a testicle to cancer, being teased about penis size, having a rectal exam, being diagnosed as sterile, being left by an intimate partner, and being seen naked by male friends (Morman 2000).

Prostate cancer is the most common cancer in America, even more common than breast cancer. The prostate is a walnut-sized gland located between the bladder and the penis and positioned in front of the rectum. Urine and semen must pass through the prostate before leaving the body. The Prostate Cancer Foundation website (*www.prostatecancerfoundation.org*) includes the following statistics:

- 80 percent of all prostate cancers are in men over 65

- African American men are 65 percent more likely to develop prostate cancer than Caucasian men, and when African American men do get prostate cancer, it is more likely to be a severe form of the disease

- Prostate cancer is most prevalent in North America and northwestern Europe, with a lower incidence in Asia, Central America, and South America

- Diet is suspected to be a major factor in these racial differences

Screening for prostate cancer is performed by a blood test and a digital rectal examination. Treatments for prostate cancer include prostatectomy (the surgical removal of the prostate gland), chemotherapy, and radiation. Some potential side effects of prostate cancer and its treatment are incontinence, impotence, and loss of libido. These side effects, as well as the fears of anal penetration during a rectal examination, discourage men from being screened for prostate cancer. Ironically, interviews from Britain and Australia have found that men's perceived ideas about confronting impotence through prostate treatments are often different than their real-life experiences (Chapple and Ziebland 2002; Oliffe 2005). According to one study,

The results . . . suggest that while the ability to have an erection may be an important part of male identity, men whose treatment only affects their sexual function were able to reframe this as "a small price to pay." . . . The greatest sense of loss is described by men who have had hormone treatments that are described as affecting their interest in sex as well as their physical function. (Chapple and Ziebland 2002, 837)

Another view is expressed by Richard Wassersug, who was chemically castrated as a result of treatment for advanced prostate cancer. A professor in the department of Anatomy and Neurobiology at Dalhousie University in Halifax, Canada, Dr. Wassersug has come out as a "eunuch"—an "emale." His body is no longer masculine—he has breasts and shrunken genitals, but he has a beard and says that he only looks different without clothes. His personality, though, has also changed, for the better, in his view—he is more emotional and empathic and sensually responsive to both men and women. In gender terms, he said, "Being free of hormonal compulsion, a modern eunuch can elect whatever gender orientation he wishes. If men are from Mars and women from Venus, then eunuchs can tour the whole solar system!" (2003).

The Male Circumcision Controversy

In some Western societies, circumcision (removal of the foreskin) of newborns in hospitals for nonreligious reasons became routine in the twentieth century. The United States has had the highest rate—about 64 percent; in Canada, about 48 percent of males are circumcised (AAP 1999). Nonritual circumcision is uncommon in Asia, South and Central America, and most of Europe. In the United States, rates vary by mother's education level and by racial category, with Whites at 81 percent, Blacks at 65 percent, and Hispanics at 54 percent (Laumann, Masi, and Zuckerman 1997).

A review of the benefits by the American Academy of Pediatrics found that the rate of urinary tract infections in the first year of life is from 7 to 14 of 1,000 uncircumcised male infants and from 1 to 2 of 1,000 circumcised male infants; however, the absolute risk of an uncircumcised male infant developing a urinary tract infection in the first year of life is less than 1 percent (AAP 1999). Neonatal circumcision offers some protection from cancer of the penis in later life; here, the overall risk is even lower—from 9 to 10 cases per year per 1 million men. In contrast, the risks of the circumcision itself (accidental injury, hemorrhaging, and infection) were 1 out of 476 in one study (Christakis et al. 2000). In 1999, the AAP concluded that the incidence of urinary tract infection and penile cancer in the United States is too low to warrant routine circumcision of male infants and now recommends that parents be informed of the potential benefits and risks of circumcision and that it is a strictly elective procedure.

A different picture of the benefits of circumcision occurs in sub-Saharan Africa, where circumcision has been shown to be highly effective in protecting men from the risk of HIV infection through heterosexual transmission (Lemle 2005; O'Farrell and Egger 2000; Weiss, Quigley, and Hayes 2000). There seem to be several reasons for this protection. One is that the foreskin is vulnerable to lesions, tears, and ulceration, which increase the likelihood of transmission of the AIDS virus and other sexually transmitted diseases. Second, the foreskin contains a high density of cells that may be the primary target for HIV infection (Szabo and Short 2000).

A volatile issue in the circumcision debate is whether removal of the foreskin diminishes sexual sensation. In the nineteenth century, circumcision (and clitorectomy in women) were recommended as deterrents to masturbation, which has led activists to argue that removal of the foreskin must deaden sexual feeling (Zoske 1998). However, data from 1,410 American men aged 18 to 59 who participated in the 1992 National Health and Social Life Survey found that self-identified circumcised men had a slightly lesser risk of experiencing sexual dysfunction, such as inability to have orgasms, especially when older (Laumann, Masi, and Zuckerman 1997). The survey also found that circumcised men engaged in more varied sexual practices and masturbated more, but the variation across ethnic groups suggested that differences were due to social factors, which correlate with likelihood of being circumcised. It is unlikely that there will ever be objective data on the differences in sexual pleasure given and received by men with and without foreskins, since these evaluations are so subjective. As Karen Ericksen Paige predicted a generation ago,

Men have debated the sexual sensitivity question for centuries. Circumcised men think that they have the more sensitive penises; uncircumcised men think that the constant exposure of the naked glans to clothes and the elements toughens it. Some men think that having a foreskin delays orgasm, giving a man more control; others think just the opposite. This discussion is never going to be settled. Sexual sensitivity appears to be in the mind of a man, not in his foreskin. (1978, 46)

Given the preoccupation with the penis, the widespread ritual practice of circumcision in male newborns or at puberty seems puzzling. For ritual circumcision, it is precisely the preciousness of the penis that underlies the rite. Male circumcision ceremonies indicate a father's loyalty to his lineage elders—"visible public evidence that the head of a family unit of their lineage is willing to trust others with his and his family's most valuable political asset, his son's penis" (Ericksen Paige and Paige 1981, 147). More symbolically, it can be seen as patriarchy embedded in the flesh, as Michael Kimmel, a professor of men's studies, felt when he and his wife decided not to circumcise their newborn son. He describes the ceremony they did have in the following excerpt.

The Kindest Uncut

Michael Kimmel
State University of New York at Stony Brook

Although it was a little late by traditional religious standards, the entire family and many friends gathered in our home three weeks after our son, Zachary, was born. We had gathered for his "bris," the moment when a young Jewish boy is first brought into the family and the community, the moment of his formal entrance into the world of Judaism. At such symbolic moments, one feels keenly the sinews of connection to family and friends that sustain a life, animate it, give it context and meaning. . . .

As family and friends drew closer together, glasses of wine and champagne in their hands, the ritual began with prayers over the wine and bread. Our first toast to this new creature who had entered all our lives. Then the mohel began the naming ceremony, and some relatives and friends offered their wishes for this young life. Amy, my wife, and I each offered a thought to the other and to Zachary as we entered this new phase of our lives as parents together. For my part, I quoted Adrienne Rich, who had written that "if I could have one wish for my own sons, it is that they should have the courage of women." I wished nothing more for Zachary—that he would have Amy's courage, her integrity and her passion.

Then it was the moment for which we had all carefully prepared, about which we had endlessly talked, debated, argued, discussed. We took a pitcher of water and a bowl to the door of the house. Amy and I carried Zachary over to the threshold. With one hand I held his little body and with the other held his tiny legs over the bowl. Amy poured some water over his feet and rubbed it in. Then she held him and I did the same. Throughout, the mohel chanted in prayer. And in that way, we welcomed Zachary into our home and into our lives.

By now you are, of course, waiting for the "real" bris to begin, for the mohel to stuff a wine-soaked handkerchief into his mouth to muffle his cries and slightly anesthetize him, and then circumcise him, cutting off his foreskin in fulfillment of God's commandment to Abraham that he mark his son, Isaac, as a sign of obedience.

Sorry to disappoint, but that's the end of our story. Or at least the end of the story of Zachary's bris. There was no circumcision on that day. We had decided not to circumcise our son. Although he enters a world filled with violence, he would enter it without violence done to him. Although he will no doubt suffer many cuts and scrapes during his life, he would not bleed by our hand.

This was not an easy decision, but we had plenty of time to prepare—nine months to be exact. From the moment we saw the sonogram and read the results of the amniocentesis, the debate had been joined. Would we or wouldn't we? How would we decide? . . .

Pros and Cons

We heard a lot of arguments, for and against. To be sure, there is no shortage of arguments in favor of circumcision. Some are aesthetic, and offer a psychological theory based on that aesthetic. He will look different from his father, and thus develop shame about his body. He will look different from other Jewish boys, especially in our heavily Jewish neighborhood, thus be subject to ridicule and teasing, and develop a sense that he does not belong. . . .

And, of course, the weight of family, history, and culture do not rest lightly on the shoulders of the new parent. As Jews we knew full well the several-thousand-year-old tradition of following one of the most fundamental of God's commandments to Abraham—that "every male among you shall be circumcised . . . and that shall be a sign of the covenant between Me and you."

In the end, though, none of the arguments in favor of circumcision was fully persuasive. Taken together, however, they raised issues that spoke to the core of our identities as a man and a woman, as parents, as feminists, and as Jews. . . .

The Psychological Aesthetics of Difference

That he would look different from his father was easily negotiated. We decided that we will simply tell him that Daddy had no choice about his own body and especially his penis, but that now, as parents, we loved him so much that we decided we didn't want to hurt him like that—turning something that could be a cause of embarrassment into a source of pride.

And he will look more and more *like* the other boys rather than different. Circumcision of newborns is decreasingly popular, performed routinely only in the United States (and here as a medical procedure in the hospital) and Israel, where it remains a significant religious ceremony. (Adolescent circumcision remains the norm in most Islamic nations.) . . . Over four-fifths of all men in the world are uncircumcised. . . .

The Weights of Tradition

The combined weights of family and religious culture were not so easily negotiated. As predicted, the future grandmothers were somewhat more sanguine about the prospect of non-circumcision than were the future grandfathers. It's ironic that it's always been women—even within Judaism—who have opposed circumcision as a violence done to their babies, and circumcised males who have supported it. Perhaps it is analogous to fraternity or military initiation ceremonies, where the salutary outcomes of feeling a sense of belonging to the larger homosocial group is deemed worth any price, including the removal of a third of one's potential sexual pleasure.

In our case, neither Amy nor I felt any strong compulsion towards circumcision, but I was more strongly opposed on moral grounds. Amy's opposition would come later, when she first held Zachary in her arms and she felt a visceral rage that anyone would do anything that would ever hurt this new creature. In very gender stereotyped terms, Amy's opposition grew from her emotional, visceral connection to the baby; mine grew first from a principled opposition grounded in a sense of justice and ethics. . . .

But what was ultimately decisive for us was the larger symbolic meaning of circumcision, and particularly the gendered politics of the ritual. After all, it is not circumcision that makes a man Jewish; one can certainly be Jewish without it. Religious membership is passed on through the mother: if the mother is Jewish then the baby is Jewish and nothing that the baby does—or that is done to him or her—can change that basic fact. A rabbi is trained to counsel parents of mixed religious backgrounds (in which the man is Jewish and the woman is not) that circumcision does not make their son Jewish, but that only the mother's conversion will make it so.

No, the circumcision means something else: the reproduction of patriarchy. Abraham cements *his* relationship to God by a symbolic genital mutilation of his son. It is on the body of his son that Abraham writes his own beliefs. In a religion marked by the ritual exclusion of women, such a marking not only enables Isaac to be included within the community of men—he can be part of a minyan, can pray in the temple, can study Torah—but he can also lay claim to all the privileges to which being a Jewish male now entitles him. Monotheistic religions invariably worship male Gods, and exhibit patriarchal political arrangements between the sexes. (Looked at this way, since both Judaism and Islam practice circumcision, it is really Christianity that is the deviant case, and it would be worth exploring how Christianity justified its evasion of the practice since it is certain that Jesus was circumcised.)

Circumcision, it became clear, is the single moment of the reproduction of patriarchy. It's when patriarchy happens, the single crystalline moment when the rule of the fathers is reproduced, the moment when male privilege and entitlement is passed from one generation to the next, when the power of the fathers is enacted upon the sons, and which the sons will someday then enact on the bodies of their own sons. To circumcise our son, then, would be, unwittingly or not, to accept as legitimate four thousand years not of Jewish tradition, but of patriarchal domination of women.

Our choice was clear.

We welcomed Zachary into our family on that morning without a circumcision. We decided that we want him to live in a world without violence, so we welcomed him without violence. We decided that we want him to live in a world in which he is free to experience the fullness of the pleasures of his body, so we welcomed him with all his fleshy nerves intact. And we decided that we want him to live in a world in which male entitlement is a waning memory, and in which women and men are seen—in both ritual and in reality—as full equals and partners. So we welcomed him equally, his mother and I, in the time-honored way that desert cultures have always welcomed strangers to their tents: We washed his feet.

Reprinted from Michael Kimmel, "The Kindest Uncut: Feminism, Judaism, and My Son's Foreskin," *Tikkun* May–June 2001, pp. 43–44, 47–48. Copyright © Michael Kimmel, 2001. Reprinted by permission.

Critical Summary

Although this chapter started with a description of idealized and homogeneous male bodies, we saw that alternative male bodies could also be valorized. Black male "cool" swaggering is one variation, a variation that is appropriated by high-status White males as a means to amplify their masculinity. Another type of male body is that of the metrosexual—a heterosexual man whose use of cosmetics and attention to clothes borders on the "queer eye." Bears are one subset of gay men whose body types are large, hairy, and cuddly and whose clothes style is down-market and working-class. Clearly, desirable male bodies are differentiated by the norms of the subcultures in which men claim membership. However, despite subcultures that celebrate diverse male body expressions, all men are still monitored by the larger patriarchal, heteronormative, and economically and racially stratified social structure of Western societies.

The proud penis and rampant sexuality celebrated in the Don Juan imagery is celebrated somewhat differently in male circumcision rituals, but then recurs in anti-circumcision, pro-sexuality rhetoric. The challenges of prostate cancer and male contraception call for a different vocabulary—an emphasis on relational, instead of penetrative, sexuality. The prediction is that in the twenty-first century, hegemonic masculinity may be more fluid and heterogeneous—leaving open the possibility of transgressing the rigid categories of dichotomous embodied genders. The grounds for optimism, R. W. Connell says, is the diversity of masculinities itself: "As this diversity becomes better known, men and boys can more easily see a range of possibilities for their own lives, and both men and women are less likely to think of gender inequality as unchangeable" (2005, 1817).

References and Recommended Readings

Bass, Barry. 2001. "The Sexual Performance Perfection Industry and the Medicalization of Male Sexuality." *Family Journal: Counseling and Therapy for Couples and Families* 9, 337–340.

Bordo, Susan R. 1999. *The Male Body: A New Look at Men in Public and Private.* New York: Farrar Straus Giroux.

Cameron, Deborah. 1992. "Naming of Parts: Gender, Culture, and Terms for the Penis Among American College Students." *American Speech* 67, 367–382.

Bourdieu, Pierre. 2001. *Masculine Domination.* Stanford, CA: Stanford University Press.

Collins, M. A., and L. A. Zebrowitz. 1995. "The Contributions of Appearance to Occupational Outcomes in Civilian and Military Settings." *Journal of Applied Social Psychology* 25, 129–163.

Connell, R. W. 1995. *Masculinities.* Berkeley: University of California Press.

———. 2005. "Change Among the Gatekeepers: Men, Masculinities, and Gender Equality in the Global Arena." *Signs* 30, 1801–1825.

Friedman, David M. 2003. *A Mind of Its Own: A Cultural History of the Penis.* New York: Penguin USA.

Hatoum, Ida Jodette, and Deborah Belle. 2004. "Mags and Abs: Media Consumption and Bodily Concerns in Men." *Sex Roles* 51, 397–407.

Kimmel, Michael S. 1996. *Manhood in America: A Cultural History.* New York: Free Press.

Kirby, David. 2004. "Party Favors: Pill Popping as Insurance." *New York Times,* Men & Health, 21 June, F1, 11.

Lee, P. A. 1996. "Survey Report: Concept of Penis Size." *Journal of Sex and Marital Therapy* 22, 131–135.

Loe, Meika. 2004. *The Rise of Viagra: How the Little Blue Pill Changed Sex in America.* New York: New York University Press.

Luciano, Lynne. 2001. *Looking Good: Male Body Image in Modern America.* New York: Hill and Wang.

Majors, Richard, and Janet Mancini Billson. 1992. *Cool Pose: The Dilemmas of Black Manhood in America.* New York: Lexington Books.

McCabe, Marita, and Lina Ricciardelli. 2004. "Body Image Dissatisfaction Among Males Across the Lifespan: A Review of Past Literature." *Journal of Psychosomatic Research* 56, 675–685.

Mueller, Ulrich, and Allan Mazur. 1996. "Facial Dominance of West Point Cadets as a Predictor of Later Military Rank." *Social Forces* 74, 823–850.

Nazario, Brunilda. 2003. Book Review of *Metrosexuals: It's a Guy Thing!* by Richard Trubo. *www.webmd.com*, 28 July.

Pope, Harrison G., Jr., Katharine A. Phillips, and Roberto Olivardia. 2000. *The Adonis Complex: The Secret Crisis of Male Body Obsession.* New York: Free Press.

Riska, Elianne. 2004. *Masculinity and Men's Health: Coronary Heart Disease in Medical and Public Discourse.* Lanham, MD: Rowman and Littlefield.

Rosenfeld, Dana, and Christopher Faircloth (eds.). 2006. *Medicalized Masculinities.* Philadelphia: Temple University Press.

Tiefer, Leonore. 1994. "The Medicalization of Impotence: Normalizing Phallocentrism." *Gender & Society* 8, 363–377.

Tuller, David. 2004. "Racing for Sales, Drugmakers Cast Erectile Dysfunction in Youthful Terms." *New York Times,* Men & Health, 21 June, F1, 10.

Wassersug, Richard. 2003. "I Am a Eunuch." *OUT Magazine,* September. *www.eunuch.org/Alpha/C/ea_195222castrati.htm*

Watson, Jonathan. 2000. *Male Bodies: Health, Culture, and Identity.* Buckingham, UK: Open University Press.

Circumcision

AAP (American Academy of Pediatrics) Task Force on Circumcision. 1999. "Circumcision Policy Statement." *Pediatrics* 103, 686–693.

Benatar, Michael, and David Benatar. 2003. "Between Prophylaxis and Child Abuse: The Ethics of Neonatal Male Circumcision." *American Journal of Bioethics* 3, 35–48.

Christakis, Dimitri A., Eric Harvey, Danielle M. Zerr et al. 2000. "A Trade-Off Analysis of Routine Newborn Circumcision." *Journal of the Ambulatory Pediatric Association* (Supplement) 105, 246–249.

Ericksen Paige, Karen. 1978. "The Ritual of Circumcision." *Human Nature* May, 40–48.

Ericksen Paige, Karen, and Jeffrey M. Paige. 1981. *The Politics of Reproductive Ritual.* Berkeley: University of California Press.

Lemle, Marina. 2005. "Circumcised Men Less Likely to Get HIV, Says Study." *Science Development Network,* 29 July.

Laumann, Edward O., Christopher M. Masi, and Ezra W. Zuckerman. 1997. "Circumcision in the United States." *Journal of the American Medical Association* 277, 1052–1057.

O'Farrell, N., and M. Egger. 2000. "Circumcision in Men and the Prevention of HIV Infection: A Meta-analysis Revisited." *International Journal of Sexually Transmitted Diseases and AIDS* 11, 137–142.

Szabo, R., and R. V. Short. 2000. "How Does Male Circumcision Protect Against HIV Infection?" *British Medical Journal* 320, 1592–1594.

Weiss, H. A., M. A. Quigley, and R. J. Hayes. 2000. "Male Circumcision and Risk of HIV Infection in Sub-Saharan Africa: A Systematic Review and Meta-analysis." *AIDS* 14 (October 20), 2361–2370.

Zoske, Joseph. 1998. "Male Circumcision: A Gender Perspective." *Journal of Men's Studies* 6, 189–208.

Prostate and Testicular Cancer

Chapple, Alison, and Sue Ziebland. 2002. "Prostate Cancer: Embodied Experience and Perceptions of Masculinity." *Sociology of Health and Illness* 24, 820–841.

Clarke, Juanne N. 1999. "Prostate Cancer's Hegemonic Masculinity in Select Print Mass Media Depictions (1974–1995)." *Health Communication* 11 (1), 59–74.

Gray, Ross. 2003. *Prostate Tales: Men's Experiences With Prostate Cancer.* Harriman, TN: Men's Studies Press.

Gurevich, Maria, Scott Bishop, Jo Bower, Monika Malka, and Joyce Nyhof-Young. 2004. "(Dis) Embodying Gender and Sexuality in Testicular Cancer." *Social Science and Medicine* 58, 1597–1607.

Morman, M. T. 2000. "The Influence of Fears Appeals, Message Design, and Masculinity on Men's Motivation to Perform the Testicular Self-Exam." *Journal of Applied Communication Research* 28, 91–116.

Oliffe, John. 2005. "Constructions of Masculinity Following Prostatectomy-Induced Impotence." *Social Science and Medicine* 60, 2249–2259.

Internet Sources

Circumcision Information and Resource Pages
www.cirp.org

Eunuch Archive
www.eunuch.org

European Menprofeminist Network
www.europrofem.org

Gay Men's Health Crisis
www.gmhc.org

Men, Masculinity, Gender Politics
www.xyonline.net

Men's Bibliography
www.mensbiblio.xyonline.net

Men's Health Network
www.menshealthnetwork.org

National Organization of Men Against Sexism (NOMAS)
www.nomas.org
National Organization to Halt the Abuse and Routine Mutilation of Males
www.noharmm.org
National Prostate Cancer Coalition
www.pcacoalition.org
Prostate Cancer Foundation
www.prostatecancerfoundation.org
Prostate.org
www.prostatitis.org/prostateorg
World Congress on Men's Health and Gender
www.ismh.org/wcmh/website ✦

Chapter 6

Ambiguous Bodies

Transgender and Intersex

Key concepts: female-to-male (FtM), intersexuality, male-to-female (MtF), politics of ambiguity, transgendered people, transgressing and gender queerness

In the last two chapters, we discussed some of the ways that gendered norms and expectations pressure all of us to present an appearance appropriate to our gender, and most of us work hard to comply most of the time. But there are people who can't or won't fit into one of the two sexes and two genders: the transgendered and the intersexed. Trans-gendered people who want to change their assigned gender and intersexed people whose genitalia and procreative organs are a biological mix of female and male present a challenge to the binary sex/gender system. Western societies do not have third genders or sexes. We expect people to be "women" or "men," "female" or "male," not "other." We organize society on a two-gender system that most people believe is based on a clear-cut two-sex biology. Sex-difference proponents believe that all gendered behavior naturally emerges from this biology. The many processes that go into the production of what are gender (not sex) differences and the gendered social order are not seen as powerful forces.

Then what do we do about people who feel that they are boys when their birth certificate says female, or girls when their birth certificate says male? What do we do about infants whose genitalia don't appear clearly male or female? They challenge the prevailing beliefs in two and only two sexes and genders. They are similar to people who are multi-racial. We may think that racial categories, especially Black/White, are clear and natural, but DNA testing shows that practically all of us are genetically multiracial. If many people were genetically sex-typed, we'd also find a variety of chromosomal, hormonal, and anatomical patterns unrecognized by our two sex categories (Shrage 2005).

Established categories impose an artificial uniformity on natural heterogeneity. They are bureaucratic, medical, or legal statuses imposed according to a limited set of physical characteristics; in the case of sex and its social equivalent, gender, on the basis of the appearance of the genitalia at birth. If the genitalia don't look clearly female or male, there may be further testing for chromosome type or for internal procreative organs (uterus, ovaries, testicles). But despite the chromosomal, organ, or genital evidence of intersexuality, the pressures of the binary sex/gender system encourage early surgical alteration of the puzzling genitalia into what most closely conforms to a "female" or "male" appearance (Kessler 1998). The child is then designated a girl or a boy on the birth certificate and named, dressed, and raised according to gender-appropriate norms and expectations. At puberty, testosterone is administered to those who were designated as boys to produce additional category markers—facial and body hair and a low-toned voice. Estrogen is administered to those who were designated as girls so that they will develop breasts and round hips. Further genital surgery may be recommended to remove scar tissue or improve appearance. In this way, intersexed children whose genitalia are not clearly female or male, or whose internal organs or chromosome patterns don't match the external genitalia's appearance of female or male, are surgically and medically constructed into "normal" boys and girls. Through this intervention, their intersexuality is erased. By altering ambiguous bodies to fit into the pre-existing categories, the binary legal sex/gender categories retain their integrity.

The surgical and hormonal processes used with intersexed children are the same processes with which transgendered adults or teens change their bodies from female to male (FtM) or male to female (MtF). Transgendered people feel that their bodies do not match their true gender identity. Some may take hormones to start the process of physical change. Some, but not all, have their breasts or penises removed and vaginas, breasts, or penises constructed. Some do only "top surgery" and leave their genitalia intact. Most legally change their names and gender status to their chosen gender and change their appearance and the way they dress, talk, and act. Most male-to-female transgendered people live as women; most female-to-male transgendered people live as men. They want to be accepted as full-fledged members of their chosen gender community.

As with intersexed people, transgendered people have the potential for significantly challenging the binary sex/gender system. But most don't, because intersexed infants are designated one or the other sex and surgically altered to fit, and most transgendered people change themselves to fit their chosen gender. Otherwise, they would suffer legal hassles, social outrage, and violence.

It is almost impossible to live as a "transgender" or an "intersex." In most languages, you cannot refer to people in a way that does not indicate a gender. In face-to-face interaction, the biological or genetic components of sex are taken for granted as congruent with the individual's gendered self-presentation. Let us suppose that "Alice" meets what she thinks is a Latina "Maria." Without ever having physical evidence of Maria's biology or genetics, Alice believes that Maria is from Latino parentage, that she was born with and continues to have a vagina, uterus, and ovaries, and that she produces estrogen and is chromosomally XX. These are all assumptions that guide how Alice communicates with, understands, and treats Maria. Interaction takes place on the basis of the initial attribution of gender and racial ethnic category. This interaction is one of the main aspects of "doing gender" and "doing difference" (West and Fenstermaker 1995; West and Zimmerman 1987). Since we constantly "do gender" and "do race," it makes a lot of difference if you are in the company of someone like you or unlike you. The assumption of like/unlike is built into the predominant racial categories and the binary gender categories, despite constant evidence that people come in a wide variety of body dimensions, skin colors, behaviors, attitudes, and emotions, and that individuals change these variables over time.

The way we interact with others of the same or different gender reflects the "natural attitude," which assumes that there are two and only two sexes, that everyone is naturally one sex or the other no matter how they dress or act and will be that sex from birth to death, and that you can't really change your "natural" sex (Kessler and McKenna 1978, 113–114).

This belief in the bodily basis of social gender is what persuades parents of intersexed children to surgically alter their genitalia to look appropriately female or male so the appearance of the genitalia won't contradict the way the child is being brought up. It is also the reason that transgendered people, who want to live as a member of a gender different from the one they were brought up in, feel they must surgically and hormonally alter their bodies.

Living on the Boundaries

The pressure to have a body that is congruent with one's social status is reinforced in myriad small and constant ways. Boxes on forms in which individuals must place themselves in M or F categories make indicating a sex compulsory; the information that is required is exclusively binary. Those whose bodies are most congruent with the established categories still have to learn to use them in socially appropriate ways, as we have seen in the gendering of bodies. Those whose bodies are significantly incongruent have to accept or resist placement in one category rather than another. If they accept the conventional categorization, they end up hiding something significant about themselves. If they resist conventional categorization, they are left in social limbo unless there is a recognized "other" or "inter" category.

Some intersexed people are fighting the common use of "clarifying" surgery on infants with ambiguous genitalia and are mounting campaigns to establish a legal status that is neither M nor F. Some transgendered people who have gone from one category to another do not wish to "pass," but instead want recognition as a "third gender." The experiences of the category resisters and refusers illuminate the arbitrariness of the categories and the social control over bodies.

A common form of category control are sex-designated public bathrooms. Bathrooms are a major hassle for transgendered and intersexed people and even for women who look masculine or men who look feminine. For example, Betsy Lucal (1999), a six-foot tall, large-bodied woman, refuses to wear feminine clothing, cosmetics, jewelry, and hair style, so she is usually taken for a man. She is challenged in women's bathrooms, and her credit cards and proofs of identity are looked at suspiciously. She wears bright red nail polish when she travels, so she doesn't get hassled over her passport, but otherwise, she has chosen to live on the gender boundaries as a way of challenging conventional views of what women should look like. She doesn't want to do away with gender categories; she wants to subvert their narrowness so that she, too, can be seen as a woman.

Transgendered and intersexed people, like people with multiracial parentage, live on the boundaries or in multiple categories. They have an outsider/insider viewpoint. Those who move between racial designations or genders encounter racism and sexism as members of both privileged and oppressed groups. One female-to-male transgender who continued to work at the same job was told by a client that he was so glad "Susan" was fired, because she was incompetent, while he, "John," was so good at the work. Of course, "Susan" and "John" were the same worker (Schilt 2005).

Transgendering

Most of the early sex/gender changers were male to female, and their goal was to pass successfully as a feminine woman. Passing both normalizes and disrupts conventional gender categories. Those who construct their bodies against their birth sex assignment through hormones and surgery and change their legal gender status reaffirm the conventional categories of man and woman. They typically dress conservatively—if MtF, in dresses and skirts, and if FtM, in suits and ties. They learn to talk, walk, and gesture in "feminine" or "masculine" ways.

Against this almost essentialist perspective, their own behavior sabotages the essentiality of the categories. In Marjorie Garber's words, anyone who passes successfully (by crossing any boundaries) possesses "extraordinary power . . . to disrupt, expose, and challenge, putting in question the very notion of the 'original' and of stable identity" (1992, 16). Transgendered people who pass as normal women or men achieve a successful transformation, but their achievement (and the gender resistance it entailed) remain a secret. As Patricia Gagné and Richard Tewksbury said of their transgendered respondents, the need to come to terms with and publicly proclaim an alternative gender identity outweighed the fear of rejection and desire for self-preservation. But the need to avoid social erasure compelled a complete (even if temporary) transformation. For most, identity achievement entailed the public expression of gender in ways that reflected an internalized sense of self, not one externally imposed upon them. Often this required enacting the gender of the "opposite" sex/gender category, the only known possibility available. (1998b, 86)

More recently, some transgendered people have subverted binary gender and sexual categories through a mixture of clothing, makeup, jewelry, hair styles, behavior, names, and use of language. They are often fluid in their choice of sexual partners. As women with penises and men with breasts, they flaunt their gender queerness.

The consequences of changing gender for status and interaction can be unexpected. FtM transgendered people may gain economic advantages and men's privileges, but to many who are feminists, their new enhanced status is a bittersweet prize, since it is at the expense of women. Black FtMs find they have acquired an intimidating persona—a Black man. Asian FtMs find just the opposite—if they are short and slender, they are denigrated as men, as are gay FtMs. The privileges of manhood and whiteness are reserved for White heterosexual FtMs.

These were the findings of Raine Dozier's intensive interviewing of 18 born-female, trans-identified people aged 20 to 45. Fourteen were white, one was African American, one was Chinese American, and two were Latino. The study should be seen as case histories rather than a representative survey, but it gives an insider view of what it is like to live first as a woman and then as a man. As the following excerpt from the study shows, gender attribution created a gendered scenario for interaction. Dozier, a sociologist, is described in the article as "transgendered, born female, with no immediate plans to transition" (p. 304).[1]

Beards, Breasts, and Bodies

Raine Dozier
University of Washington, Seattle

As I listened to interviewees, the tension and balance between behavior and appearance, between acting masculine and appearing male, became evident. In general, interviewees confirmed Nicholson's (1994) assertion that (perceived) sex is an important aspect of the construction of gender and that perceived sex is a lens through which behavior is interpreted. However, particular sex characteristics such as a penis or breasts are not as crucial to the perception of sex as their meanings created in both social and sexual interaction.

Generally, after taking hormones, interviewees were perceived as men regardless of behavior and regardless of other, conflicting sex signifiers including breasts and, in the case of one interviewee, even when nine months pregnant.[1] The physical assertion of sex is so strong through secondary sex characteristics that gender identity is validated. Interviewees find certain sex characteristics to be particularly important to their social identity as male: "I think its all about facial hair. It's not about my fetish for facial hair, but socially, when you have facial hair, you can pass regardless of what your body looks like. I mean, I was nine months pregnant walking around and people were like, 'Ooh, that guy's fat'" (Billy).

Another interviewee also finds facial hair to be particularly important to initial gender/sex attribution. In reply to the question, "For you, what is the most important physical change since transitioning," he responds, "Probably facial hair, because nobody even questions facial hair. . . . I've met FTMs that have these huge hips. I mean this guy, he was [shaped] like a top, and he had a full beard. Nobody questioned that he had huge hips, so that is the one key thing. And probably secondary is a receding hairline. Even with a high voice, people accept a high voiced man" (Joe).

As the interviewees became socially recognized as men, they tended to be more comfortable expressing a variety of behaviors and engaging in stereotypically feminine activities, such as sewing or wearing nail polish. The increase in male sex characteristics creates both greater internal comfort with identity and social interactions that are increasingly congruent with sex identity. As a result, some FTMs are able to relax their hypermasculine behavior.

> I went through a phase of thinking every behavior I do is going to be cued into somehow by somebody. So, I've got to be hypervigilant about how many long sentences I say, does my voice go up at the end of a sentence, how do I move my hands, am I quick to try and touch someone. . . . And I got to a point where I said, This is who I am. . . . There are feminine attributes and there are masculine attributes that I like and I am going to maintain in my life. . . . If that makes people think, "Oh you're a fag," well great, all my best friends are fags. . . . But when I was first coming out, it was all about "I've got to be perceived as male all the time, no matter what." That bone-crushing handshake and slapping people on the back and all of that silliness. I did all that. (Rogelio).

Like Rogelio, Pete finds transitioning gave him the freedom to express his feminine side:

> "It was very apparent how masculine a woman I was . . . and, now it's like I've turned into this flaming queen like 90 percent of the time. And so my femininity, I had an outlet for it somehow, but it was in a kind of gay way. It wasn't in a womanly kind of way, it was just femininity. Because I don't think that female equals femininity and male equals masculinity" (Pete).

Sex category and gendered behavior, then, are compensatory; they are both responsible for the social validation of gender identity and require a particular balance. When sex is ambiguous or less convincing, there is increased reliance on highly gendered behavior. When sex category is obvious, then there is considerably more freedom in behavior, as is evident when talking to FTMs about the process of transitioning.

For two interviewees, gay men are particularly valuable role models in deconstructing traditional masculinity and learning to incorporate "feminine" behavior and expression into a male identity:

> So, those fairly feminine men that I have dated have been very undeniably male, but they haven't been a hundred percent masculine all the time, and I think I've learned from my relationships with them to sort of relax. Lighten up a little; nail polish isn't going to kill anybody. I think that I'm more able to be at peace with all of the aspects of myself. . . . [Now] I'm not going to go out of my way to butch it up. I'm male looking enough to get away with it, whereas when I did that kind of stuff before I transitioned people were like, "Well, you're not butch enough to be a man." (Billy)

FTMs transition for many reasons, but aligning external appearance with internal identity and changing social interaction were the chief reasons given by my interviewees. "Doing gender" (West and Zimmerman 1987) in a way that validates identity relies on both internal and external factors. Being able to look like one feels is key to the contentment of many FTMs. More than interacting with the social world as a man, comfort in one's body can be a chief motivator for FTMs, especially when seeking chest surgery. "I'd say that having a flat chest really seems right, and I really like that. I can throw a T-shirt on and feel absolutely comfortable instead of going [hunching shoulders]. And when I catch my reflection somewhere or look in the mirror, it's like, 'Oh, yeah' instead of, 'Oh, I forgot,' and that's been the most amazing thing . . . recognizing myself" (Trevor).

Some interviewees believed they would be content to live without any medical treatment or with chest surgery but not hormones, as long as they were acknowledged as transgendered by themselves and their social circle. Even for those who were able to achieve a reasonable level of internal comfort, social interaction remained an ongoing challenge. Feeling invisible or not being treated in congruence with their gender identity motivated them to take hormones to experience broader social interaction appropriate to their gender identity. Some FTMs reported the desire to be seen as trans by other FTMs as an important factor in their decision to transition. For others, being called "ma'am" or treated as a woman in public was particularly grating. Being "she'd" was a constant reminder of the incongruence between social identity and internal gender identity.

> And the longer I knew that I was transgendered, the harder it got to live without changing my body. It's like the acknowledgment wasn't enough for me, and it got to a point where it was no longer enough for the people who knew me intimately to see my male side. It just got to be this really discordant thing between who I knew I was and who the people in my life knew I was . . . because

I was perceived as a woman socially. I was seen as a woman and was treated differently than how I was treated by my friends and the people that I loved. . . . So finally after a couple of years . . . I finally decided to take hormones. (Billy)

The potential impact on social interaction is key to the decision to transition. Although for some FTMs, gaining comfort in their body is the crucial element in decision making, for most interviewees, the change in social interaction is the motivating factor. Being treated as a man socially is important enough to risk many other things including loss of family, friends, and career. For other interviewees, though, not wanting to be treated as a man in all social situations motivated them not to transition. "In some ways, I wouldn't really want to give up my access to woman's space, and I think that would be a big reason why I wouldn't do it because I like being around women. I don't feel like I'm women identified, but I'm women centered. So in that sense, I wouldn't want to give up being able to spend a lot of time with women in different contexts that I might lose if I passed as a man" (Jay).

Some interviewees also worried that appearing as a biological man would make them no longer identifiable as trans or queer, making them invisible to their communities. As well, for some of those not transitioning, the potential loss of friends and family outweighed their desire to transition.

As expected, social interaction changed radically after transitioning, but sometimes in ways not anticipated. Whether these changes were positive or negative, expected or not, they still provided FTMs with social validation of their gender identity and the clear message that they were passing.

Changing Interaction

Many transmen found being perceived as a man enlightening. The most often noted changes to social interaction included being treated with more respect, being allowed more conversational space, being included in men's banter, and experiencing an increase in women's fear of them. Some FTMs realized that they would be threatening to women at night and acted accordingly while others were surprised to realize that women were afraid of them. "I remember one time walking up the hill; it was like nine o'clock, and this woman was walking in front of me, and she kept looking back, and I thought, 'What the hell is wrong with that girl?' And then I stopped in my tracks. When I looked at her face clearly under the light, she was afraid. So I crossed the street" (Joe).

For many FTMs, becoming an unquestioned member of the "boys' club" was an educational experience. The blatant expressions of sexism by many men when in the company of each other was surprising to these new men.

I was on one of the school shuttles on campus and it was at a time when there weren't a lot of people on. There was a male bus driver, myself, and a young woman on the bus, and she had long blonde hair, a very pretty girl. She got off the bus, and there was just me and the bus driver, and the bus driver was reading me as a guy and totally being a sexist pig. I did not know how to deal with it or how to respond, let alone call him on his shit because I wasn't particularly, at this point, feeling like I wanted to get read or anything. So I basically just nodded my head and didn't say anything. (Ted)

One nontransitioned FTM who is usually taken for a man at work also feels pressure to conform and to ward off suspicion by either ignoring or contributing to sexist and homophobic comments when among coworkers. This is in direct contrast to Pete's experience, who became known as an outspoken advocate for women and minorities at his job after transitioning: "I feel like I'm one of the guys, which is really kind of odd. In some ways, it's really affirming, and in some ways, it's really unsettling. In Bellevue [his former job], it was a joke. 'Pete's here, so you better shut up!' Because they're sexist, they're homophobic, they're racist. And I would say, 'This is not something I think you should be talking about in the lunch room.' So I was constantly turning heads because I'm kind of an unusual guy" (Pete).

Acting like a "sensitive new age guy" did not challenge Pete's masculinity or essential maleness but simply defined him as "kind of an unusual guy." He was able to assume this role because his gender was established and supported through his unquestionably male appearance.

Interviewees found that their interactions with both men and women changed as they transitioned. After transitioning, a few FTMs, like the previously quoted interviewee, maintained strong feminist ideals and worked hard to change to appropriate behavior for a feminist man. This was an effort as behavioral expectations for men and butch lesbians differ radically, and what may be attributed to assertiveness in a masculine woman becomes intolerable in a man:

> I found that I had to really, really work to change my behavior. Because there were a lot of skills that I needed to survive as a butch woman in the world that made me a really obnoxious guy. There were things that I was doing that just were not okay. Like in school, talking over people. You know when women speak, they often speak at the same time with each other and that means something really different than when a guy speaks at the same time. And so it wasn't that I changed, it was that people's perceptions of me changed and that in order to maintain things that were important to me as a feminist, I had to really change my behavior. (Billy)

The perception that behavior had not really changed, but people's assignation of meaning to that behavior had, was common in the interviews. That is, what is masculine or feminine, what is assertive or obnoxious, is relative and dependent on social context. And the body—whether one appears male or female—is a key element of social context. These interviews suggest that whether a behavior is labeled masculine or feminine is highly dependent on the initial attribution of sex.

Besides gaining information as insiders, FTMs also felt they gained permission to take up more space as men. Many FTMs transition from the lesbian community, and most in this sample had been butch identified. As a result, they were used to having what they perceived to be a comfortable amount of social space even though they were women. As they transitioned, however, they were surprised at how much social privilege they gained, both conversationally and behaviorally. Terry, a previously high-profile lesbian known for her radical and outspoken politics, reported, "I am getting better service in stores and restaurants, and when I express an opinion, people listen. And that's really weird because I'm not a shy person, so having people sort of check themselves and make more conversational space than they did for me before is really kind of unsettling" (Terry).

As well as being allowed conversational space, many of these new men received special attention, and greater respect from heterosexual women because their behavior was gender atypical yet highly valued. They were noticed and rewarded when confronting sexist remarks, understanding women's social position and performing tasks usually dominated by women. Billy reports an experience in a women's studies class where he was the only man siding with the female students' point of view: "A woman came up to me after class and said, 'Wow, you know you're the most amazing feminist man I've ever met.' I just did not have the heart to ruin that for her. I was just like, you know, there are other guys out there who are capable of this, and it's not just because I'm a transsexual that I can be a feminist" (Billy).

. . . The assumption of a rise in status after sex reassignment also rests largely on the assumption of whiteness. Through my limited sample and conversations with friends, it appears that becoming a Black man is often a step down in status. Rogelio talks about the change in his experience as he becomes more consistently taken for a man:

> I am a Black male. I'm the suspect. I'm the one you have to be afraid of. I'm the one from whom you have to get away, so you have to cross the street, you have to lock your doors. You have to clutch whatever you've got a little closer to your body. . . . It's very difficult to get white FTMs to understand that. . . . [As a Black person], if I go into a store, I am followed. Now I am openly followed; before it was, "Oh, let's hide behind the rack of bread or something so that she won't see us." Now it's, "Oh, it's a guy, he's probably got a gun; he's probably got a knife. We have to know where his hands are at all times." (Rogelio)

Although it is an unpleasant experience, he reports that at least he knows he is consistently passing as a man by the rude treatment he receives from other men in social situations.

Another group of FTMs also experiences being perceived as male as a liability, not a privilege. Even though FTMs can have feminine behavior without calling their maleness into question, feminine behavior does lead to an increase in gay bashing and antigay harassment. FTMs who transitioned from being very butch to being perceived as male generally experienced a radical decline in harassment. Two of these butches were even gay bashed before transitioning because they were perceived to be gay men. With additional male sex characteristics, however, they were no longer perceived to be feminine men. For these men, the transition marked a decline in public harassment and intimidation. However, for more feminine FTMs, the harassment increased after transitioning. Appearing as small, feminine men made them vulnerable to attack.

Conclusion

. . . Trans people are in the unique position of experiencing social interaction as both women and men and illustrate the relativity of attributing behavior as masculine or feminine. Behavior labeled as assertive in a butch can be identified as oppressive in a man. And unremarkable behavior for a woman such as shopping or caring for children can be labeled extraordinary and laudable when performed by a man. Although generally these new men found increased social privilege, those without institutional privilege did not. Becoming a Black man or a feminine man were social liabilities affecting interaction and increasing risk of harassment and harm. Whether for better or worse, being perceived as a man changed social interaction and relationships and validated gender identity.

In addition to illustrating the relativity of assignation of meaning to behavior, these interviews illustrate the relativity of sexual orientation. Sexual orientation is based not exclusively on object attraction but also on the gendered meanings created in sexual and romantic interaction. Sexual orientation can be seen as fluid, depending on both the perceived sex of the individuals and the gender organization of the relationship.

This study of a small group of FTMs helps clarify the relationship between sex and gender because it does not use sex as the initiating point for gender and because most respondents have experienced social interaction as both men and women. Much sociological theory regarding gender assumes that gender is the behavioral, socially constructed correlate of sex, that gender is "written on the body." Even if there are case studies involving occasional aberrations, gender is generally characterized as initiating from sex. With this study, though, the opposite relationship is apparent. Sex is a crucial aspect of gender, and the gendered meaning assigned to behavior is based on sex attribution. People are not simply held accountable for a gender performance based on their sex (see West and Zimmerman 1987); the gendered meaning of behavior is dependent on sex attribution. Whether behavior is defined as masculine or feminine, laudable or annoying, is dependent on sex category. Doing gender, then, does not simply involve performing appropriate masculinity or femininity based on sex category. Doing gender involves a balance of both doing sex and performing masculinity and femininity. When there is not confusion or ambiguity in the sex performance, individuals are able to have more diverse expressions of masculinity and femininity. This balance between behavior and appearance in expressing gender helps explain the changing behavior of FTMs as they transition as well as the presence of men and women with a diversity of gendered behaviors and display.

Note

1. After taking testosterone, an individual appears male even if he or she discontinues use. The interviewee who became pregnant discontinued hormones to ovulate and continue his pregnancy, then began hormones again after childbirth.

References

Nicholson, Linda. 1994. Interpreting gender. *Signs: Journal of Women in Culture and Society* 20: 79–105.

West, Candace, and Don Zimmerman. 1987. Doing gender. *Gender & Society* 1: 125–51.

Intersexuality

Intersexed people are born with genitalia that by conventional standards look neither clearly male nor female. They also frequently have divergent combinations of chromosomes, hormones, and physiology, whose effects may not show up until puberty, but these future effects are not at issue for choosing the sex of a newborn with ambiguous genitalia. In Western societies, intersexed infants are assigned a sex and usually undergo "clarifying" surgery; they are then brought up in the assigned sex. The choice of sex is significantly influenced by culture and the views of mostly men surgeons.

Suzanne Kessler (1998), a psychologist, interviewed pediatric plastic surgeons working with intersexed infants. Her research found that what sex the child with ambiguous genitalia is assigned depends on the size of the penis/clitoris. According to her research, only if the surgeon feels that he (and it is usually a he) can make an adequate-sized penis will the child be designated a boy; otherwise, the sex assignment will be "female." Kessler points out that this social determination of the sex of the child and its construction through surgery is glossed over by medical rhetoric. The doctors' message to the parents is that the child has a true sex that is female or male, and that the surgery is needed to make the anomalous genitals match the true sex. In actuality, the sex is socially constructed, because the child usually ends up with a combination of male and female biology but is designated male or female and socialized in the norms of the assigned sex and gender.

About 1.7 percent of all infants are born with anomalies of sex chromosomes, internal procreative organs, and external genitalia in a variety of combinations (Fausto-Sterling 2000, 50–54). The surgical procedures for dealing with intersexed infants were developed in the 1920s and 1930s by a urologist, Hugh Hampton Young (Chase 1998). In the 1950s, John Money, the noted Johns Hopkins sex researcher, and Lawson Wilkins, the founder of pediatric endocrinology, instituted the practices of immediate postbirth intervention, and their protocol was widely adopted in hospitals in the United States. The theory behind the early intervention is John Money's contention that gender identity is not established until the child is about two years old but then becomes fixed. As Cheryl Chase, founder of the Intersex Society of North America, described the still-used Johns Hopkins model,

> the birth of an intersex infant today is deemed a "psychosocial emergency" that propels a multidisciplinary team of intersex specialists into action. Significantly, they are surgeons and endocrinologists rather than psychologists, bioethicists, representatives from intersex peer support organizations, or parents of intersex children. The team examines the infant and chooses either male or female as a "sex of assignment," then informs the parents that this is the child's "true sex." Medical technology . . . is then used to make the child's body conform as closely as possible to that sex. (1998, 191)

Internal organs and hormonal input are usually left to be treated at adolescence, when the intersexed child often must undergo additional extensive surgery along with medical treatments in order to produce a physiology and anatomy that will match the previously assigned sex and gender (Minto and Creighton 2001).

In the last few years, there has been an intersex movement that protests against "clarifying" surgery on infants. This movement argues that such surgery is genital mutilation that ruins future sexual pleasure. Activists against genital surgery in infancy or childhood recommend that any surgery be left until adolescence, when informed consent is feasible (Chase 2000; Kipnis and Diamond 1998). Yet even if ambiguous genitalia are not reconstructed to look female or male at infancy, most babies and children will of necessity be gendered (Zucker 1999). A gender-neutral or androgynous person is a weird anomaly when there are no "third genders," as there are in some societies. Since our worlds are so divided by gender, and genitalia are the physical signals of gender, it is not surprising that parents of intersexed infants feel they have no choice but to let surgeons construct appropriate-looking genitalia. In their eyes, it would be psychologically damaging for a child to grow up with ambiguous or wrong-looking genitals, which could lead to shaming by peers and rejection by potential sexual partners.

The underlying purpose of neonatal surgery is to create genitals that are supposed to look "normal" and give a clear signal about the person's sex that affirms his or her gender status. These genitals do not necessarily conform to hormonal or genetic sex. To look different in the locker room (the site always given as the source of danger) is potentially stigmatizing (Preves 1998). Here again, medicine serves dominant gender norms. The intersexed child undergoing "clarifying" genital surgery is actually undergoing social control that perpetuates the conditions of gender conformity.

In 1997 and 1998, Sharon Preves (2003) interviewed 37 intersexed adults she found through intersex support groups, internet postings, and professionals who work in the field of sexuality. Her criteria for choosing participants were that they be over 18 years old and have ambiguous genitalia, sexual organs, or sex chromosomes. Her interviewees were aged 20 to 65, mostly Caucasian and college-educated. Of the 84 percent who were sexually active, 46 percent had same-gender partners, which included other intersexed people. In her book about her research, Preves described herself as "a white Jewish woman who was born and raised unambiguously female in a wealthy suburb of Minneapolis" (p. 160). She had urinary infections and urological surgery as a child, which she felt was an important bond with the people she interviewed. All but two had had surgery as infants or children.

Preves' interview topics covered sex/gender identity and its development, challenges as an intersexed person, and responses to those challenges. The surgery, hormonal treatment, and repeated medical examinations and procedures they all had as children and teenagers had pathologized them and had given them feelings of shame and inadequacy. Most of Preves' informants were given misleading or euphemistic explanations during childhood and adolescence. For many, their sense of stigma was dispelled by the intersex activist movement, which gave them knowledge, group social support, and feelings of pride and power. The following excerpt from Preves' book, *Intersex and Identity*, describes their "coming out."

Intersex Pride

Sharon E. Preves
Hamline University, St. Paul, Minnesota

Politicizing identity was important to a number of the participants in this study, regardless of the type of support group with which they were associated. Some of the groups were committed to working on improving current medical treatment, as seen in the efforts undertaken by the Androgen Insensitivity Syndrome Support Groups. Others who were equally committed to effecting medical change worked from outside the medical establishment; for example, Hermaphrodites with Attitude picketed the 1996 Annual Meeting of the American Academy of Pediatrics in Boston.[1] Study participants demonstrated various means of stating both their pride and their politics. For example, recall that 27 percent of those interviewed chose to use their real names for the study. Furthermore, another 24 percent changed their first and sometimes last names as a form of reclaiming themselves.[2]

Many participants spoke of the importance of experiencing a sexual awakening at the same time that they came to terms with their intersexuality. For some, this was perhaps viewed as a political act, in that 14 percent of the sample was sexually active with other intersexuals. Regarding the development of a broader concept of self, participants spoke of being unable to freely explore their sexuality until they had overcome the barriers inherent to secrecy and shame. These barriers were heightened for participants who were repeatedly subjected to genital scrutiny. Breaking free from shame and inhibitions was often associated with learning about and acknowledging one's intersexuality. As Kiira illustrates,

> I was asexual and anorgasmic until I was thirty-two years old. Then I discovered my sexuality, my identity as an intersexed person, and I learned how to become orgasmic. I'd never had any sexual feelings, but it was almost like my sexuality just kind of awakened at that time in my life. Before, I would think about sex and go, "Oh, people like me don't have sex."

Similarly for Greta and Claire, learning to accept and respect their bodies for, and not in spite of their differences, led to enhanced self-confidence and freedom of sexual expression. In Greta's experience, coming to terms with her intersexuality dissipated her earlier fears of inadequacy and inauthenticity. In her own words, "I love having sex. I'm not afraid to let myself go. My response is very normal, so I know that I'm not a freak, as I at one point thought." Claire also articulates the deeper level of trust and appreciation she developed for her body after accepting her intersexuality. In her words,

> And then I came to really love my sexual self. The way I felt, and the way I smelled, and the way I responded, and the way I tasted. I came to love my body that way without any judgment about how it looked in a societal way or how it performed or what it could and couldn't do. I just loved its "itness" for what it was.

While recognizing one's sexual awakening as a form of politcal actvism was important to some study participants, others were engaged in forms of activism that were more explicitly political. Several spoke to their commitment of being "out" and visibly intersexed in an effort to overcome their experiences with shame and isolation. In Julian's words,

> Closets are bad. Closets are awful. Closets are the enemy. Sometimes they can be necessary for short periods of time, but one should always be working towards getting out of the closet, no matter what you have to do. It's so much easier to be out than to be consumed with shame. When you're in the closet it

looks horrible to be out. But when you're out, you look back at digging in the closet and you say, "Why did I do that? Why was I such an idiot for so long?"

But being "out" as an intersexual can sometimes take effort because similar to other types of "invisible" difference, such as some forms of learning disability or chronic illness, intersexuals are often assumed to be typical women and men because clothing quite easily conceals intersex ambiguity. Some participants spoke of wanting to be accurately categorized as intersexed, and as a result, they occasionally engaged in political acts of destabilizing and subverting their social identity by intentionally living in opposition to normative gender roles and expectations.[3] For example, in young Constance's experience,

Who I am, is a person that doesn't have to conform because in my very DNA I don't agree with the societal norm. There's just no way I could fit either [gender] role. Then why the hell should I bother to try? Why don't I have a little fun? It's been a really freeing experience. I'm a lot happier. I don't blend in ever, so I may as well have fun if I'm gonna get noticed anyway. I might as well get noticed for what I really want to be.

And in Julian's case,

Part of the reason I'm out is I want people to know what I am. I want people to know that I'm gender ambiguous. I don't feel female, but I don't necessarily feel male either. I feel like I am in the middle and feel that very solidly. And that seems very natural. When people say, "Do you identify as male or female?" [I hear,] "What do you pretend to be?" I don't pretend. I just am what I am, which is something in between.

Many participants spoke directly to the importance of using social visibility as a strategy for destigmatization and empowerment. Here Tiger speaks of his appearances on television talk shows in an effort to educate lay audiences about intersex and to externalize his feelings of shame.

Becoming a person who is comfortable standing up in public, literally on television and saying, "No matter what you think of how I look or how I speak, no matter what I've done to fit into this world, I am not male or I am not female. And probably neither are you," to be in the position [of] making those kinds of statments and having all the signs and facts to back up my position, it's very exciting. This is a dramatic level of self-acceptance that I have fought with and been tortured by all my life. And to have come to a place where I realize that mine is a position of strength, not of disadvantageous exclusion, which is all it had ever been before . . . it's a good place to come to.[4]

Some participants also spoke openly about their strategies to reappropriate particular words and activities that were formerly associated with medical trauma and social stigma. For example, some members of intersex support groups find it important to not only meet others like themselves, but also to see each other's bodies as they search for validation of their own social and biological experiences. For example, upon meeting another woman with AIS for the first time, Jenny asked:

"Do I look intersexed?" [The other woman said,] "What do you mean?" [Again, Jenny asked,] "Do I look intersexed?" "No, what do you mean? Do I?"

"No." She goes, "Oh yeah, that's right. This is the first time you're meeting any-body. How does that feel to know that no one can walk down the street and 'make' you?" [Jenny] said, "It's like really a relief."

As I have noted throughout this book, most forms of intersex are visible only when an individual is undressed. Participants consistently demonstrated that fully acknowledging one's difference with others who have been similarly out-cast is validating and transforming. Some participants involved in intersex retreats wanted not only to meet and compare themselves to others, but also to see and show others what it was about their bodies that had caused them to be cast as different. Those who described how they participated in these encounters of "genital show and tell" said the experience was empowering for them simply because they had choice regarding when and to whom they exposed their bodies. For many, being able to exert choice increased their sense of autonomy. In addition, seeing other bodies that had been similarly medicalized or had not been medicalized at all provided even further validation for some. For example, speaking of his intersexed partner's body, Tiger said,

My partner is somebody who escaped surgery. So when I look at the genitals on my partner, it's like, "Oh, I see." It really wasn't until just a year ago now that I had my experience with my current partner and it's like, this is what I've been missing. This is what I have hoped for. This is what being with someone who is like me is like.

In addition to these experiences, many study participants found the medical terminology associated with their difference to be shameful and distressing. Moreover, many participants felt that they lacked appropriate language to express their difference in ways that were free of negative connotations. Oftentimes, the ability to express themselves without shame resulted from their association with intersex support and advocacy organizations. For example, in Gaby's experience, "It is only in the last three to four years that I've been able to have the vocabulary to express myself as an intersexual." For many, the term *hermaphrodite* itself was particularly painful. In a rather gutsy and subversive move, the founding director of the Intersex Society of North America chose to embrace the word in the group's newsletter title. Speaking of her decision to do so, Cheryl said,

I was so tickled with the fact that we had made this incredibly traumatic thing into something with humor in it. And we came up with the name Hermaphrodites with Attitude. I thought of myself as incredibly subversive here. Here are all these little subversive messages winding their way out into the world. And [the newsletter] got all over the place. So many people told me, "I just saw the words Hermaphrodites with Attitude and it changed my life in that moment. I was petrified and traumatized; that word had been so painful and yet, there it was out there. Just out there and then I picked up the newsletter and it was my story on every page."

Notes

1. Beck 1997–1998.
2. Fifty-six percent of the sample who changed their names also chose to use their real names in the study.

3. Seidman 1995.
4. Several participants made media appearances in various print, radio, television, and film venues.

References

Beck, Max. 1997/1998. "Hermaphrodites with Attitude Take to the Streets." *Chrysalis: The Journal of Transgressive Gender Identities* 2 (5) (Fall/Winter): 45–46, 50.

Seidman, Steven. 1995. "Identity and Politics in a 'Postmodern' Gay Culture: Some Historical and Conceptual Notes." In *Fear of a Queer Planet: Queer Politics and Social Theory,* ed. Michael Warner, 105–142. Minneapolis: University of Minnesota Press.

The Politics of Ambiguity

Advocates for intersexed people are particularly adamant about surgery on infants and children. They want society to view genital variations "as an expansion of what is meant by female and male" (Kessler 1998, 131). Kessler said,

> A more radical intersexual agenda would make intersex identities moot. There would just be women with large clitorises or fused labia or men with small penises or misshapen scrota—phenotypes with no particular clinical or identity meaning. (1998, 90)

Another possibility, urged by some intersexual and transgender activists, is to have a legal "third gender." That would mean being treated as a person with rights to specially designated public spaces and accommodations, such as showers, dorm rooms, beds in homeless shelters, and bathrooms, and protection from physical danger and violations of personal integrity. The downside is that it would add another category, with its own criteria for who belongs in it, excluding others.

As with other stigmatized identities, the choices for those with marginalized gender and sex statuses are assimilation or blending into the mainstream as much as possible, separate identities with demands for rights based on respect for differences, and activist challenges to the categories that force them to modify their bodies to be "normal."

The first choice, *assimilation,* can be political if the mainstream is forced to make changes in attitudes and environment in order to accept those who are different, as has happened with the disability rights movement, which tries to teach us that ability and disability, bodily integrity and bodily dysfunction are a continuum, not a dichotomy. However, assimilation often results in a false universality with hidden stigmas, so that transgendered people never reveal their early biographies, and intersexed people hide their anomalous genitalia or medical histories.

Separatism maintains distinctive identities, but adds new categories: intersex, transgender, multiracial. Separatism may also sustain the inequality among groups, unless the differences that mark the new identity-based groups are valorized as equivalent to the dominant group's characteristics. Separatism can be protective and a way to do activist politics, but it often produces boundary fights over who belongs in the new group, especially among transgendered people. Do those who have not had surgery qualify as transgendered people? Only top surgery?

Attacking the boundaries of "normal" and "other" directly by refusing to choose one of the conventional sex, sexual, gender, or racial identities is *transgressive*, but needs a follow-up agenda to be truly *transformative* of status hierarchies. How does one live as a transgendered, intersexed, interracial, or sexually queer person when all the norms and expectations are binary?

In the following excerpt, Johanna E. Foster, a White sociologist with a multiracial child, lays out some of the paradoxes of identity politics. She found parallels between the politics of intersex and multiracial movement activists. She argued that they straddle the contradictions between fighting for identity-based rights and fighting against the narrowness of conventional identities with a politics based on "strategic ambiguity"—identity disruption combined with identity affirmation.

Paradoxes of Identity Politics

Johanna E. Foster
Monmouth University, West Long Branch, New Jersey

When my daughter was nearly a year old, she and I found ourselves at the playground one afternoon when a preschooler approached us and asked of my daughter, "Is she black?" Trying consciously to "disrupt" everyday assumptions about race, I responded, "She is black and white. Her Dad is black and her Mom is white. I'm her Mom. How about you? What's your race?" Perhaps somewhat bewildered by how a supposedly yes or no question became slightly more complicated and then redirected, the young, "obviously" white child said, "Oh, I'm just a girl." I was not surprised that our new young friend had already come to know the "clearly obvious" markers of blackness well enough to question my daughter's "ambiguous" racial identity. I was also not surprised that she took for granted that while her own privileged racial identity goes unmarked in American society, her gender identity does not. What did surprise me was my own response: Even as I deliberately tried to challenge what I sensed was this child's belief in particular "commonsense facts" (Garfinkel 1967) about race, I, myself, re-asserted the conventional assumption that race is clearly a matter of biological ties when I turned to my daughter's biological parentage to make sense of her racial identity. . . .

Strategic Ambiguity and the Identity Claims of Multiracial and Intersex Activists

The multiracial movement data is peppered with explicit charges that racial classifications in the United States do not merely reflect the objective reality of race "out there" in America, but are instead reflective of "arbitrary distinctions," "fictions," or "social constructions." Ramona Douglass, president of the Association for Multiethnic Americans, highlights the openly articulated movement sentiment that race is produced in ongoing social interactions when, in at least three separate places in social movement documents, she conceptualizes race as "a conversation" (e.g., Douglass 1997). Similarly, and taking aim at the conceptualization of race as biological, immutable, and self-evident, Valerie Wilkins-Godbee, founding president of Multi-ethnic Women for Media Fairness and representative for A Place for Us New York, argues in her speech at the first Multiracial Solidarity March in Washington, D.C. that "[r]acial identity is neither simple nor fixed but complex and fluid—always changing across time" (Wilkins-Godbee 1996).

Multiracial movement activists are certainly not alone in their overt claims to the social basis of identity. Intersex activists also disrupt the conventional conceptualization of gender as necessarily grounded by essential biological criteria when they suggest that children who are not easily classified using normative biological sex categories should nonetheless be assigned to one of the two socially accepted gender categories of "girl" or "boy." Intersex advocates are also adamant that intersexed children should be afforded the freedom to choose for themselves whether or not they want to use surgery or hormonal treatments to "align" their sex and gender identities once they have reached the age where they can make informed decisions. As such, intersex activists thus take a rather overt stand against the inevitability of particular bodily criteria serving as the basis of gender identity.

Along with rejecting the essence of race as biological purity and the essence of gender as a particular configuration of genitalia, multiracial and intersex activists directly problematize the inevitable operationalization of race and sex [re: not gender] as discrete and/or dichotomous categories. In each case, activists justify the reasonableness of their demands by citing historical, cross-cultural, and sub-cultural evidence of changing or varied patterns of racial and sex classification (e.g., Fausto-Sterling 1993; Root 1992, 1996). For example, multiracial movement activists make claims to the ever-shifting classification of race in the U.S. Census, which has failed to use the same racial classification schema twice since the first recorded Census in 1690 (see Welland 2003). In doing so, multiracial movement activists send a central message: Racial purity is a fiction as evidenced by the very existence of multiracial people throughout history and across cultures. Hence, if racial purity is a fiction, then the notion of essentially discrete racial identity categories is unfounded and must also be abandoned. . . .

Like multiracial movement activists, intersex activists call into question assumptions about the operationalization of identity boundaries, in this case, the dichotomous categories of male and female, when they cite evidence of hermaphroditism in other cultural and historical contexts (e.g., Dreger 1998). One of the first steps intersex activists have taken to combat the medical management of intersexuality is the seemingly simple but powerful assertion that intersex people are not mythical. In an issue of *Hermaphrodites With Attitude,* the newsletter of the Intersex Society of North America, activist Kiira Triea responds to stereotypes about intersexuality by explaining, "Intersexed people, real hermaphrodites, really do exist" (Triea 1995). Deployed as a successful counter to the larger cultural belief—enforced by both the law and the medical establishment—that a two-party sex system is natural and inevitable, intersex activists make clear that intersexed individuals are not in so infrequent numbers as one might expect. Like multiracial movement advocates, intersex activists claim recognition as a people who are "neither male nor female," "both male and female," "both/neither," "intergendered," "sexually intermediate," or "mixed." Indeed, the very retention of the term "mixed" by both the intersex movement and the multiracial movement, as well as the deployment of sometimes competing identifiers such as "biracial," "multiracial," "multiethnic," "intersex," "sexually intermediate," and "hermaphrodite," suggest that activists in both cases openly embrace the permeability of supposedly discrete identity categories.[1]

More importantly for ongoing debates in critical theory, not only do activists in each case openly deconstruct popular conceptualizations and operationalizations of racial and sex identity, they critique the social construction of binary and/or discrete identity categories as a mechanism of social injustice. The most obvious examples of multiracial and intersex advocates expressly politicizing the production of "commonsense facts" about race and sex are the consistent, and respective, charges that multiracialism is a fundamental challenge to white supremacy and intersexuality a fundamental challenge to patriarchy. For instance, multiracial movement activists have tied much of their demands for an official multiracial identifier to their analysis that both past and present racial classifications are nothing more than state-sanctioned practices of maintaining white supremacy. . . .

In the same way that multiracial activists challenge the naturalness of racial classifications by arguing that they are social constructs invented to sustain white privilege, intersex activists also argue that so-called "corrective" surgeries and hormonal treatments are fundamentally performed to relieve cultural anxieties over gender and sexual transgressors that deeply threaten a patriarchal sex and gender system. This charge that the medical management of intersexuality is a form of patriarchal social control is comprised of three specific claims that are somewhat distinct. Activists argue that such procedures are used (1) to protect an arbitrary two-party sex system; (2) to devalue women's bodies; and (3) to enforce compulsory heterosexuality. For example, in *Hermaphrodites Speak!* (ISNA 1997), the first documentary by intersexed people about the intersex movement, activists explicitly discuss intersex treatment as a "deliberate institutionalized effort to maintain gender polarization." . . .

Implicitly Rearticulating the Boundaries of Race, Sex, and Gender

In overtly theorizing the relationship between the reification of identity categories and unjust social practices, however, activists also essentialize the very same identity categories they find problematic when they attempt to legitimate the normalcy of multirace and intersex itself. Embedded in activists' openly deconstructionist claims are interrelated assumptions about multiracialism and intersexuality as true, inherent, ever-present (albeit denied), obvious, fixed identities attached to individuals, and with meanings that are consistent across cultural contexts and historical periods. Of course, these are some of the very same assumptions about race and sex identity that have justified the construction of discrete, exhaustive and/or binary categories of identity that foreclose the possibility of multiraciality and intersexuality in the first place.

For instance, one of the most paradoxical discursive effects of strategic ambiguity is the production of multiracialism and intersexuality as distinct, "real" and "true" identities naturally given by the body rather than ones made possible by social practices of classification that activists so poignantly argue are the source of all sorts of physical and psychological harm (see also Spencer 1997). Multiracial movement activists' repeated use of terms and phrases such as "the reality is," "the truth is," "forced to lie," "we need a true and accurate account," and "forced to commit fraud" expose a more complicated position that there is nothing fictional about multiracial identity even if race itself is "a conversation." Indeed, some multiracial movement activists suggest that while they are "clear" about race, "traditional" civil rights activists who oppose the multiracial movement are "blind" to or "confused" about the "truth" about race. Over and over again, activists assert that multiraciality is a "true identity" in comparison to the "false identity" that multiracial people must claim when they are forced to check only one racial category on various federal and state forms. Unintentionally illustrating this interplay between claims to a core identity and claims to the social construction of identity, multiracial movement advocate Vandon Jenerette explained in his speech at the first Multiracial Solidarity March, "In one lifetime . . . a student . . . went from Negro to Afro-American to African-American—but has a white grand-mother and an Indian grandmother—and no one asked him about all these changes—every time he fills out a form he has to lie and deny" (Jenerette 1996). In one pass, then, Jenerette recognizes the variability of racial clas-sifications in U.S. history while also appealing to some "truth" to the iden-tity categories that constitute racial classification systems. To be clear, it is not that multiracial activists routinely claim all people lie about their true racial identities on official forms, a position that would be more consistent with their deliberate claims that race is a fiction. Rather, the implication is that only multiracial people are forced to be fraudulent when they must choose from a list full of inapplicable identities. . . .

This same tension between claims to the arbitrariness of identity cate-gories and claims to some pre-discursive quality to "both and/or neither" identities is apparent in claims made by intersex activists. In the same way that multiracial movement activists reify the very "monoracial" categories that they claim are invalid when they reconstruct the biological founda-tions of race, intersex activists reify the boundaries of "male" and "female" when they claim that intersex identity is an identity that must no longer be denied. For example, like multiracial movement advocates who claim to be denied a true identity given by genetic ties, intersex movement activists reject surgical and hormonal interventions on infants born with ambiguous genitalia. They do so, in part, by implying that each infant has a unique identity that is given to them at birth, one that is thus "stolen" as a result of unethical "corrective" treatment.[2]

This paradoxical invocation of social constructionist arguments to rein-force the biological foundations of identity is also what Rainier Spencer argues occurs in multiracial advocacy, "Dressing the mythology of biologi-cal race in the garb of socially designated race is a transparent artifice that does nothing to resolve the fact that the socially designated racial catego-ries are precisely the same as the biological classifications upon which they are based" (1997, 95). In this case, although intersex advocacy disrupts the notion that certain genitals and gender categories should *match*, re-artic-ulation occurs as activists do not publicly and explicitly question the cul-tural practice of using genital (or hormonal, or chromosomal) distinctions as foundational to social identities in the first place. Instead, intersex advocacy affirms the use of genitals to mark sex categories, just as long as they are not interpreted in a way that denies the legitimacy of inter-sexuality. . . .

Taken together, these illustrations suggest that while multiracial move-ment activism shifts the debate to which biological ties are marked rather than refutes the use of biological ties in general, intersex activism shifts the focus from a particular set of biological markers of sex/gender/sexuality to others without fundamentally challenging the use of biology to naturalize identities. By asserting that the very boundaries between conventional race and sex categories are not as impassable as we would like to believe because there is a "true" or "real" multirace or intersex identity that has been denied, activists deploy a kind of strategic ambiguity, or a set of explicit social constructionist claims about identity that then paradoxically help solidify new boundaries around "clearly" distinct both and/or neither identities. Indeed, the very embrace of the names "multiracial" and "intersexual" suggests that activists see themselves as something different than "monoracial" and "monosexed" people. In doing so, identity boundaries are shifted, but not necessarily weakened.

Notes

1. The deployment of what could be competing signifiers by both activists and academicians alike is worth addressing since "crossing" boundaries may not be the same as occupying a space "in-between," living as "both and/or neither," in a "liminal" or dynamic state of becoming, as a "hybrid" or "mixture" of supposedly essentially distinct elements, as constantly "in flux," or as something else entirely.
2. The data suggest that intersex advocates are not always aligned in their perceptions of whether it is sex, gender and/or sexual identity that is denied by "corrective" treatment. These findings alone are significant because they mirror the complicated perceptions about these categories in the larger culture.

References

Douglass, R. 1997. Testimony before the House Subcommittee on Government Management, Information, and Technology of the Committee on Government Reform and Oversight, May 22, 1997, *Hearing on Federal Measures of Race and Ethnicity and the Implications for the 2000 Census.* 105th Cong., 1st Sess., 23 April and 2 May, 1997.

Dreger, A. D. 1998. *Hermaphrodites and the Medical Invention of Sex.* Cambridge, MA: Harvard University Press.

Fausto-Sterling, A. 1993. "The Five Sexes: Why Male and Female Are Not Enough." *The Sciences* 33 (2), 20–25.

Garfinkel, H. 1967. *Studies in Ethnomethodology.* Englewood Cliffs, NJ: Prentice Hall.

ISNA. 1997. *Hermaphrodites Speak!* Documentary produced by the Intersex Society of North America.

Jenerette, V. 1996. "The New Face of America—Moving Beyond Race." Speech at Multiracial Solidarity March I. Washington, D.C.

Root, M. P. P. (ed.). 1992. *Racially Mixed People in America.* London: Sage.

——. (ed.). 1996. *The Multicultural Experience: Racial Borders as the New Frontier.* Thousand Oaks, CA: Sage.

Spencer, R. 1997. "Theorizing Multiracial Identity Politics in the United States," Doctoral Dissertation, Emory University. Ann Arbor, MI: UMI Dissertation Services.

Triea, K. 1995. "The Awakening." *Hermaphrodites With Attitude!* Newsletter of the Intersex Society of North America, Winter.

Welland, S. 2003. "Being Between." *ColorLines: Race, Culture, Action.* Summer, 31–33.

Wilkins-Godbee, V. 1996. Untitled Speech. Multiracial Solidarity March I, Washington, D.C.

Critical Summary

The complexities of intersex and transgender identities are fault lines in the social order that can be exploited for progressive social change. Multiple genders, sexes, and sexualities show that the conventional categories are not universal or essential, nor are the social processes that produce dominance and subordination. Border crossers and those living on borders have opened a social dialogue over the power of categories, and their resistances, refusals, and transgressions have encouraged political activism.

The goals and political uses of community and identity have not been uniform. Those whose bodies don't conform to norms—hefty, tall women and short, slender men—don't want to change their bodies or their gender; they want gender norms to expand. Some MtF and FtM transgendered people want to pass as a member of their chosen category. They modify their bodies surgically and hormonally and learn to walk, talk, dress, and gesture convincingly in order to embody femininity or masculinity. They support rather than challenge the gendered social order. Other transgendered people are gender benders who modify some of their bodies, taking hormones or having "top surgery" but not altering genitalia and often choosing both men and women as sex partners. They "queer" sex/gender categories.

Intersex activism has centered on combating genital surgery on infants with ambiguous genitalia and pressuring for a recognition of intersex as a legal status. Both goals would disrupt the binary sex/gender system by undermining its biological rationale. However, the political pressure to recognize a "third identity" adds another category, with boundaries and borders that contain and exclude.

Rather than weakening the power of categories to control heterogeneous and diverse lives, the establishment of another category starts the cycle of boundary definition and border disputes all over again. New categories also enter the political arena with demands for social recognition and distribution of rewards and privileges. Older identity-based political groups of gays, lesbians, transgendered, and intersexed people argue that the new groups undercut their claims of discrimination and siphon off economic resources.

Ambiguity politics that add new categories of people offer a place for those who don't fit into conventional categories, but the hierarchical system of social recognition and resource distribution is not overthrown. If heterosexual, White, and prosperous people are at the top of the hierarchical distribution of social power, and homosexual, poor, and Black people at the bottom, transgendered and intersexed people might fit into the middle, or, intersected with disadvantaged racial and economic statuses, may become the new bottom layer of multiple oppressions.

Note

1. Researchers and writers in the areas of intersex and transgender usually indicate where they are located in the politics of identity, as a way of alerting the reader to their standpoint, sympathies, and possible biases.

References and Recommended Readings

Colker, Ruth. 1996. *Hybrid: Bisexuals, Multiracials, and Other Misfits Under American Law.* New York: New York University Press.

Gamson, Joshua G. 1995. "Must Identity Movements Self-Destruct? A Queer Dilemma." *Social Problems* 42, 390–407.

——. 1997. "Messages of Exclusion: Gender, Movements, and Symbolic Boundaries." *Gender & Society* 11, 178–199.

——. 1998. *Freaks Talk Back: Tabloid Talk Shows and Sexual Nonconformity.* Chicago: University of Chicago Press.

Garber, Marjorie. 1992. *Vested Interests: Cross-Dressing and Cultural Anxiety.* New York: Routledge.

Herdt, Gilbert (ed.). 1994. *Third Sex Third Gender: Beyond Sexual Dimorphism in Culture and History.* New York: Zone Books.

Kessler, Suzanne J., and Wendy McKenna. 1978. *Gender: An Ethnomethodological Approach.* Chicago: University of Chicago Press.

Lorber, Judith. 1999. "Crossing Borders and Erasing Boundaries: Paradoxes of Identity Politics." *Sociological Focus* 32, 355–369.

——. 2001. "It's the 21st Century—Do You Know What Gender You Are?" In *An International Feminist Challenge to Theory, (Advances in Gender Research Vol. 5)* edited by Marcia Texler Segal and Vasilike Demos. Greenwich, CT: JAI.

Lucal, Betsy. 1999. "What It Means to Be Gendered Me: Life on the Boundaries of a Dichotomous Gender System." *Gender & Society* 13, 781–797.

Shrage, Laurie. 2005. "Is Female to Male as Black Is to White? Sex and Miscibility." Paper presented at McGill University, University of Sheffield, and California State University, Northridge.

West, Candace, and Sarah Fenstermaker. 1995. "Doing Difference." *Gender & Society* 9, 8–37.

West, Candace, and Don Zimmerman. 1987. "Doing Gender." *Gender & Society* 1, 125–151.

Intersexuality

Chase, Cheryl. 1998. "Hermaphrodites With Attitude: Mapping the Emergence of Intersex Political Activism." *GLQ: A Journal of Lesbian and Gay Studies* 4, 189–211.

——. 2000. "Genital Surgery on Children Below the Age of Consent: Intersex Genital Mutilation." In *Psychological Perspectives on Human Sexuality*, edited by L. Szuchman and F. Muscarella. New York: Wiley.

Domurat Dreger, Alice. 1998. *Hermaphrodites and the Medical Invention of Sex*. Cambridge, MA: Harvard University Press.

——. (ed.). 1999. *Intersexuality in the Age of Ethics*. Hagerstown, MD: University Publishing Group.

Fausto-Sterling, Anne. 2000. *Sexing the Body: Gender Politics and the Construction of Sexuality*. New York: Basic Books.

Foucault, Michel. 1980. *Herculine Barbin: Being the Recently Discovered Memoirs of a Nineteenth-Century French Hermaphrodite*. (Trans. Richard McDougall). New York: Pantheon.

Hird, Myra J. 2000. "Gender's Nature: Intersexuals, Transsexuals, and the 'Sex'/'Gender' Binary." *Feminist Theory* 1, 347–364.

——. 2003. "Considerations for a Psychoanalytic Theory of Gender Identity and Sexual Desire: The Case of Intersex." *Signs* 28, 1067–1092.

Kessler, Suzanne J. 1998. *Lessons From the Intersexed*. New Brunswick, NJ: Rutgers University Press.

Kipnis, Kenneth, and Milton Diamond. 1998. "Pediatric Ethics and the Surgical Assignment of Sex." *Journal of Clinical Ethics* 9, 398–410.

Minto, Catherine, and Sarah Creighton. 2001. "Objective Cosmetic and Anatomical Outcomes at Adolescence of Feminising Surgery for Ambiguous Genitals Done in Childhood." Research Letter. *Lancet* 358 (July 14), 124–125.

Preves, Sharon E. 1998. "For the Sake of the Children: Destigmatizing Intersexuality." Special Issue on Intersex, *Journal of Clinical Ethics* 9 (4), 411–420.

——. 2003. *Intersex and Identity: The Contested Self*. New Brunswick, NJ: Rutgers University Press.

——. 2004. "Out of the O.R. and Into the Streets: Exploring the Impact of Intersex Activism." *Research in Political Sociology* 13, 179–223.

Zucker, Kenneth J. 1999. "Intersexuality and Gender Identity Differentiation." *Annual Review of Sex Research* 10, 1–69.

Transgender

Ames, Jonathan (ed.). 2005. *Sexual Metamorphosis: An Anthology of Transsexual Memoirs.* New York: Vintage.

Atkins, Dawn (ed.). 1998. *Looking Queer: Body Image and Identity in Lesbian, Bisexual, Gay, and Transgender Communities.* New York: Haworth Press.

Bernstein, Fred A. 2004. "On Campus, Rethinking Biology 101." *New York Times* Sunday Styles, 7 March, 1, 6.

Bolin, Anne. 1988. *In Search of Eve: Transsexual Rites of Passage.* South Hadley, MA: Bergin & Garvey.

Bornstein, Kate. 1994. *Gender Outlaw: On Men, Women, and the Rest of Us.* New York: Routledge.

Brown, Patricia Leigh. 2005. "A Quest for a Restroom That's Neither Men's Room Nor Women's Room." *New York Times,* 4 March, A14.

Butler, Judith. 2001. "Doing Justice to Someone: Sex Reassignment and Allegories of Transsexuality." *GLQ: A Journal of Lesbian and Gay Studies* 7, 621–636.

Califia, Pat. 1997. *Sex Changes: The Politics of Transgenderism.* San Francisco: Cleis Press.

Cromwell, Jason. 1999. *Transmen and FTMs: Identities, Bodies, Genders, and Sexualities.* Chicago: University of Chicago Press.

Denny, Dallas (ed.). 1997. *Current Concepts in Transgender Identity.* New York: Garland.

Devor, Holly [Aaron Devor]. 1989. *Gender Blending: Confronting the Limits of Duality.* Bloomington: Indiana University Press.

———. 1997. *FTM: Female-to-Male Transsexuals in Society.* Bloomington: Indiana University Press.

Dozier, Raine. 2005. "Beards, Breasts, and Bodies: Doing Sex in a Gendered World." *Gender & Society* 19, 297–316.

Ekins, Richard. 1997. *Male Femaling: A Grounded Theory Approach to Cross-Dressing and Sex-Changing.* New York and London: Routledge.

Epstein, Julia, and Kristina Straub (eds.). 1991. *Body Guards: The Cultural Politics of Gender Ambiguity.* New York: Routledge.

Feinberg, Leslie. 1996. *Transgender Warriors: Making History From Joan of Arc to Dennis Rodham.* Boston: Beacon Press.

Gagné, Patricia, and Richard Tewksbury. 1998a. "Conformity Pressures and Gender Resistance Among Transgendered Individuals." *Social Problems* 45, 81–101.

———. 1998b. "Rethinking Binary Conceptions and Social Constructions: Transgender Experiences of Gender and Sexuality." In *Advances in Gender Research,* Vol. 3, edited by Marcia Texler Segal and Vasilikie Demos. Greenwich, CT: JAI.

———. 1999. "Knowledge and Power, Body and Self: An Analysis of Knowledge Systems and the Transgendered Self." *Sociological Quarterly* 40, 59–83.

Gagné, Patricia, Richard Tewksbury, and Deanna McGaughey. 1997. "Coming Out and Crossing Over: Identity Formation and Proclamation in a Transgender Community." *Gender & Society* 11, 478–508.

Halberstam, Judith. 1998. *Female Masculinity.* Durham, NC: Duke University Press.

Hale, C. Jacob. 1998. "Consuming the Living, Dis (re) membering the Dead in the Butch/FTM Borderlands." *Journal of Gay and Lesbian Studies* 4, 311–348.

Hausman, Bernice L. 1995. *Changing Sex: Transsexualism, Technology, and the Idea of Gender.* Durham, NC: Duke University Press.

Heyes, Cressida J. 2003. "Feminist Solidarity After Queer Theory: The Case of Transgender." *Signs* 28, 1093–1120.

Hines, Sally. 2005. "'I Am a Feminist but . . .': Transgender Men and Women and Feminism." In *Different Wavelengths: Studies of the Contemporary Women's Movement,* edited by Jo Reger. New York: Routledge.

Jacobs, Sue-Ellen, Wesley Thomas, and Sabine Lang (eds.). 1997. *Two-Spirit People: Native American Gender Identity, Sexuality, and Spirituality.* Urbana: University of Illinois Press.

Mason-Schrock, Douglas. 1996. "Transsexuals' Narrative Construction of the True Self." *Social Psychology Quarterly* 59, 176–192.

Meyerowitz, Joanne. 2002. *How Sex Changed: A History of Transsexuality in the United States.* Cambridge, MA: Harvard University Press.

Middlebrook, Diane Wood. 1998. *Suits Me: The Double Life of Billy Tipton.* Boston: Houghton Mifflin.

Najmabadi, Afsaneh. 2005. *Women With Mustaches and Men Without Beards: Gender and Sexual Anxieties of Iranian Modernity.* Berkeley: University of California Press.

Namaste, Viviane. 2000. *Invisible Lives: The Erasure of Transsexual and Transgendered People.* Chicago: University of Chicago Press.

Prosser, Jay. 1998. *Second Skin: The Body Narratives of Transsexuality.* New York: Columbia University Press.

Raymond, Janice G. 1979. *The Transsexual Empire: The Making of the She-male.* Boston: Beacon.

Roen, Katrina. 2002. "'Either/Or' and 'Both/Neither': Discursive Tensions in Transgender Politics." *Signs* 27, 501–522.

Rubin, Gayle S. 1992. "Of Catamites and Kings: Reflections on Butch, Gender, and Boundaries." In *The Persistent Desire: A Femme-Butch Reader,* edited by Joan Nestle. Boston: Allyson Publications.

Schilt, Kristen Rose. 2005. "Just One of the Guys? FTMs, Male Privilege, and the Workplace." Paper presented at the American Sociological Association Annual Meetings, Philadelphia.

Schrock, Douglas, Lori Reid, and Emily M. Boyd. 2005. "Transsexuals' Embodiment of Womanhood." *Gender & Society* 19, 317–335.

Stone, Sandy. 1991. "The *Empire* Strikes Back: A Posttranssexual Manifesto." In *Body Guards: The Cultural Politics of Gender Ambiguity,* edited by Julia Epstein and Kristina Straub. New York: Routledge.

Wickman, Jan. 2001. *Transgender Politics: The Construction and Deconstruction of Binary Gender in the Finnish Transgender Community.* Åbo, Finland: Åbo Akademi University Press.

Wilchins, Ricky Anne. 1997. *Read My Lips: Sexual Subversion and the End of Gender.* New York: Firebrand Books.

Internet Sources

Intersexual

Bodies Like Ours—Intersex Information and Peer Support
www.bodieslikeours.org

International Foundation for Gender Education
www.ifge.org

Intersex Initiative
www.intersexinitiative.org

Intersex Society of North America
www.isna.org

Transgender

National Transgender Advocacy Coalition
www.ntac.org

Sexual Minority Youth Assistance League
www.smyal.org/main.php

Sylvia Rivera Law Project
www.srlp.org

Transgender at Work
www.tgender.net/taw

Transgender Care
www.transgendercare.com

Transgender Forum
www.tgforum.com

Transgender Guide
www.tgguide.com

Transgender Law and Policy Institute
www.transgenderlaw.org ✦

Chapter 7

You Don't Need Arms and Legs to Sing

Gender and Disability

Key concepts: continuum of physical functioning, gendering and disabling, "sitpoint," social construction of "disability," transcending the body

Throughout this book, we have focused on the ways that the body is socially and culturally constructed, showing how human bodies are given meanings beyond the biological. We have focused on how the body is gendered—made masculine or feminine—according to social norms. We have interwoven racial ethnic and social class effects in the gendering processes and argued that women's and men's bodies are not uniform, but vary by both physical characteristics and social patterning. Now we bring in another crucial way that bodies vary—on a continuum of physical functioning and on the social construction of the meaning of that continuum.

Consider the following recent newspaper accounts: A description of *Murderball*, a documentary of quadraplegic athletes playing wheelchair rugby, in which the players "perform remarkable feats of wheeling and spinning, executing artful feints and lobbing courtwide passes to one another" (McGrath 2005, D7). A description of a concert by Thomas Quasthoff, a bass-baritone who "will be introduced as a distinguished artist, a Grammy Award winner and popular recitalist who appears regularly with the major orchestras of the world"; nothing will be said about his "abnormally short legs and vestigial arms, a result of his mother's having taken thalidomide when she was pregnant"—he used to talk about it but now "considers it irrelevant" (Tommasini 2004, E1). A description of Matt Fraser, "a handsome, six-foot-tall English actor, singer and sometime drummer with pouty lips, a black belt in karate," who was about to star in *The Flid Show,* a stage drama about "a British nightclub singer who was born with abnormally fore-shortened arms"; Fraser's "flipper arms" are also a result of his mother having taken thalidomide (Schillinger 2005, 8). Fraser has not only appeared as himself; he previously played a heroin dealer in a British TV series, *Metrosexuality.*

It's not only successful men with paralyzed or missing limbs who are newsworthy. The obituaries of Diana Golden Brosnihan, who died of cancer at 38, called her life "remarkable" (Araton 2001, D1). A skier from the age of five, she developed bone cancer when she was 12 and resumed skiing six months after her right leg was amputated above the knee. Skiing on one leg with regular ski poles, she competed against two-legged skiers and won a gold medal in the giant slalom in the 1988 Winter Olympics, as well as 10 world and 19 U.S. championships from 1986 to 1990, skiing against others with disabilities (Litsky 2001). Golden Brosnihan didn't want to be admired because she had overcome a disability. "She wanted admiration for her technique, her skill, for how she had discarded disabled ski equipment for regular ski poles to produce faster times and fought successfully to compete in the same races with the nonhandicapped" (Araton 2001, D1). In recognition of her fight for equal status, her citation when she was inducted into the Women's Sports Foundation International Hall of Fame in 1997 read, "She persuaded the ski world to treat all athletes the same, regardless of ability or, in her case, disability" (Litsky 2001, D7).

Athletes and performers use their bodies in their work; people whose careers rely on their minds need to surmount their bodies. Stephen Hawking is a famous 63-year-old physicist who has had amyotrophic lateral sclerosis (Lou Gehrig's disease) since he was 21. An incurable, progressive neurological disease, ALS has confined Hawking's paralyzed body to a wheelchair and 24-hour nursing care. To enable him to speak and write, colleagues in Britain and the United States have devised a computer program and voice synthesizer system attached to his wheelchair. He has written groundbreaking, best-selling books, such as *The History of Time,* teaches at Cambridge University in Great Britain, and gives scientific lectures and popular talks. He is married and has three children and one grandchild.

What Is a Disability?

Given these accounts, we could well ask what a disability is. Each of us is likely, at some time in our lives, to become disabled—temporarily for an acute episode through illness or accident or permanently for all or the rest of our lives through congenital conditions, injuries, chronic illnesses, or the debilities of aging. The World Health Organization defines disability, physical and mental, in three ways: *impairment,* any loss or abnormality of psychological, physiological, or anatomical structure or function; *disability,* any functional restriction (resulting from an impairment) or lack of ability to perform an activity within the range considered normal for a human being; and *handicap,* the relationship between impaired and/or disabled people and their surroundings affecting their ability to participate normally in a given activity and putting them at a disadvantage.

It is difficult to obtain global estimates on disability, but during 2005–2006, the United Nations and World Health Organization worked on developing a way to measure the global prevalence of disability. One important finding of their research so far is that "at a global level, women live on average 3.9 years longer than men, but lose the equivalent of 1.9 extra years of good health to the non-fatal consequences of diseases and injuries. In other words, although women live longer, they spend a greater amount of time with disability" (Mathers et al. 2001, 1689). They also spend a greater amount of time as caretakers of aging and disabled male partners and other family members.

Having a permanent disability may not be an identity or a role for the person concerned; instead, it may be hidden because it is stigmatizing. Conversely, when diminished body functioning is heroically compensated by athletic, creative, or intellectual feats, the stigma is converted to a charismatic aura. Sometimes, just living a full life—going to college, having a good job, getting married, having children—is the cause for celebration. Diana DeVries, born without arms or legs, refused prostheses as a child and lived such a full life as a proud "Venus on wheels" (Frank 2000). In Trafalgar Square in London, there is a prominently displayed statue, which will be there until 2007:

> The statue, 11 feet 7 inches of snow-white Carrara marble, shows the naked, eight-and-a-half-month-pregnant figure of 40-year-old Alison Lapper, a single mother who was born with shortened legs and no arms. Ms. Lapper is a friend of the sculptor, Marc Quinn, who has said that Nelson's Column, the focal point of Trafalgar Square, is "the epitome of a phallic male moment" and that he thought "the square needed some femininity." (Lyall 2005, E1)

Ironically, Admiral Horatio Nelson, a famous British eighteenth-century naval commander in the Napoleonic Wars, was also disabled—he lost an arm and was blinded in one eye during the battles he fought. His statue at the top of the column shows him with a pinned sleeve, but it is so high up that it is hard to see without binoculars.

The stories of public heroes don't often tell us about the caregivers and technologists that make it possible for them to thrive, if not to live. Just like the rest of us, people with lesser physical functioning are embedded in relationships, as a feminist ethics of care points out. We are all, at one time or another, care receivers or caregivers, and sometimes both simultaneously. According to Joan Tronto, a feminist philosopher,

> The care perspective requires that we think about the moral dimension of receiving care as well as that of giving care. It requires that we reflect upon the place of dependency, illness, insecurity, and death in human life. These have not been the central concerns of moral philosophy and political theory. Furthermore, exploring the personal provision of care makes clear how limited our individual capacities are and how much we depend upon others for guidance and direction. (Tronto 2006, 431)

In addition to an ethics of care, feminists have contributed other concepts to disability studies: the intersection of body functioning with gender and sexual orientation in discrimination patterns; the standpoints of people of different body and social statuses, especially gender, racial ethnic group, class, and age; the gendered social construction of disabling processes; gendered discourse and language as shaping how we think about body functioning; a systemic view of "disability" as subordinating and silencing, especially for women (Garland Thomson 2005).

Gendering and Disabling

How does gendering intersect with processes of disabling? Is the process of disabling different for women and men? Gendering separates women and men in their work and family roles and thus affects the extent to which disabling modifies work opportunities, living arrangements, family life, and a person's sense of self differently for women and men. People with physical impairments certainly resist and reshape social expectations about what they can or cannot do, but the behavior of physicians, families, and professional and lay caretakers often reflects conventional ideas about what women and men can do when disabled. These beliefs about "normal" gendered behavior lead them to encourage or discourage surmounting or giving in to body limitations.

In a widely cited paper, Michelle Fine and Adrienne Asch (1985) argued that women with disabilities face "sexism without the pedestal." Compared with men of a similar level of physical functioning, women are less likely to find jobs that allow them to be economically independent. They are also less likely to have a lifetime partner, because they need the care and attention that women are expected to give to others. Lesbians may be better able to find a life partner or a circle of women caregivers.

In the traditional husband role, a man expects care from his wife and expects to support and protect her and their children. Therefore, as long as a man with disabilities can earn an income, he can fulfill his family role obligations. However, sexuality and its machismo qualities are particularly devastating minefields for men with disabilities, as it is for men who have had prostate surgery and older men. As we have seen, the immense popularity of Viagra and similar drugs indicates that actual or imagined sexual dysfunction is very widespread, even among healthy men. In short, despite the conventional wisdom that "'disabled man' is a self-contradiction, because men are stereotypically supposed to be 'able,' strong, and powerful" (Tolmach Lakoff 1989, 368), a man with disabilities may be quite able to function well as a husband, father, and lover.

A woman with disabilities can run a household, take care of her children, and also work outside the home, yet gynecologists are more likely to suggest a hysterectomy than help with getting pregnant. Women with quite severe physical limitations have devised ways of caring for small children: "One mother who could not use her arms found that her two children both learned to scramble up her and hang around her neck" (Lonsdale 1990, 79). Carrie Killoran says of her own parenting, "People with disabilities are already accustomed to doing everything differently and more slowly, and caring for children is no different" (1994, 122). Nonetheless, because she is viewed as not being able to be the chief caretaker in a household, a woman with disabilities is often discouraged from having children. Interviews with 31 women aged 22 to 69, with a variety of disabilities and of different racial ethnic groups, well-educated and highly productive, revealed "the common experience of having their reproductive needs undervalued. Many said their physicians treated them as asexual, thought they should not be having children, and assumed that they would not be having children and that they did not want menstrual periods. In many cases, the first recommendation offered was to have a hysterectomy" (Nosek et al. 1995, 512).

The conventional norms of masculinity push men to find ways of feeling independent, even when they need to rely on white canes (Kudlick 2005). Looking at masculinity and physical disability in the lives of ten men, Thomas Gerschick and Adam Stephen Miller (1994) found that those who subscribed to conventional ideals of masculinity felt they had to demonstrate physical strength, athleticism, sexual prowess, and independence. Their self-image was tied in to heroics and risk taking, but they often felt inadequate and incomplete because they couldn't do what they wanted or go where they wanted. The men who reformulated these norms defined their ways of coping with their physical limitations as demonstrations of strength and independence. For example, two quadriplegics who needed round-the-clock personal care assistants did not feel they were dependent on others but had hired helpers whom they directed and controlled. The men who rejected the standard version of masculinity put more emphasis on relationships than on individual accomplishments, were comfortable with varieties of sexuality, and felt they were nonconformists.

Disability and Gendered Sexuality

Irving Kenneth Zola, a sociologist who had difficulty walking as a result of polio, said that "our society does not like to picture people who are weak, sick, and even dying, having needs for sexual intimacy" (1982a, 214). From personal experience, he found that there were few apartments for couples in an otherwise comprehensive living facility in the Netherlands, and that a Swedish project that encouraged the sexual involvement of able-bodied counselors with people with severe disabilities was discontinued because the counselors "actually began to find these very physically disabled people attractive, and *that* was regarded as shocking if not sick" (p. 215).

Conceptions of masculine sexuality as assertive and penetrative in effect "unman" an adult male with physical impairments. Although he conceded that there were many ways to make love, Robert Murphy, a paraplegic, bleakly assessed his future sexuality:

> Most forms of paraplegia and quadriplegia cause male impotence and female inability to orgasm. But paralytic women need not be aroused or experience orgasmic pleasure to engage in genital sex, and many indulge regularly in intercourse and even bear children, although by Caesarean section. . . . Paraplegic women claim to derive psychological gratification from the sex act itself, as well as from the stimulation of other parts of their bodies and the knowledge that they are still able to give pleasure to others. . . . Males have far more circumscribed anatomical limits. Other than having a surgical implant that produces a simulated erection, the man can no longer engage in genital sex. He either becomes celibate or practices oral sex—or any of the many other variations in sexual expression devised by our innovative species. Whatever the alternative, his standing as a man has been compromised far more than has been the woman's status. He has been effectively emasculated. (1990, 96)

Irving Kenneth Zola's version of sexuality is much more diffuse and emotional. In the following excerpt, he described mutual lovemaking with a severely paralyzed woman, an activity that began with his doing all her physical care, as well as the more conventional undressing, and ended with him feeling that she had made love to him as well.

Tell Me, Tell Me

Irving Kenneth Zola

Now I was the one who was nervous. Here we were alone in her room thousands of miles from my home.

"Well, my personal care attendant is gone, so it will all be up to you," she said sort of puckishly, "Don't look so worried! I'll tell you what to do."

This was a real turn-about. It was usually me who reassured my partner. Me who, after putting aside my cane, and removing all the clothes that masked my brace, my corset, my scars, my thinness, my body. Me who'd say, "Well, now you see 'the real me.'" How often I'd said that, I thought to myself. Saying it in a way that hid my basic fear—that this real me might not be so nice to look at . . . might not be up to 'the task' before me.

She must have seen something on my face, for she continued to reassure me, "Don't be afraid." And as she turned her wheelchair toward me she smiled at me that smile that first hooked me a few hours before. "Well," she continued, "first we have to empty my bag." And with that brief introduction we approached the bathroom.

Anger quickly replaced fear as I realized she could get her wheelchair into the doorway but not through it.

"Okay, take one of those cans," she said pointing to an empty Sprite, "and empty my bag into it."

Though I'd done that many times before it wasn't so easy this time. I quite simply couldn't reach her leg from a sitting position on the toilet and she couldn't raise her foot toward me. So down to the floor I lowered myself and sat at her feet. Rolling up her trouser leg I fumbled awkwardly with the clip sealing the tube. I looked up at her and she laughed, "It won't break and neither will I."

I got it open and her urine poured into the can. Suddenly I felt a quiver in my stomach. The smell was more overpowering than I'd expected. But I was too embarrassed to say anything. Emptying the contents into the toilet I turned to her again as she backed out. "What should I do with the can?" I asked.

"Wash it out," she answered as if it were a silly question. "We try to recycle everything around here."

Proud of our first accomplishment we headed back into the room. "Now comes the fun part . . . getting me into the bed." For a few minutes we looked for the essential piece of equipment—the transfer board. I laughed silently to myself. I seemed to always be misplacing my cane—that constant reminder of my own physical dependency. Maybe for her it was the transfer board.

When we found it leaning against the radiator I reached down to pick it up and almost toppled over from its weight. Hell of a way to start, I thought to myself. If I can't lift this, how am I going to deal with her? More carefully this time, I reached down and swung it onto the bed.

She parallel parked her wheelchair next to the bed, grinned, and pointed to the side arm. I'd been this route before, so I leaned over and dismantled it. Then with her patient instructions I began to shift her. The board had to be placed with the wider part on the bed and the narrower section slipped under her. This would eventually allow me to slip her across. But I could do little without losing my own balance. So I laid down on the mattress and shoved the transfer board under her. First one foot and then the other I lifted toward me till she was at about a 45 degree angle in her wheelchair. I was huffing but she sat in a sort of bemused silence. Then came the scary part. Planting myself as firmly as I could behind her, I leaned forward, slipped my arms under hers and around her chest and then with one heave hefted her onto the bed. She landed safely with her head on the pillow, and I joined her wearily for a moment's rest. For this I should have gone into training, I smiled silently. And again, she must have understood as she opened her eyes even wider to look at me. What beautiful eyes she has, I thought, a brightness heightened by her very dark thick eyebrows.

"You're blushing again," she said.

"How can you tell that it's not from exhaustion?" I countered.

"By your eyes . . . because they're twinkling."

I leaned over and kissed her again. But more mutual appreciation would have to wait, there was still work to be done.

The immediate task was to plug her wheelchair into the portable recharger. This would have been an easy task for anyone except the technical idiot that I am.

"Be careful," she said. "If you attach the wrong cables you might shock yourself."

I laughed. A shock from this battery would be small compared to what I've already been through.

But even this attaching was not so easy. I couldn't read the instructions clearly, so down to the floor I sank once more.

After several tentative explorations, I could see the gauge registering a positive charge. I let out a little cheer.

She turned her head toward me and looked down as I lay stretched out momentarily on the floor, "Now the real fun part," she teased. "You have to undress me."

"Ah, but for this," I said in my most rakish tones, "we'll have to get closer together." My graceful quip was, however, not matched by any graceful motion. For I had to crawl on the floor until I could find a chair onto which I could hold and push myself to a standing position.

As I finally climbed onto the bed, I said, "Is this trip really necessary?" I don't know what I intended by that remark but we both laughed. And as we did and came closer, we kissed, first gently and then with increasing force until we said almost simultaneously, "We'd better get undressed."

"Where should I start?" I asked.

My own question struck me as funny. It was still another reversal. It was something I'd never asked a woman. But on those rare occasions on which I'd let someone undress me, it was often their first question.

"Wherever you like," she said in what seemed like a coquettish tone.

I thought it would be best to do the toughest first, so I began with her shoes and socks. These were easy enough but not so her slacks. Since she could not raise herself, I alternated between pulling, tugging, and occasionally lifting. Slowly over her hips, I was able to slip her slacks down from her waist. By now I was sweating as much from anxiety as exertion. I was concerned I'd be too rough and maybe hurt her but most of all I was afraid that I might inadvertently pull out her catheter. At least in this anxiety I was not alone. But with her encouragement we again persevered. Slacks, underpants, corset all came off in not so rapid succession.

At this point a different kind of awkwardness struck me. There was something about my being fully clothed and her not that bothered me. I was her lover, not her personal care attendant. And so I asked if she minded if I took off my clothes before continuing.

I explained in a half-truth that it would make it easier for me to get around now 'without all my equipment.' "Fine with me," she answered and again we touched, kissed and lay for a moment in each other's arms.

Pushing myself to a sitting position I removed my own shirt, trousers, shoes, brace, corset, bandages, undershorts until I was comfortably nude. The comfort lasted but a moment. Now I was embarrassed. I realized that she was in a position to look upon my not so beautiful body. My usual defensive sarcasm about 'the real me' began somewhere back in my brain but this time it never reached my lips. "Now what?" was the best I could come up with.

"Now my top . . . and quickly. I'm roasting in all these clothes."

I didn't know if she was serious or just kidding but quickness was not in the cards. With little room at the head of the bed, I simply could not pull them off as I had the rest of her clothes.

"Can you sit up?" I asked.

"Not without help."

"What about once you're up?"

"Not then either . . . not unless I lean on you."

This time I felt ingenious. I locked my legs around the corner of the bed and then grabbing both her arms I yanked her to a sitting position. She made it but I didn't. And I found her sort of on top of me, such a tangle of bodies we could only laugh. Finally, I managed to push her and myself upright. I placed her arms around my neck. And then, after the usual tangles of hair, earrings and protestations that I was trying to smother her, I managed to pull both her sweater and blouse over her head. By now I was no longer being neat, and with an apology threw her garments toward the nearest chair. Naturally I missed . . . but neither of us seemed to care. The bra was the final piece to go and with the last unhooking we both plopped once more to the mattress.

For a moment we just lay there but as I reached across to touch her, she pulled her head back mockingly, "We're not through yet."

"You must be kidding!" I said, hoping that my tone was not as harsh as it sounded.

"I still need my booties and my night bag."

"What are they for?" I asked out of genuine curiosity.

"Well my booties—those big rubber things on the table—keep my heels from rubbing and getting irritated and the night bag . . . well that's so we won't have to worry about my urinating during the night."

The booties I easily affixed, the night bag was another matter. Again it was more my awkwardness than the complexity of the task. First, I removed the day bag, now emptied, but still strapped around her leg and replaced it with the bigger night one. Careful not to dislodge the catheter I had to find a place lower than the bed to attach it so gravity would do the rest. Finally, the formal work was done. The words of my own thoughts bothered me for I realized that there was part of me that feared what "work" might still be ahead.

She was not the first disabled woman I'd ever slept with but she was, as she had said earlier, "more physically dependent than I look." And she was. As I prepared to settle down beside her, I recalled watching her earlier in the evening over dinner. Except for the fact that she needed her steak cut and her cigarette lit, I wasn't particularly conscious of any dependence. In fact quite the contrary, for I'd been attracted in the first place to her liveliness, her movements, her way of tilting her head and raising her eyebrows: But now it was different. This long process of undressing reinforced her physical dependency.

But before I lay down again, she interrupted my associations. "You'll have to move me. I don't feel centered." And as I reached over to move her legs, I let myself fully absorb her nakedness. Lying there she somehow seemed bigger. Maybe it was the lack of muscle-tone if that's the word—but her body seemed somehow flattened out. Her thighs and legs and her breasts, the latter no longer firmly held by her bra, flapped to her side. I felt guilty a moment for even letting myself feel anything. I was as anxious as hell but with no wish to flee. I'm sure my face told it all. For with her eyes she reached out to me and with her words gently reassured me once again, "Don't be afraid."

And so as I lay beside her we began our loving. I was awkward at first, I didn't know what to do with my hands. And so I asked. In a way it was no different than with any other woman. In recent years, I often find myself asking where and how they like to be touched. To my questions she replied, "My neck . . . my face . . . especially my ears. . . ." And as I drew close she swung her arms around my neck and clasped me in a suprisingly strong grip.

"Tighter, tighter, hold me tighter," she laughed again. "I'm not fragile. . . . I won't break."

And so I did. And as we moved I found myself naturally touching other parts of her body. When I realized this I pulled back quickly, "I don't know what you can feel."

"Nothing really in the rest of my body."

"What about your breasts," I asked rather uncomfortably.

"Not much . . . though I can feel your hands there when you press."

And so I did. And all went well until she told me to bite and squeeze harder, then I began to shake. Feeling the quiver in my arm, she again reassured me. So slowly and haltingly where she led, I followed.

I don't know how long we continued kissing and fondling, but as I lay buried in her neck, I felt the heels of her hands digging into my back and her voice whispering, "tell me . . . tell me."

Suddenly I got scared again. Tell her what? Do I have to say that I love her? Oh my God. And I pretended for a moment not to hear.

"Tell me . . . tell me," she said again as she pulled me tighter. With a deep breath, I meekly answered, "Tell you what?"

"Tell me what you're doing," she said softly, "so I can visualize it." With her reply I breathed a sigh of relief. And a narrative voyage over her body began; I kissed, fondled, carressed every part I could reach. Once I looked up and I saw her with her head relaxed, eyes closed, smiling.

It was only when we stopped that I realized I was unerect. In a way my penis was echoing my own thoughts. I had no need to thrust, to fuck, to quite simply go where I couldn't be felt.

She again intercepted my own thoughts—"Move up, please put my hands on you," and as I did I felt a rush through my body. She drew me toward her again until her lips were on my chest and gently she began to suckle me as I had her a few minutes before. And so the hours passed, ears, mouths, eyes, tongues inside one another.

And every once in a while she would quiver in a way which seemed orgasmic. As I thrust my tongue as deep as I could in her ear, her head would begin to shake, her neck would stretch out and then her whole upper body would release with a sigh.

Finally, at some time well past one we looked exhaustedly at one another. "Time for sleep," she yawned, "but there is one more task—an easy one. I'm cold and dry so I need some hot water."

"Hot water!" I said rather incredulously.

"Yup, I drink it straight. It's my one vice."

And as she sipped the drink through a long straw, I closed my eyes and curled myself around the pillow. My drifting off was quickly stopped as she asked rather archly, "You mean you're going to wrap yourself around that rather than me?"

I was about to explain that I rarely slept curled around anyone and certainly not vice-versa but I thought better of it, saying only, "Well, I might not be able to last this way all night."

"Neither might I," she countered. "My arm might also get tired."

We pretended to look at each other angrily but it didn't work. So we came closer again, hugged and curled up as closely as we could, with my head cradled in her arm and my leg draped across her.

And much to my surprise I fell quickly asleep—unafraid, unsmothered, and more importantly rested, cared for, and loved.

Excerpted from Irving Kenneth Zola, *Ordinary Lives: Voices of Disability and Disease*, pp. 208–216. Copyright © 1982 by Apple-wood Books, Inc.

Community and Isolation

Heterosexual women with disabilities do not find it easy to be sexual. One study comparing heterosexual women with and without disabilities found that women with a disability have less sexual knowledge and less experience with intercourse, and they are less satisfied with their sexual situation, since they have the same sexual desires and fantasies as women without a disability (Vansteenwegen, Jans, and Revell 2003). If they are in a relationship, though, they are equally sexually involved.

Some writers have pointed out the parallels in the experiences of nondisabled lesbians and gays and heterosexuals with disabilities (Sherry 2004). Both are often isolated from families and subject to stereotyping and discrimination. Both have to make difficult choices about trying to pass as "normal" or being up front about who they are. The feelings of isolation are compounded for lesbian women and gay men with disabilities.

For women and men of any sexual orientation who have disabilities, social life is complicated by difficulties in dating, going to parties, and casual socializing. One lesbian who lost her eyesight long after she came out writes of missing terribly "regular validation of my status through visual interaction with other dykes"—the winks and smiles exchanged with strangers who recognize they are members of the same community (Peifer 1999, 33). She has the alienating sense of living in two disparate worlds. A lesbian mother with no hearing feels that she and her nonhearing school-age daughter live in communities that have little overlap and, sometimes, little tolerance of diversity (D'aoust 1999). These communities are the world of the physically challenged (she uses a wheelchair for mobility), the Deaf, White mothers of adopted non-White children, and lesbians. She says of her daughter that she "is part of a community that welcomes Deaf people as members but does not have the same history of dealing with other differences" (p. 117).

In the following excerpt, Eli Clare, a transgender poet, essayist, and disability activist, describes a weekend encounter and its effect on a sense of isolation and connection.

Flirting With You

Eli Clare
University of Vermont, Burlington

All weekend we have been shouting slogans, singing songs, blockading doorways, being rude to cops, making as much noise as possible with the intent of disrupting the national Hemlock Society convention. Fifty crips and our nondisabled allies in all, we make it known in no uncertain terms that physician-assisted suicide and euthanasia put our disabled lives at risk. We say "NO" loud and clear to Dr. Faye Girsh, head of Hemlock Society USA, who has said in support of "mercy killing":

> A judicial determination should be made when it is necessary to hasten the death of an individual whether it be a demented parent, a suffering, severely disabled spouse or a child.

We call ourselves "Not Dead Yet," and when all the other slogans and songs dwindle away, we simply chant and sign, "We're not dead yet. We're not dead yet."

Amid all the chaos—making placards, strategizing, figuring out how to get into their conference rooms, passing out handcuffs to wheelchair users so that they can lock their chairs together—you and I keep returning to each other. We flirt and joke and talk: talk about class, disability, queerness, writing, the freak show as crip history. Talk and talk and talk. You—a fat, queer, radical crip femme—as our blockade progresses, you park your three-wheeler among the jam of wheelchairs, lock your brakes and defiantly fold your arms across your chest. No one can get around you. Me—a gimpy butch, shaved head and one ear pierced, shaky hands and slow speech—I'm a walkie: a crip who walks rather than rolls. Today the cops would love to arrest a walkie, easier than finding wheelchair-accessible transportation to the police department, easier than figuring out how to unlock wheelchair brakes and steer the power chairs of noncompliant gimps. So I hang back and watch, do support work, shoot the breeze with our lawyer, scope out which entrances are still unlocked. This is civil disobedience crip style.

Through it all, you and I can't get enough of talking, laughing, trading stories about queer community. I walk you back to your van at the end of the day. You call me a gallant butch. I give you shit for generalizing about femmes. You tell me about growing up white trash. I talk about being taunted. Your eyes take me in. I smile in return, my wide lopsided smile.

Sunday, as the convention winds down, we sit outside the hotel and make noise using whistles, air horns, tambourines; our voices hoarse after two days of protesting. You and I watch Sean, a six-year-old kid with cerebral palsy (CP) in his bright red power chair. He wears a "Crip Cool" baseball cap. His brothers hitch rides on the back of his chair. His nondisabled father wears an ADAPT T-shirt and has trouble keeping up as Sean motors through the crowd of gimps. We both know he could be another Tracy Latimer, a twelve-year-old girl with severe cerebral palsy, killed by her father, who says he did it only to end her unbearable suffering.

Something about how Sean moves—his wrists bent at odd angles, arms pulled tight against body, tremors catching his head—feels so familiar to me. His CP and mine are so far apart, and yet in him I can see my reflection—hands trembling, body slightly off center, right shoulder braced. You lean over and ask, "What would it have been to grow up like Sean in the middle of crip community?" I can almost hear all the stories rise untold around us. I say, joking, "Don't push it. You'll make me cry, which I don't do often and never in public." You respond, laughing, "That's what all butches say. But I know, you just need a pair of loving arms." I try to banter but can't, feel a lump form in my throat. I just look at you and start chanting again, "We're not dead yet.". . .

After the action is over, a group of us roll and walk and drive to the mall to find some lunch. Sunday afternoon, an upscale mall, five trips, two service dogs, one nondisabled lover riding on her boyfriend's lap, and one very out dyke personal attendant: This is material for a hilarious comedy. People gawk; people turn their heads; people get out of our way. We meet the staring head on, seven of us taking up so much space.

Over pizza and root beer, you ask me, "Do you pass," then smile, "I mean, as nondisabled," both of us knowing I never pass as straight. I don't know how to answer. I could tell you about the brief moments before I open my mouth and folks hear my slurred speech, before my hands start shaking, before I take the stairs carefully, one by one, using the handrail for balance. In those moments I probably do pass, but then they're gone. I could tell you about not knowing why people stare at me. Are they gawking at the cripple, trying to figure out what's "wrong" with me, or at the transgendered butch, trying to figure out whether I'm a man or a woman? Or are they simply admiring my jean jacket, my stubbly red hair, my newly polished boots? I could tell you about how I mostly don't see people gawking at me. I have built the stone wall so high. I could tell you about all the years I wanted to pass, and failed, but tried to believe that I was succeeding.

I no longer want to pass; that much is easy. Fifteen years after answering Mary Wall's taunts with my fists, I made my first friend with another crip, slowly finding my way into disability community. I've come to appreciate the tremoring arm, the gnarly back, the raspy breath, the halting speech, the thin legs, the milky eyes, the language that lives not in tongues but in hands. Somewhere in there, my desire to pass as nondisabled—really to be nondisabled—reluctantly let go but at the same time left its mark. Today, even as I sit here laughing with you, queer humor sliding across crip humor, all my close friends, the people I call chosen family, are nondisabled. Often I feel like an impostor as I write about disability; feel that I'm not disabled enough, not grounded deeply enough in disability community. Isolation and connection tug against each other.

I never feel this way about queer community. Even as a rural-raised, mixed-class (working class/lower middle class) person in a largely urban, middle-class community, a gimp in a largely nondisabled community, even when I feel queer among queer folk, I know without a doubt I belong. My butchness, my love of dykes and queer culture, my gender transgressiveness all make my connection to queer community unambiguous. But with disability community, it's a different story.

Inside your seemingly simple query—*Do you pass as nondisabled*—live a dozen questions. What does it mean to be disabled? Which experiences shape a disability identity? What are the differences between me and you: me a walkie and you using a chair, me disabled all at once at birth and you disabled in progressive steps through your adulthood, me securely employed right now but with a long history of trouble finding work and you fighting with Medicaid and SSI? How does my college education, shaped in part by the early decision to mainstream me, impact my experience of disability? How do I answer these questions honestly without separating myself from other disabled people?

It would be easy to call myself a privileged crip and leave it at that. After all, I have a decent job at a time when some of us work in sheltered workshops, earning only a few dollars a day, when the unemployment rate among disabled people is seventy-four percent. After all, I live in a house of my own choosing when many of us are homeless or locked away in nursing homes, group homes, state-run institutions, our own parents' back rooms. After all, I don't struggle daily with issues of accessibility—I can always get into the building, use the restroom, board the bus, use the phone without a TTD, read the signs not in Braille. It would be easy to call myself a privileged crip, but since when are housing, decent jobs and basic accessibility privileges? Are these not rights we should all have? Instead I'm faced with finding my place in a community with a complex criss-cross of differences and similarities. Where do my privileges exist? Where do they not?

Sitting here, being loud and rowdy with other crips, our food eaten but no one wanting to leave, I feel connected. I feel at peace with being a crip. Sitting here with you, I realize I'm not the only queer gimp in the room. It's so familiar, being the only gimp in a crowd of queer folk, the only queer in a room of disabled folk, the only crip in my daily life. I catch your eye again. You raise an eyebrow as if to say, "What next?" I simply grin.

I feel connected here, but yet when I go home tonight, the action done, these rabble-rousing gimps headed back to their homes all over the country, I'll slip back into the nondisabled world with relative ease, an ease that reflects yet another difference between us. This morning before we started making noise outside the convention, you came back from Burger King fuming. Some snot-nosed manager had given you and your service dog grief about blocking the entryway with your three-wheeler, had been barely willing to serve you, a simple trip to get a junk-food breakfast turning into a royal pain-in-the-ass. Unlike me, you rarely slide smoothly into the nondisabled world.

But once I am in that world, I often feel alone, different, the only one. I am reminded over and over that I move more slowly, talk more slowly, carry myself in ways different from everyone around me, and reminded that difference is not valued but mocked, not respected but used as leverage to give certain groups power and to marginalize others. Alone, different, the only one. Me the butch so deeply embedded in queer community—I feel the legacy, the legacy of being the first one in that backwoods school to be mainstreamed, the shadow of my deep desire to be "normal," even as I flirt with you, gimpy butch to gimpy femme.

Reprinted from Eli Clare, "Flirting With You: Some Notes on Isolation and Connection," pp. 127–128, 133–135. In Victoria A. Brownworth and Susan Raffo (eds.), *Restricted Access: Lesbians on Disability.* Copyright © 1999 by Victoria Brownworth. Reprinted by permission.

Transcending the Body

With all the mainstreaming, bravery, skillful care taking, and innovative technology, the body itself persists. In the summer of 2005, a middle-aged nursing home attendant suffered a mini-stroke, and a 20-year-old accomplished horsewoman and college student suffered traumatic head injuries when she fainted and fell off her horse. Both were left with lack of muscle control and loss of memory. Unable to study, work, or drive, both had their lives turned upside down. With therapy, they both recovered much of their functioning, but they could never forget how much their bodies govern their lives.

Susan Wendell, a philosopher who has had myalgic encephalomyelitis, or chronic fatigue immune dysfunction syndrome, since 1985, experiences "constant muscle pain, muscle weakness. . . , periods of profound fatigue. . . , overlapping periods of dizziness and/or nausea and/or depression, headaches lasting for several days, and intermittent problems with short-term memory, especially verbal recall" (1996, 3). She has creative work, a good income, a prestigious position, and a loving partner, but her need to accomodate her body, she says, gives her and others defined as disabled a point of view different from those whose bodies give them little trouble. This perspective is a standpoint, or what Nancy Mairs, a wheelchair user, calls "sitpoint." As with other standpoints, it comes from experiences in a social, cultural, and physical world, and it constitutes "a significant body of knowledge" (Wendell 1996, 73). In the following excerpt, Wendell challenges feminism's call for women to valorize and exert control over their bodies. For her, living through her body entails a form of transcendence.

The Suffering and Limited Body

Susan Wendell
Simon Fraser University, Burnaby, B.C., Canada

Feminism's continuing efforts on behalf of increasing women's control of our bodies and preventing unnecessary suffering tend to make us think of bodily suffering as a socially curable phenomenon. Moreover, its focus on alienation from the body and women's bodily differences from men has created in feminist theory an unrealistic picture of our relationship to our bodies. On the one hand, there is the implicit belief that, if we can only create social justice and overcome our cultural alienation from the body, our experience of it will be mostly pleasant and rewarding. On the other hand, there is a concept of the body which is limited only by the imagination and ignores bodily experience altogether. In neither case does feminist thought confront the experience of bodily suffering. One important consequence is that feminist theory has not taken account of a very strong reason for wanting to transcend the body. Unless we do take account of it, I suspect that we may not only underestimate the subjective appeal of mind-body dualism but also fail to offer an adequate alternative conception of the relationship of consciousness to the body. . . .

Attempting to transcend or disengage oneself from the body by ignoring or discounting its needs and sensations is generally a luxury of the healthy and able-bodied. For people who are ill or disabled, a fairly high degree of attention to the body is necessary for survival, or at least for preventing significant (and sometimes irreversible) deterioration of their physical conditions. Yet illness and disability often render bodily experiences whose meanings we once took for granted difficult to interpret, and even deceptive. Barbara Rosenblum described how a "crisis of meaning" was created by the radical unpredictability of her body with cancer:

> In our culture it is very common to rely on the body as the ultimate arbiter of truth. . . . By noticing the body's responses to situations, we have an idea of how we "really feel about things." For example, if you get knots in your stomach every time a certain person walks into the room, you have an important body clue to investigate. . . . Interpretations of bodily signals are premised on the uninterrupted stability and continuity of the body. . . . When the body, like my body, is no longer consistent over time . . . when something that meant one thing in April may have an entirely different meaning in May, then it is hard to rely on the stability—and therefore the truth—of the body. (Butler and Rosenblum 1991, 136–37)

Chronic pain creates a similar (but more limited) crisis of meaning, since, to a healthy person, pain means that something is wrong that should be acted upon. With chronic pain, I must remind myself over and over again that the pain is meaningless, that there is nothing to fear or resist, that resistance only creates tension, which makes it worse. When I simply notice and accept the pain, my mind is often freed to pay attention to something else. This is not the same as ignoring my body, which would be dangerous, since not resting when I need to rest can cause extreme symptoms or a relapse into illness that would require several days' bed rest. I think of it as a reinterpretation of bodily sensations so as not to be overwhelmed or victimized by them. This process has affected profoundly my whole relationship to my body, since fatigue, nausea, dizziness, lack of appetite, and even depression are all caused by my disease from time to time, and thus all have changed their meanings. It is usually, though not always, inappropriate now to interpret them as indications of my relationship to the external world or of the need to take action. Unfortunately, it is often much easier to recognize that something is inappropriate than to refrain from doing it.

For this reason, I have found it important to cultivate an "observer's" attitude to many bodily sensations and even depressive moods caused by my illness. With this attitude, I observe what is happening as a phenomenon, attend to it, tolerate the cognitive dissonance that results from, for example, feeling depressed or nauseated when there is nothing obviously depressing or disgusting going on, accommodate to it as best I can, and wait for it to pass. . . .

In general, being able to say (usually to myself): "My body is painful (or nauseated, exhausted, etc.), but I'm happy," can be very encouraging and lift my spirits, because it asserts that the way my body feels is not the totality of my experience, that my mind and feelings can wander beyond the painful messages of my body, and that my state of mind is not completely dependent on the state of my body. Even being able to say, "My brain is badly affected right now, so I'm depressed, but I'm fine and my life is going well," is a way of asserting that the quality of my life is not completely dependent on the state of my body, that projects can still be imagined and accomplished, and that the present is not all there is. In short, I am learning not to identify myself with my body, and this helps me to live a good life with a debilitating chronic illness.

I know that many people will suspect this attitude of being psychologically or spiritually naive. They will insist that the sufferings of the body have psychological and/or spiritual meanings, and that I should be searching for them in order to heal myself (Wilber [and Wilber] 1988). This is a widespread belief, not only in North America but in many parts of the world, and . . . I do not reject it entirely. I too believe that, if my stomach tightens every time a particular person enters the room, it is an important sign of how I feel about her/him, and I may feel better physically if I avoid or change my relationship to that person. But, having experienced a crisis of meaning in my body, I can no longer assume that even powerful bodily experiences are psychologically or spiritually meaningful. To do so seems to me to give the body too little importance as a cause in psychological and spiritual life. It reduces the body to a mere reflector of other processes and implicitly rejects the idea that the body may have a complex life of its own, much of which we cannot interpret.

When I look back on the beginning of my illness, I still think of it, as I did then, as an involuntary violation of my body. But now I feel that such violations are sometimes the beginnings of a better life, in that they force the self to expand or be destroyed. Illness has forced me to change in ways that I am grateful for, and so, although I would joyfully accept a cure if it were offered me, I do not regret having become ill. Yet I do not believe that I became ill *because* I needed to learn what illness has taught me, nor that I will get well when I have learned everything I need to know from it. We learn from many things that do not happen to us because we need to learn from them (to regard the death of a loved one, for example, as primarily a lesson for one-self, is hideously narcissistic), and many people who could benefit from learn-ing the same things never have the experiences that would teach them.

When I began to accept and give in to my symptoms, when I stopped searching for medical, psychological, or spiritual cures, when I began to develop the ability to observe my symptoms and reduced my identification with the transient miseries of my body, I was able to reconstruct my life. The state of my body limited the possibilities in new ways; but it also presented new kinds of understanding, new interests, new passions, and projects. In this sense, my experience of illness has been profoundly meaningful, but only because I accepted my body as a cause. If I had insisted on seeing it primarily as reflecting psychological or spiritual problems and devoted my energy to uncovering the "meanings" of my symptoms, I would still be completely absorbed in being ill. As it is, my body has led me to a changed identity, to a very different sense of myself even as I have come to identify myself less with what is occurring in my body.

References

Butler, Sandra, and Barbara Rosenblum. 1991. *Cancer in Two Voices.* San Francisco: Spinster Book Company.

Wilber, Ken, and Treya Wilber. 1988. "Do We Make Ourselves Sick?" *New Age Journal* Sep-tember/October 50–54, 85–90.

Critical Summary

The stories of people with disabilities convey mixed messages. One is that body limitations can be overcome through one's own efforts and the help of other people. The other message is that body limitations become part of one's status because of the way other people see you. The gendering of physical disability makes men less masculine, reduc-ing them to the status of women. Zola said,

Whoever I was, whatever I had, there was always a sense that I should be grateful to someone for allowing it to happen, for like women, I, a handicapped person, was perceived as dependent on someone else's largesse for my happiness, or on someone else to *let* me achieve it for myself. (1982a, 213)

In order to restore their public personae of masculinity, men often go to great lengths to try to make their disabilities irrelevant to their identities. At a time when disability was much more stigmatizing than it is today, Franklin Delano Roosevelt, a polio victim who served as president of the United States from 1933 to 1945, masked his inability to walk or to stand without supports, and the press respected his privacy (Gallagher 1985). In contrast, John Hockenberry, a paraplegic due to an automobile accident, has gone around the world as a reporter in his wheelchair, flaunting his physical state (Hockenberry 1995).

While men with disabilities try to project masculine strength, women with disabilities cannot come across as conventionally feminine because it might exaggerate their dependence. So, paradoxically, they do what the men now do—project an image of strength in adversity. As Nancy Mairs said,

People—crippled or not—wince at the word "cripple," as they do not at "handicapped" or "disabled." Perhaps I want them to wince. I want them to see me as a tough customer, one to whom the fates/gods/viruses have not been kind, but who can face the brutal truth of her existence squarely. As a cripple, I swagger. (1986, p. 9)

People with disabilities may be praised for the heroic ways in which they live "normal" lives, but there is always an undercurrent of "difference." It is this difference, a combination of the physical and the social, that gives those with permanent or long-term body problems a special standpoint (or "sitpoint"), a way of looking at the world that is different from those safely on the right side of "normal." It is an "outsider" viewpoint, just as women have an outsider viewpoint on the male-dominated world, and people of color have an outsider viewpoint on the White world. It necessitates fighting for a place in the hegemonic world and not taking any privileges for granted. A person who is at the intersection of several outsider statuses—a lesbian with cerebral palsy, a Black man in a wheelchair—has complex knowledge that could be very special to convey because it shows "normals" how much they take for granted that their environment will be physically accessible and socially welcoming.

References and Recommended Readings

Adelson, Betty M. 2005. *The Lives of Dwarfs: Their Journey From Public Curiosity Toward Social Liberation.* New Brunswick, NJ: Rutgers University Press.

Araton, Harvey. 2001. "A Champion Slips Away Unnoticed." *New York Times,* 30 August, D1.

Barnartt, Sharon N., and Richard Scotch (eds.). 2001. *Disability Protests: Contentious Politics, 1970–1999.* Washington, DC: Gallaudet University Press.

Blumenfeld, Warren J. (ed.). 1999. Queer and Dis/Abled. Special issue of *International Journal of Sexuality and Gender Studies* 4, 1–123.

Brownworth, Victoria A., and Susan Raffo (eds.). 1999. *Restricted Access: Lesbians on Disability.* Seattle, WA: Seal Press.

Clare, Eli. 1999. *Exile and Pride: Disability, Queerness, and Liberation.* Cambridge, MA: South End Press.

D'aoust, Vicky. 1999. "Complications: The Deaf Community, Disability and Being a Lesbian Mom—A Conversation With Myself." In *Restricted Access: Lesbians on Disability,* edited by Victoria A. Brownworth and Susan Raffo. Seattle, WA: Seal Press.

Deutsch, Helen, and Felicity Nussbaum (eds.). 2000. *"Defects": Engendering the Modern Body.* Ann Arbor: University of Michigan Press.

Fine, Michelle, and Adrienne Asch. 1985. "Disabled Women: Sexism Without the Pedestal." In *Women and Disability: The Double Handicap,* edited by Mary Jo Deegan and Nancy A. Brooks. New Brunswick, NJ: Transaction Books.

———. (eds.). 1988. *Women With Disabilities: Essays in Psychology, Culture, and Politics.* Philadelphia: Temple University Press.

Frank, Geyla. 2000. *Venus on Wheels: Two Decades of Dialogue on Disability, Biography, and Being Female in America.* Berkeley: University of California Press.

Gallagher, Hugh Gregory. 1985. *FDR's Splendid Deception.* New York: Dodd Mead.

Garland Thomson, Rosemarie (ed.). 1996. *Freakery: Cultural Spectacles of the Extraordinary Body.* New York: New York University Press.

———. 1997. *Extraordinary Bodies: Figuring Physical Disability in American Culture and Literature.* New York: Columbia University Press.

———. 2005. "Feminist Disability Studies." *Signs* 30, 1557–1587.

Gerschick, Thomas J., and Adam Stephen Miller. 1994. "Gender Identities at the Crossroads of Masculinity and Physical Disability." *Masculinities* 2, 34–55.

Grealy, Lucy. 1994. *Autobiography of a Face.* New York: Perennial Press.

Hall, Kim (ed.). 2002. "Feminist Disability Studies," special issue of *NWSA Journal* 14 (3).

Hawking, Stephen. "My Experience With ALS." *www.hawking.org.uk/disable/dindex.html*

Hillyer, Barbara. 1993. *Feminism and Disability.* Norman: University of Oklahoma Press.

Hockenberry, John. 1995. *Moving Violations: War Zones, Wheelchairs, and Declarations of Independence.* New York: Hyperion.

Killoran, Carrie. 1994. "Women With Disabilities Having Children: It's Our Right, Too." *Sexuality and Disability* 12, 121–126.

Kittay, Eva, Alexa Schriempf, Anita Silvers, and Susan Wendell (eds.). 2001. Feminism and Disability: Part I. Special issue of *Hypatia* 16 (4).

——. 2002. Feminism and Disability: Part II. Special issue of *Hypatia* 17 (3).

Kudlick, Catherine. 2005. "The Blind Man's Harley: White Canes and Gender Identity in America." *Signs* 30, 1549–1606.

Linton, Simi. 1998. *Claiming Disability: Knowledge and Identity.* New York: New York University Press.

Litsky, Frank. 2001. "Diana Golden Brosnihan, Skier, Dies at 38." *New York Times,* 28 August, D7.

Lonsdale, Susan. 1990. *Women and Disability.* New York: St. Martin's Press.

Lorber, Judith. 2000. "Gender Contradictions and Status Dilemmas in Disability." In *Expanding the Scope of Social Science Research on Disability,* edited by Barbara M. Altman and Sharon N. Barnartt. Stamford, CT: JAI.

Lyall, Sarah. 2005. "In Trafalgar Square, Much Ado About Statuary." *New York Times,* 10 October, E1, 7.

Mairs, Nancy. 1986. *Plaintext.* Tucson: University of Arizona Press.

——. 1996. *Waist-High in the World: A Life Among the Nondisabled.* Boston: Beacon.

Mathers, Colin D., Ritu Sadana, Joshua A. Salomon, Christopher J. L. Murray, and Alan D. Lope. 2001. "Healthy Life Expectancy in 191 Countries, 1999." *Lancet* 357, 1685–1691.

McGrath, Charles. 2005. "Hell on Wheels." *New York Times,* 26 March, B7, 13.

McRuer, Robert, and Abby L. Wilkerson (eds.). 2003. Desiring Disability: Queer Studies Meets Disability Studies. Special issue of *GLQ: A Journal of Lesbian and Gay Studies* 9, (1–2).

Murphy, Robert F. 1990. *The Body Silent.* New York: W.W. Norton.

Noddings, Nel. 2002. *Starting at Home: Caring and Social Policy.* Berkeley: University of California Press.

Nosek, Margaret A., Mary Ellen Young, Diana H. Rintala et al. 1995. "Barriers to Reproductive Health Maintenance Among Women With Physical Disabilities." *Journal of Women's Health* 4, 505–518.

O'Brien, Ruth. 2005. *Bodies in Revolt: Gender, Disability, and an Alternative Ethic of Care.* New York: Routledge.

Peifer, Deborah. 1999. "Seeing Is Be(liev)ing." In *Restricted Access: Lesbians on Disability,* edited by Victoria A. Brownworth and Susan Raffo. Seattle, WA: Seal Press.

Rohrer, Judy. 2005. "Toward a Full-Inclusion Feminism: A Feminist Deployment of Disability Analysis." *Feminist Studies* 31, 34–63.

Rousso, Harilyn, and Michael L. Wehmeyer (eds.). 2001. *Double Jeopardy: Addressing Gender Equity in Special Education.* Albany: SUNY Press.

Saxton, Marsha. 1994. Women With Disabilities: Reproduction and Motherhood. Special issue of *Sexuality and Disability* 12 (Summer).

Saxton, Marsha, and Florence Howe (eds.). 1987. *With Wings: An Anthology of Literature by and About Women With Disabilities.* New York: Feminist Press.

Schillinger, Liesl. 2005. "Arms and the Man: The Star of 'The Flid Show.'" *New York Times* Arts & Leisure, 30 January, 8.

Serlin, David. 2003. "Crippling Masculinity: Queerness and Disability in U.S. Military Culture, 1800–1945." *GLQ: A Journal of Lesbian and Gay Studies* 9, 149–179.

Shakespeare, Tom, Kath Gillespie-Sells, and Dominic Davies (eds.). 1996. *The Sexual Politics of Disability: Untold Desires.* New York: Cassell.

Sherry, Mark. 2004. "Overlaps and Contradictions Between Queer Theory and Disability Studies." *Disability & Society* 19, 769–783.

Smith, Bonnie G., and Beth Hutchison (eds.). 2004. *Gendering Disability.* New Brunswick, NJ: Rutgers University Press.

Thomas, Carol. 1999. *Female Forms: Experiencing and Understanding Disability.* Philadelphia: Open University Press.

Tolmach Lakoff, Robin. 1989. "Review Essay: Women and Disability." *Feminist Studies* 15, 365–375.

Tommasini, Anthony. 2004. "It's the Vocal Cords That Matter Most." *New York Times,* 28 January, E1, 6.

Tremain, Shelley (ed.). 1996. *Pushing the Limits: Disabled Dykes Produce Culture.* Toronto: Women's Press.

Tronto, Joan C. 1993. *Moral Boundaries: A Political Argument for an Ethic of Care.* New York: Routledge.

———. 2006. "Moral Perspectives: Gender, Ethics, and Political Theory." In *Handbook of Gender and Women's Studies,* edited by Kathy Davis, Mary Evans, and Judith Lorber. London: Sage.

Vansteenwegen, Alfons, I. Jans, and Arlynn T. Revell. 2003. "Sexual Experience of Women With a Physical Disability: A Comparative Study." *Sexuality and Disability* 21, 283–290.

Weiss, Meira. 1994. *Conditional Love: Parental Relations Toward Handicapped Children.* Westport, CT: Greenwood Press.

Wendell, Susan. 1996. *The Rejected Body: Feminist Philosophical Reflections on Disability.* New York: Routledge.

Willmuth, Mary, and Lillian Holcomb (eds.). 1993. *Women With Disabilities: Found Voices.* New York: Haworth.

Zola, Irving Kenneth. 1982a. *Missing Pieces: A Chronicle of Living With a Disability.* Philadelphia: Temple University Press.

———. (ed.). 1982b. *Ordinary Lives: Voices of Disability and Disease.* Cambridge, MA: Apple-wood Books.

Internet Sources

Chartbook on Women and Disability in the United States
www.infouse.com/disabilitydata/womendisability/intro.php

Disability Resources, Women With Disabilities
www.disabilityresources.org/WOMEN.html

Disability World
www.disabilityworld.org

Disabled Women on the Web
www.disabilityhistory.org/dwa

Education for Disability and Gender Equity (EDGE)
www.disabilityhistory.org/dwa/edge/curriculum

Gender and Disability: A Survey of InterAction Member Agencies
www.miusa.org/publications/freeresources/genderdisability

InterAction Diversity Initiative
www.interaction.org/diversity/about.html

International Disability and Development Consortium: Gender
www.iddc.org.uk/dis_dev/specific_groups/gender.shtml

Mobility International USA (MIUSA), Women, Disability, and Development
www.miusa.org/development/archive/programs/women

Ragged Edge Magazine Online
www.ragged-edge-mag.com

Society for Disability Studies (SDS)
www.uic.edu/orgs/sds

Women's Equity Resource Center Gender and Disability Digest
www2.edc.org/WomensEquity/pdffiles/disabdig.pdf ✦

Chapter 8

Political Bodies

Violence and Violations

Key concepts: *government-sponsored violence, imprisoned bodies, military bodies, sex slaves, sexual torture, suicide bombers*

The theme we have been developing throughout this book is how bodies are constructed to be masculine or feminine, how they are shaped to conform to gendered expectations, and how these expectations are modified or resisted. When we go beyond the impact of body gendering on the lives of individual women and men, we find a more general impact—bodies in the mass. Particularly in times of conflict, bodies in the mass are subject to violent, injurious actions. They suffer bombings, war injuries, imprisonment, torture, rape, and sexual slavery. As with so much of social embodiment, violence to bodies is not "equal opportunity." Men and women suffer differently, and the poor and disadvantaged are the most likely victims.

Governments in Western societies maintain social order through masculine values—coercion, domination, and military and police strength. Men swell the ranks of military institutions and the corporations that benefit from the military—the "military industrial complex." Similarly, in the prison industrial complex, men are overwhelmingly the wardens and prison guards. Even in peacetime, nations often behave as if they are under attack by some enemy or violent criminals, which stirs up fear and anxiety among their citizens and justifies spending a large part of the national budget on the criminal justice system and the mili-

195

tary and its weapons. Nations also encourage citizens to join the military voluntarily or to submit to required military service. These are all instances of government-sponsored, legitimated violence.

The gendered issues in body violence are not straightforward. The military and prison systems are major sources of violence to bodies through injuries, physical abuse, and torture. Women as well as men are soldiers and prisoners, but the bodies that suffer are predominantly those of men. When women are the perpetrators of violence, as prison guards or suicide bombers, their rarity makes them major news. Their actions call into question the conventional and feminist views of women as nurturant, empathic caretakers. We are more familiar with women's vulnerability in times of conflict—as rape victims and sexual slaves. This familiarity often makes the violence done to their bodies invisible.

Military Bodies

In many societies, the government reserves the right to require military service of its citizens—called conscription or the draft—and most draft only men. Chile and Israel draft both men and women into required military service. In the United States, women may volunteer for the military, but if there were a national emergency requiring a draft, there would be a political issue over gender equality, because historically only men have been drafted.

In the volunteer military in the United States, Black people are overrepresented, and people of Hispanic origin are underrepresented. In 2002, 13.1 percent of the U.S. population aged 18 to 24 were categorized as Black, and 13.3 percent were categorized as Hispanic; Black people were 21.8 percent of enlisted military personnel on active duty, and 10 percent were Hispanic (Adamshick 2005, Table 1). In 2004 and 2005, the number of Black recruits declined considerably, presumably because of lack of support for the current war in Iraq (White 2005). In contrast, commissioned officers are overwhelmingly White. In 2002, 38.8 percent of the enlisted military personnel were classified as "minority," but only 19.7 percent of the officers (Adamshick 2005, Table 2).

In 2002, the percentage of U.S. women who were 18 to 24 years old and free to serve was 50.9; the percentage of the active U.S. military personnel who were women was 17.3 (U.S. Department of Defense 2002, Table 2.2). The Air Force had the highest percentage of women (24 percent) and the Marine Corps the lowest (6.8 percent). The Army had the highest percentage of Black women (28.3 percent); the Marine Corps had the highest percentage of women of Hispanic origin (16 percent). The percentage of women officers in all the branches except the Navy was similar to the percentage of enlisted personnel. In the Navy, 14.7 percent of officers were women in 2002, as were 13.8 percent of enlisted personnel (Adamshick 2005, Table 2).

Many Black and Hispanic women and men volunteer for the military as a way to attain an education and a good job or to escape violent and deteriorated inner cities. White women and men who enlist in the armed services tend to come from impoverished small towns or rural areas. The recruiters often entice poor and vulnerable young people to enlist by claiming that they can make something of themselves and see the world by joining the military. Rarely is there a discussion of battles, having to kill or be killed, losing limbs and eyes, being paralyzed, scarred, or suffering post-traumatic stress syndrome. The strategies of recruitment and staffing the ranks of the military indicate that in a class and racially stratified society, the bodies of poor people, especially those of color, are not as valuable as middle- and upper-class White bodies. Poor bodies of color may be considered more "disposable." Who better to fight and put their bodies on the line than those who uphold the society's values of achievement but don't have access to resources to achieve? Offered a legitimate way up the social ladder, many are willing to risk their bodies and lives.

Most civilians don't see the bodies that return from war dead, wounded, disabled, scarred, or injured. The dead are given a hero's funeral, but the living often suffer horrendous injuries. A journalist, Dan Baum, described one case:

> A bomb injures in many ways. The shock wave can loosen organs and leave a victim to bleed to death internally, or rake him with shrapnel. Long after the initial wounds are treated, the effects of the bomb continue to plague the victim. In Cain's case, the blast pulverized dirt, truck metal, engine fluids, and his own clothing, and drove microscopic debris deep into his muscle, macerating the tissue. Each tiny fleck had to be dug out, the pulped

flesh cut away, and the wounds cleaned and re-cleaned—a process that took twelve surgeries over three months. (Had there been any people between him and the mine, their flesh might have been atomized and driven into his, which can cause particularly dangerous infections.) (Baum 2004a, 68).

The survival rate among the U.S. military in Iraq is higher than in previous wars, but wounds are multiple and severe:

Survivors are coming home with grave injuries, often from roadside bombs, that will transform their lives: combinations of damaged brains and spinal cords, vision and hearing loss, disfigured faces, burns, amputations, mangled limbs, and psychological ills like depression and post-traumatic stress. (Grady 2006, 1)

Many of these multiple wounds are from explosions—improvised explosive devices, or I.E.D.s, mortars, bombs, and grenades. As of mid-January 2006, the Defense Department reported that 11,852 members of the U.S. military had been wounded in explosions (Grady 2006, 24).

Women in the U.S. military are not supposed to serve in combat, but there isn't a clear front line, nor are there safe areas in modern wars. In Iraq, women are drivers in supply convoys, military police, and checkpoint patrollers, where they are needed to search and question Iraqi women. In all these jobs, they are vulnerable to roadside bombs, suicide bombers, and mortar fire. The number of military women who have been killed and injured in Iraq is a higher percentage than in any other war since World War II, with 2 percent of those killed as of October 25, 2005, when the death count of U.S. military personnel reached 2,000 (Dao 2005).

A comparison of the other social characteristics of the first and second thousand U.S. troops who died in Iraq as of October 2005 showed that the percentage categorized as Black dropped from 13 to 8 percent, and the percentage of Hispanic dropped from 13 to 5 percent. The percentage of those who were 18 to 24 years old went from 52 to 54, and the percentage of enlisted personnel who had died rose from 88 to 92 (Dao 2005). The estimated number of Iraqi civilians, police officers, and soldiers who died since March 2003 was 30,051 (Tavernise 2005). Children were 10 percent of the estimate, that is, 3,000, and women, 8 percent, or 2,400.

Imprisoned Bodies

In times of high anxiety about personal and national security, there is an increase in the scope and amplitude of mechanisms of social control. These systems of social control do not treat people equally. The prison industrial complex has thrived by incarcerating particular types of bodies—primarily poor, male, and non-White (Davis 1998). Once in prison, incarcerated men are vulnerable to the violence perpetrated by other inmates and guards.

According to the U.S. Department of Justice, as of December 31, 2004, there were 2,135,901 prisoners in federal or state prisons or in local jails. At the end of 2004, among the men who were sentenced prison inmates, there were 3,218 Black, 1,220 Hispanic, and only 463 White men inmates per 100,000 men of each group in the general population.[1] Statistics from 1995 reveal that one in three Black men between the ages of 20 and 29 years old was under correctional supervision or control (Mauer and Huling 1995). Although incarceration rates for women are lower than those of men at every age, they show the same racial ethnic breakdown (Harrison and Beck 2005).

The racial ethnic disparities are due in part to differences in sentencing for non-White men and boys compared with their White counterparts. A review of forty recent studies investigating the link between race and sentence severity found evidence of direct racial discrimination that resulted in significantly longer and more severe sentences for Black and Hispanic young, unemployed men (Spohn 2000).

Racial group is a determinant in who receives the death penalty, particularly when it comes to the racial group of the victim. A study conducted by the Associated Press reviewed 1,936 indictments in Ohio from October 1981 through 2002. One of the most significant findings was that offenders facing a death penalty charge for killing a White person were twice as likely as those who had killed a Black victim to go to death row (Welsh-Huggins 2005).

These different rates of incarceration, sentencing, and receiving the death penalty are evidence that in the United States, the least valued bodies are those of Black men.

Sexual Torture

Torture is a violation of body and mind. Tortured bodies are maimed and often killed, but those who survive often suffer the psychological effects for the rest of their lives. Sexual torture specifically targets minds—the sense of oneself as a man or a woman. Torture involving the genitalia may maim or kill, but its purpose is to cause humiliation as well as excruciating pain. Men as well as women have been subject to sexual torture, although men are extremely reluctant to talk about it. The following excerpt is from a report of the Medical Centre for Human Rights. It documents the prevalence of sexual torture of men and the ways that masculinity is attacked through defiling the male body.

Sexual Torture of Men and Women

Pauline Oosterhoff
Medical Committee Netherlands Vietnam, Hanoi

Prisca Zwanikken
Royal Tropical Institute, Amsterdam

Evert Ketting
Sexual and Reproductive Health Center, Amsterdam

Rape and other forms of sexual torture are a means of terrorising and controlling a population, e.g. to terrorise an ethnic minority. Governments have probably always used it in both war and peacetime. Sexual torture of women in detention during peacetime has been documented in recent years in dozens of countries, including China, Egypt, Spain and France,[4,5] and is also common during war.[1] In every armed conflict investigated by Amnesty International in 1999 and 2000, sexual torture of women was reported, including rape.[5] Rape of male prisoners and sexual torture of homosexual men are also well documented.[6]

When sexual torture occurs, it often follows arrests and round-ups of the local population, particularly where repressive governments are faced with armed rebellion. Torture might take place in a field, a school, the victim's own house or a torture chamber or prison.[7,8] Like other forms of torture, sexual torture usually takes place during the first week of captivity, most often at night and often when guards are drunk.[8] . . .

Before World War II, rape and sexual violence were considered inevitable by-products of war or ascribed to renegade soldiers. Even at the Nuremberg trials, not a single case of rape was punished.[7]

The 1949 Geneva Conventions on the Protection of Civilians in Time of War were the first in which international law addressed wartime sexual violence. Protocol II to the Geneva Conventions explicitly outlaws "outrages upon personal dignity, in particular humiliating and degrading treatment, rape, enforced prostitution, and any form of indecent assault."[9] The 1984 Convention against Torture and Other Cruel, Inhuman or Degrading Treatment or Punishment, which in Article 1 gives the definition of torture still accepted today,[2] does not specifically mention sexual violence as a form of torture, however.

Legal recognition that sexual violence could constitute torture came as a result of the war in the former Yugoslavia, with its abundant testimony by female rape survivors. The International Criminal Tribunal for the Former Yugoslavia (ICTY) was mandated to try the perpetrators of heinous crimes (genocide, crimes against humanity, violations of the laws of war and serious breaches of the 1949 Geneva Conventions) committed during the conflict.

In its Celebici judgment, the ICTY established that sexual violence constitutes torture when it is intentionally inflicted by an official, or with official instigation, consent or tolerance, for purposes such as intimidation, coercion, punishment, or eliciting information or confessions, or for any reason based on discrimination.[3]. . .

Incidence of Sexual Torture of Men

It was not possible to calculate or even estimate the incidence of sexual torture in wartime Croatia. Only a small proportion of survivors are likely to have admitted to having been sexually tortured. Many victims may have been killed. Their remains, even if discovered, may not show evidence of sexual torture. Thus, the study was not designed to measure incidence. However, it is possible to try to develop a broad sense of whether sexual torture of men occurred often enough to be considered a regular feature of wartime violence or limited to a few exceptions.

Among the 22 male torture survivors in the International Rehabilitation Council for Torture (ICRT) Victims Programme, 14 reported having suffered some type of sexual torture, ten suffered genital beatings or electroshock, and four had been raped.

Of the 1,648 testimonies screened by Medical Centre for Human Rights (MCHR) staff, 78 self-reported sexual torture. Among the 55 survivors of sexual torture who sought help from MCHR, 24 were subjected to genital beatings or electroshock, 11 were raped, seven were forced to engage in sexual acts and 13 were fully or partially castrated. In addition, MCHR staff had found six post-mortem cases of total castration.

Comparatively few self-reported cases of sexual torture were found by the Centre for Psychotrauma. Of the 5,751 Croatian war veteran patients, nine reported having suffered genital beatings and/or electroshock, and five reported rape. Among the unknown number of male civilians, one reported having been raped and three reported genital beatings.

The data from the ICRT and the MCHR support the conclusion that sexual torture of men was a regular, unexceptional component of violence in wartime

Croatia, not a rare occurrence. The data from the Centre for Psychotrauma were probably at variance because of the nature of the sample and the attitudes of at least one therapist. . . .

An Open Secret

One of the striking points to emerge from the study is how silent male survivors of sexual torture have remained about their experiences. In the MCHR therapy group, specifically advertised as a group for male survivors of sexual torture, none of the men who showed up would initially admit to having suffered sexual torture themselves; they claimed they had come on behalf of friends. It was only after some time that group members acknowledged they had been tortured. In the ICRT group, none of the survivors mentioned sexual torture during intake interviews. Other types of torture were discussed relatively openly, but sexual torture was not broached until later in therapy, according to the therapists.

Torture is often carried out in public to demonstrate the power of the perpetrators. Narratives by male survivors show that torture was frequently perpetrated by groups and in full and deliberate view of bystanders. The example below illustrates the public nature of the sexual torture:

> "First they grabbed X and pushed him down by the road. He was the weakest. . . . Four men pushed him down and were holding his head, legs and arms. Y approached him, she had a scalpel in her hand. The men who pushed him down took his trousers off. She castrated him. We had to watch. I was watching, but I was so scared that I did not see much. . . . One of the Chetniks had a wooden stick and he hit X a few times across his neck. X showed no signs of life anymore. Then three Chetniks shot at X. The fourth took a pistol and shot him in the head." (Unpublished testimony, a soldier at MCHR)

The silence that envelopes the sexual torture of men in the aftermath of the war in Croatia stands in strange contrast to the public nature of the crimes themselves.

As shown in the literature and confirmed by our study, sexual torture of men In wartime occurs regularly. While there are certain specific differences in the sexual torture of men and women and its effects, the psychological symptoms experienced by male and female survivors seem to be substantially similar.

In fact, perpetrators seem to torture both men and women sexually. Although more women than men have reported sexual torture in some studies, lack of recognition may discourage male survivors from reporting sexual torture even more than women, and professionals may fail to recognise cases. Few men admit being sexually tortured or seek help. Health professionals, the legal system and human rights advocates have proven to be somewhat gender-biased about sexual torture and have only recently begun to acknowledge that men as well as women are potential victims. It is difficult enough for survivors of sexual torture to come forward; men should not have to face the additional problem of disbelief that it could even happen to them at all.

The occurrence of sexual torture of men during wartime and in conflict situations remains something of an open secret, although it happens regularly and often takes place in public. These shortcomings are a critical barrier for those needing treatment and legal assistance, and limit the possibility of action against the perpetrators. The challenge is to turn this open secret into a recognised fact, so that it can be deterred and prosecuted alongside the sexual torture of women.

References

1. Shanks, L, Ford N, Schull M, et al. Responding to rape. Lancet 2001; 357 (9252): 304.
2. Convention against Torture and Other Cruel, Inhuman or Degrading Treatment or Punishment, G.A. Res. 39/46, [Annex, 39 U.N. GAOR Supp. (No. 51) at 197, U.N. Doc. A/39/51 (1984)], entered into force June 26, 1987. Geneva: United Nations, 1984.
3. Celebici Judgement, Prosecutor v. Delalic, Mucic, Delic, and Landzo, Case No. IT-96-21-T, Para. 770, November 1998.
4. Amnesty International, International Centre for Human Rights and Democratic Development. Documenting Human Rights Violations by State Agents: Sexual Violence. Montreal: ICHRDD, 1999.
5. Amnesty International. Broken bodies, shattered minds, torture and ill-treatment of women. Amnesty International Index: ACT 40/001/2001: 2001. London: Amnesty International Publications, 2001.
6. Amnesty International, Crimes of hate, conspiracy of silence: torture and ill-treatment based on sexual identity. Amnesty International Index: ACT 40/016/2001. London: Amnesty International Publications, 2001.
7. Asian Legal Resource Centre. Specific contexts of sexual torture and cruel, inhuman and degrading treatment. Armed conflict, Police/Penal. At: *http://www.alrc.net*. Accessed 11 November 2002.
8. Amnesty International. A Glimpse of Hell: Reports on Torture Worldwide. Forrest, D (editor). New York: New York University Press, June 2002.
9. Geneva Conventions, Protocol II, Article 4(2)(e). Protocol Additional to the Geneva Conventions of 12 August 1949, and relating to the Protection of Victims of Non-International Armed Conflicts (Protocol II), 8 June 1977. At: *http://www.icrc.org.IHL.nsf/0/f9cbd575d47ca6c8c12563cd0051e783?OpenDocument*. Accessed 2 February 2004.

Less physically damaging but culturally and psychologically insidious has been the public documentation of American women soldiers' collaboration in the prevalent sexual humiliation of Muslim men prisoners in Iraq, Afghanistan, and Guantánamo Bay. According to an official Pentagon report,

There were several instances when female soldiers rubbed up against prisoners and touched them inappropriately. In April 2003, a soldier did that in a T-shirt after removing her uniform blouse. Following up on an F.B.I. officer's allegation that a female soldier had done a "lap dance" on a prisoner, the report described this scene from the interrogation of the so-called 20th hijacker from the 9/11 attacks: A female soldier straddled his lap, massaged his neck and shoulders, "began to enter the personal space of the subject," touched him and whispered in his ear. . . . These practices are as degrading to the women as they are to the prisoners. (Editorial 2005, A18)

Why do women soldiers agree to be "pseudo lap dancers," to smear fake menstrual blood on prisoners, to be photographed holding a naked hooded man on a leash? One feminist response to the highly publicized abuses at Abu Ghraib prison in Baghdad was that the young women soldiers "succumbed to a culture of power that they did not create and could not change, though they likely didn't try" (Enda 2004). Another rationale was that the ones who were complicit were too far down the military hierarchy, and the woman general who was in charge of the prison had no other women at her level. The "critical mass" needed to change organizational culture was missing: "On the one hand, we think that women can change things. But on the other hand, if you just have a handful of women in a very militarized system, they aren't going to be any different, unfortunately," said Sanam Naraghi Anderlini, director of the Women Waging Peace policy commission (Enda 2004). These rationales don't excuse the complicity with torture; feminists have argued that women have agency, and that means taking responsibility for one's actions. We also don't hear much about the women (and men) who did protest the torture.

Suicide Bombers

So far, we have concentrated on the victims of violence and the violations done to them. A suicide bomber—a person carrying explosives with awareness and consent to detonate them strategically to kill or damage other people or property—is a human weapon. The term suicide bomber is value laden; in different circumstances, these individuals have been called homicide bombers or martyrs. Historically, rebels and revolutionaries have planted bombs in civilian areas. Also in the past, there have been occasional suicide bombers, but since September 11, 2001, "suicide bombings have rapidly evolved into perhaps the most common method of terrorism in the world, moving west from the civil war in Sri Lanka in the 1980s to the Palestinian intifada of recent years to Iraq today" and, most recently, the bombings in London in July 2005 (Eggen and Wilson 2005, A1).

Most of the contemporary suicide bombers are men, but in 1991, a woman Tamil Tiger assassinated Prime Minister Rajiv Gandhi of India by detonating explosives strapped to her body.

Since women are not often thought of as suicide bombers, the news of the first woman Palestinian suicide bomber, 27-year-old college-educated Wafa Idris, made global headlines in January 2002. In interviews after Wafa Idris' death, many attributed her suicide bombing to her frustration and loss of hope after working as a Red Crescent Society emergency paramedic and witnessing so much pain and suffering from the Palestinian-Israeli conflict (Bennet 2000a). The second woman suicide bomber blew herself up at an Israeli checkpoint just a month later. She was a 22-year-old college student, Darin Abu Eisheh, who said she was following in the footsteps of Wafa Idris, who had been praised in some of the Arab-language press as an Islamic Joan of Arc (Bennet 2002b). Al Aqsa reportedly set up a women's unit named for Wafa Idris, and the third and fourth women suicide bombers struck a few weeks later.

The use of feminist metaphors to celebrate Idris made her a hero, but body imagery kept her very much a woman: "'She bore in her belly the fetus of a rare heroism, and gave birth by blowing herself up,' the columnist Mufid Fawzie wrote in the Egyptian Daily Al Aalam al Youm" (Bennet 2002b, A8). The videotape Darin Abu Eisheh left also used birth imagery. She stated, "Let Sharon the coward know that every Palestinian woman will give birth to an army of suicide attackers, even if he tries to kill them while still in their mother's wombs, shooting them at the checkpoints of death" (Greenberg 2002, A10).

The imagery may have been feminine, but these women also projected their commitment to the Palestinian cause. Frances Hasso, who analyzed the gendered discourse around the first four Palestinian women "suicide bombers/martyrs," noted that the three women who left videos, pictures, and messages depicted themselves in militant poses and "represented their acts as explosive and embodied action, recognizing that it was more dramatic and dangerous because they are women" (2005, 29). Two of them were long-time activists, and all were politically aware. The response by Arab men was mixed, with some of the religious leaders uncomfortable with these women's public role, but activists welcomed their joining the battle. Many young Arab women "interpreted and responded to the attacks as calls for *women's political action in defense of community*" (Hasso 2005, 30). The public memorial for Wafa Idris was attended by about 3,000 people, mostly women; the funeral procession was led by the head of the Fatah women's committees. Hasso said,

> [T]he daring of the women's acts also generated feminist pride and increased public display of militance among Arab, including Palestinian, women and girls throughout the region. . . . It is as if when they inserted themselves—by dying and killing—into a sphere of politics dominated by men, the Palestinian women militants allowed other Arab girls and women to contest their own marginality in national and regional politics. (2005, 35)

Israel is not the only place where women are using their bodies as conduits for bombs. In at least fifteen separate attacks, women have been deemed responsible for the suicide bombing of public markets, train stations, and aircraft in the Russian-Chechnyan conflict (Myers 2004). Their motives are attributed to grief over the deaths of fathers, sons, and husbands. These attributions of womanly motives of grief and empathy are in marked contrast to the nationalistic and religious motives attributed to men suicide bombers, whose masculinity is interwoven into their heroic martyrdom:

> The martyr is a young, unmarried (virgin, innocent) man, fearless and strong. He is depicted with eyes cast forward to *jihad* and the blessed state of martyrdom. His hair is dark and held back with a bandana with Qur'anic inscriptions. If depicted in full figure, he wears white, the color of a coffin, while holding a gun. Sometimes he is depicted in the foreground, leading a group of women and older male martyrs; or he is depicted in the foreground of fully veiled women and young girls, protecting them and the country's honor. (Gerami 2003, 267)

Other rationales for women suicide bombers have implied that they were forced to choose between martyrdom and an honor killing for adultery or an out-of-wedlock pregnancy. Three Chechnyan women who are suspected of bombing a plane were said to have been divorced because they couldn't have children, a severe stigma in Muslim society (Myers 2004).

Amal Amireh, who frequently writes about Arab women and Arab literature, argued that these Western denigrations of Muslim women suicide bombers are a form of "death by culture," an erasure of their choice to be martyrs for national liberation. In the following excerpt, she critiqued the Western feminist view.

Palestinian Women Suicide Bombers Through Western Eyes

Amal Amireh
George Mason University, Fairfax, Virginia

The female suicide bomber challenges the image of Muslim and Arab women as docile bodies that is dominant in the Western context. While this image of docility has its roots in the long history of Orientalist stereotypes of Muslim women, it has become more visible in recent years. Certainly, in the aftermath of September 11th, the veiled and beaten body of the Afghan woman under the Taliban was deployed on a massive scale and came to stand for Muslim and Arab women generally. U.S. feminists played a key role in disseminating this profile, when the Feminist Majority, a prominent U.S. feminist organization, joined forces with the Bush Administration to "liberate" the bodies of the downtrodden women of Afghanistan. The oppressed body of the Muslim woman was inserted into debates about American national security and was offered as an important reason to justify a war. In contrast to this image, the female suicide bomber's body is far from being dormant or inactive, passively waiting for outside help. It is purposeful, lethal, and literally explosive. Sometimes veiled, sometimes in "Western" dress, this body moves away from home, crosses borders, and infiltrates the other's territory. It is a protean body in motion and, therefore, needs a translation.

Another reason the woman suicide bomber poses a challenge to feminists in particular is the ambivalent view feminists have concerning women's relationship to nationalism. Despite recent scholarship that attempts to provide a nuanced analysis of women's connection to national institutions, the dominant view continues to see women of the Third World as victims of nationalism, simultaneously embodied by their governments, countries, and cultures. While U.S. feminists may acknowledge that American women have a complex relation to their country and its patriarchal institutions (such as the military), they often deny that same kind of relationship to Arab and Muslim women, who are usually seen as a monolithic group always tainted with victimhood. As a result, the nationalist Arab and Muslim woman, with the suicide bomber as her most sensational embodiment, urgently needs an explanation.

To make this incomprehensible woman figure accessible to a Western readership, some U.S. feminists have deployed what Uma Narayan has called, in the context of her critique of Western feminist discourse on *sati* a "death by culture" paradigm.[1] This paradigm abstracts Palestinian women suicide bombers from any historical and political context and places them exclusively in a cultural one. Culture is opposed to politics and is seen as "natural," "organic," "essential," and therefore unchanging.[2] Doomed to this cultural context, Palestinian women are seen as victims of an abusive patriarchal Arab culture that drives them to destroy themselves and others.[3] Thus, their violent political act is transformed into yet another example of the ways Arab culture inevitably kills its women.[4]. . .

This Western feminist discourse on Arab women has a chilling effect, particularly on the relationship between Arab and Arab-American feminists, on the one hand, and their American counterparts on the other. Arab-American feminists and activists have long shouldered a double burden: not only do they work against sexism and patriarchy in their communities, but they also have to contend with the harmful stereotypes propagated about them and their Arab culture in the mass media. Due to their hard work and their forming of important alliances with other women of color in the U.S., who also had to struggle against the racism and classism of mainstream white feminists, their voices have made some impact and better channels of communication have been opened. However, since the tragic events of September 11th, these little gains in feminist solidarity seem to have been eroded in the face of the mobilizing of U.S. feminists in the service of nationalism and militarism. The discourse on Palestinian women suicide bombers, just like that on Afghan women, is bound to widen the gap separating Arab-Americans from feminists. . . .

But beyond feminist solidarity, invoking the "death by culture" paradigm to understand why some women become suicide bombers leads to a dead end, for this understanding implies a Kurtzian "exterminate all the brutes" solution, the "brutes" in this case being all those who are made by Arab or Palestinian culture. For those who do not believe this is a viable solution, it is crucial to acknowledge that suicide bombings by women, just like those by men, are, first and foremost, forms of political violence. The culture that is implicated in this phenomenon is not a fetishized, oppressive "Arab culture," but rather a culture of militarization whose effects are by no means limited to Palestinian society. The recognition of suicide bombing as a political form of violence neither trivializes nor idealizes the suicide bomber/*el isteshhadeya*. On the contrary, seeing her as a political agent is a first and necessary step for launching a feminist critique of women, militarization, and nationalism that goes beyond casting Palestinian women as demons, angels, or victims of a killer culture.

Notes

1. Sati refers to the practice of widow burning in India. The word also refers to the woman who engages in such an act. For insightful work on sati, see Mani.
2. In this context, culture is equivalent to "nature" in the nature/culture dichotomy that second wave feminists have engaged with much passion.
3. This is the favorite propaganda argument of Israeli security. See, for instance, "The Role of Palestinian Women in Suicide Terrorism" *http://www.mfa.gov.il*

4. In fact, Phyllis Chesler, a Zionist radical feminist, declares that suicide bombing by women is "another form of Arab honor killing." FrontPageMagazine.com, January 22, 2004. *http://www.frontpagemag.com/Articles/ReadArticle.asp?ID=11855*

Reprinted from Amal Amireh, "Palestinian Women's Disappearing Act: The Suicide Bomber Through Western Feminist Eyes," *MIT Electronic Journal of Middle East Studies,* 5 (Spring): 230–231, 240. Copyright © 2005 The MIT Electronic Journal of Middle East Studies. Reprinted by permission.

Women's Vulnerability

Women suicide bombers and sexual humiliators show that women's experiences of violent conflict are not all the same. During World War II, women were concentration camp victims and members of the resistance in Nazi-occupied countries. German women were concentration camp guards and victims of rape by the Russian and American postwar occupation armies. Korean women were abducted into military sexual slavery for Japanese soldiers, and Japanese women who survived the atom bombing of Hiroshima and Nagasaki were sterile and badly scarred.

Women may be combatants, prison guards, and resistance fighters, but they are more commonly ordinary citizens vulnerable to rape, forced pregnancy, and sexual slavery. In the twentieth century, nine out of ten people killed in wars were civilians, and these were overwhelmingly women and children (Hynes 2004). As the United Nations Security Council on Women and Peace and Security reported in 2004:

> Gender-based violence is a form of discrimination that seriously inhibits the ability of women to enjoy their rights and freedoms on a basis of equality with men. The unacceptable violence against women and girls in peacetime is further exacerbated during armed conflict and in its aftermath. Both State and non-State actors are responsible for severe violations of women's human rights, including killings, abductions, rape, sexual torture and slavery, as well as denial of access to food and health care, with dramatic consequences. (U.N. Security Council 2004, 16)

In many destabilized and devastated countries, women often end up becoming prostitutes through coercion or economic necessity to help their families survive. Much of the global trafficking in sex workers since the fall of communism has been from countries in the former Soviet Union to Western Europe, Israel, and the United States. There is a concentration of child and teenage sex workers in Asia and South America; some are boys but most are girls.

In the following piece, Grace Cho, a sociologist, describes the situation of women in South Korea after World War II. In 1945, Korea was liberated from 35 years of Japanese rule by the Russians and Chinese in the north and the Americans in the south. Aided by the Chinese, the North Koreans invaded South Korea in 1950, driving U.S. forces almost to the sea and starting the three-year Korean War, which killed two million people and left the country divided and economically devastated. During the war and in its aftermath, young women in American-occupied South Korea became prostitutes to earn money for themselves and their families. Like the dead Iraqi civilians and coffins of the American military dead of today and the 200,000 Korean sexual slaves of the Japanese military in World War II, these Korean prostitutes are invisible violated bodies.

Prostituted and Invisible Bodies

Grace M. Cho
College of Staten Island, City University of New York

Each day in the United States, we hear about military and civilian casualties in Iraq, suicide bombings, people being shot mistakenly at checkpoints, and incidents of "friendly fire" in which American troops shoot each other or non-Iraqi allies. Every few weeks, we hear news about how that particular day is the bloodiest or deadliest day in Iraq since the war began, indicating that the war continues to get bloodier and deadlier, despite its official ending. Yet there is a striking absence of actual dead bodies in the U.S. media. The visual images of dead soldiers' bodies are replaced by images of caskets draped in American flags. Thus, the material destruction of war and the grief embodied in the remains literally gets covered up with symbols of patriotic fervor. Consistent with the way in which the American news media represent casualties, the only bodies we can even imagine beneath this cloak of patriotism are American. If the only bodies that count as casualties of the war are those of American soldiers, often pictured as male, then one must ask, which bodies are obscured from our sight? Why are some bodies put on display, while others are made invisible?

Gendered Visibility

The Iraqi bodies that have been exposed, indeed overexposed, in the U.S. media are those of Abu Ghraib prisoners forced into positions of submission by U.S. military personnel. The circulation of these images of the tortured and feminized male Arab body struck a deep chord with American viewers, but it reinforced the narrative that such instances of abuse were exceptional. Thus, the images implied that similar abuses do not occur and could not routinely be perpetrated by a democratic nation. The hypervisibility of the tortured Iraqi body also evokes the trope of the occupied nation as a feminized other, thereby situating the U.S. military in a dominant position, at least at the level of the collective unconscious. The figure of the tortured Iraqi prisoner has come to embody one of the contradictions of the Iraq war. Entangled in the discourse of democracy and freedom are the physical and psychic wounds inflicted upon the liberated.

This wounding is unequally distributed because the way in which bodies are subjected to war is gendered. Although those who are on the front lines of war are typically figured as men, women's bodies have been both overt military targets and sites of "collateral damage." Rape and sexual exploitation have been unintended consequences of war in some contexts and strategic forms of warfare in others. Women's bodies are not only subjected to practices of war; they are constituted by these very practices.

Out of the ruins of war, new bodies emerge. They are stigmatized bodies that are reminders of collective trauma, such as Darfur's "babies of rape," and they are embodiments of a disrupted social order in which women are exposed to a wider range of both freedoms and dangers. To illustrate the way in which new bodies are created out of the conditions of war, I now turn to the example of the South Korean military prostitute (*yanggongju*) and the Korean War as the ground against which she becomes enfigured.

The Korean War and the Embodiment of Trauma

Articulated in terms of a collective failure to remember, the Korean War is often called the "forgotten war" in the United States. Yet the Korean War that divided Korea into North and South Korea is not over in geopolitical terms, and the events that took place on the peninsula between 1950 and 1953 continue to haunt diasporic South Koreans. Some survivors continue to mourn, while others remain unable to even remember their traumas, although they are deeply affected by them.

The *yanggongju* is one of the bodies produced by the legacy of the Korean War. Literally meaning "Western princess," *yanggongju* is also translated as "Yankee whore," "G.I. bride," or "U.N. lady." The varied translations of *yanggongju* demonstrate how the figure occupies contradictory and shifting positions of privilege in the South Korean imagination, evoking a sense of American luxury and political power at the same time as it evokes sexual subordination and moral decay. Not only does *yanggongju* refer to women who are sexual laborers for U.S. military personnel; the label is also used much more broadly for women who are marked by the stigma of the West—women who date or marry American men regardless of whether or not that woman is a known sex worker.

Above all, the *yanggongju* is an embodiment of the traumas and losses of the Korean peninsula and the diaspora of its people during the past century—the loss of language and indigenous culture under Japanese colonialism, the loss of autonomy under U.S. military dominance since 1945, the decimation of the peninsula during the Korean War through the destruction of every major town and city, and the massive loss of human lives. In 1950, the population of the Korean peninsula was about 30 million; by 1953, at least 10 percent were dead, and the vast majority of survivors were homeless. The casualties of the war included 3 million civilians killed, 2 million missing or wounded, and 10 million separated from their families by division and displacement.

The failure to resolve the war serves as the geopolitical rationale for the continued U.S. troop presence in South Korea, and therefore the continuation of military prostitution. Having arisen from these conditions, the *yanggongju* is both a creation of the war and a painful reminder of it. In other words, military prostitutes are "living symbols of the destruction, poverty, bloodshed, and separation from family of Korea's civil war" (Moon 1997, 8).

The war's obliteration of normal ways of life disrupted traditional gender roles and created the economic necessity that would lead South Korean civilians to the bases to look for employment. Thus, the psychic and material conditions were set in place for the beginning of U.S. military prostitution as an institutional practice. Some women were allowed more freedoms under these conditions, even as they were made more vulnerable.

During the first months of the Korean war, there was mounting anxiety about American soldiers' capacity to kill and rape, and thus South Koreans began the practice of hiding their daughters, or alternatively, offering them up to pacify American soldiers. The fear of American men's sexual appetites served as a rationalization for many South Koreans to condone prostitution as a necessary evil that would prevent the rape of "innocent" women and girls. At the same time that American soldiers were feared, American bases became centers of survival, where South Korean men and women bought or begged for leftovers, ate garbage from the mess halls, and sought medical care and employment. The public fear of rape coupled with the will to survive and a desire for American goods created the conditions for the rise of the *yanggongju*.

The Prostitute Body and U.S.–South Korean Relations

In survivors' early memories of the Korean War, the woman who made a living from dating American soldiers was excused as a victim under duress of the war, or as a price to be paid for American protection. It was during the postwar period that women who consorted with Americans became associated with the image of the "Western princess" because of their access to American products. But while American goods were the most valuable form of currency for postwar South Koreans, these new objects also became ambivalent symbols of the way in which U.S. aggression and benevolence are conflated in cultural memory.

The *yanggongju*, as the primary consumer of American products, became the screen upon which South Koreans projected their feelings of fear and resentment of the United States, along with their desire to become part of the American dream. The *yanggongju* intensified collective feelings of shame, not only because of her affiliation with the U.S. military but also for her status as a morally bankrupt woman who violates Confucian gender norms. Yet the phenomenon of military prostitution was tolerated so that the *yanggongju* could be the buffer between respectable South Korean citizens and the "beast-like" American GI's. Military prostitution became the only form of legal prostitution in South Korea, and it was highly regulated by both governments, despite its absence from official U.S. military documents.

The sexual labor of more than one million South Korean women who have worked in the bars and brothels around U.S. military bases since the Korean War has been one of the unacknowledged forces behind the U.S.–South Korean relationship and South Korea's economic miracle, as Katharine Moon (1997) documents in her study of camptown prostitution during the 1960s and 1970s. During this period, the South Korean government began to recognize the role that camptown prostitutes played in building South Korea's economy. Government officials tried to construct a new identity for the military sex worker, changing her depiction from a struggling woman negotiating the poverty of postwar South Korea to a "diplomat" fulfilling her patriotic duties by keeping U.S. interests engaged. But in practice, military sex workers continued to be disposable bodies whose deaths were not officially documented. In interviews with military sex workers and in memoirs of children growing up around U.S. military bases, there are stories of unidentified bodies found in dumpsters, women who were killed by clients and pimps, or women who simply disappeared (Fenkl 1996; Moon 1997; Pollock Sturdevant and Stoltzfus 1992).

Manipulation of Bodies as a Practice of Nationalism

While the bodies of real women have been made invisible under the regime of officially sanctioned militarized prostitution in South Korea, the *yanggongju* is also symbolic of a more widespread manipulation and disappearing of women's bodies during times of war. The example of the *yanggongju* offers insight into the process by which new bodies are created out of conditions of war, particularly as women's bodies become more vulnerable to sexual exploitation. Like the *yanggongju,* the soldier is another kind of body in service of national security whose life is sacrificed, but by virtue of their immersion in a culture of militarized masculine aggression, male soldiers occupy very different positions of institutional power vis-à-vis local women. The uncounted casualties of war continue to be women whose lives are sacrificed for the fantasy of nation.

The bodies that suffer injury and death that no one sees, the tortured bodies that are displayed as examples of exceptionalism, and the bodies that are returned home covered in American flags are all indicative of the ways in which grief and destruction get muted by the rhetoric of national security. Bodies of women and men are subjected to a variety of militarized practices, and through these practices, new bodies and social conditions are produced.

Thus, histories of militarized violence do not remain fixed in the past, but are carried forward as embodied everyday experiences in the stigma of the prostitute, in the nightmares of the tortured, and in the long and painful rehabilitation of amputees. Bodies, then, are not only material but also texts of psychic and social histories that continue to be lived in the present.

References

Fenkl, Heinz Insu. 1996. *Memories of My Ghost Brother.* New York: Dutton.

Moon, Katharine H. S. 1997. *Sex Among Allies: Military Prostitution in US-Korea Relations.* New York: Columbia University Press.

Pollack Sturdevant, Saundra, and Brenda Stoltzfus. 1992. *Let the Good Times Roll: Prostitution and the U.S. Military in Asia.* New York: The New Press.

Original article commissioned for this book.

Critical Summary

The history and current practices of body violation and violence during and after armed conflict are very well documented—we have barely touched on the subject. We have seen that the violence is government-sponsored and also perpetrated by insurgents against governments. We may not think of imprisonment as a form of body violence, but beyond deprivation of liberty, people in prison are subject to physical abuse by guards and beatings and killing by other prisoners. Most of those imprisoned in the United States are Black and Hispanic men. They are most likely to be arrested even if they have not committed a crime, and if convicted, they receive longer sentences than White men. They are also more likely to get the death penalty, especially if the murder victim is White.

Women and girls are the victims of different body violations than are men. They are often referred to as the spoils of war. In wartime, they are not only subject to killing, maiming, and sexual torture, as men are, but also to rape, sexual slavery, and forced pregnancies. In many countries, men are drafted into the military and trained to be violent. In other countries, men volunteer, as do women, and in two countries, Chile and Israel, women are drafted. Women can be the violators—sexual humiliation is a mild form of what women are asked to do as members of the military and what they did as Nazi concentration camp guards.

Governments, the military, and insurgencies are dominated by men and men's valorization of violence, but women do have agency and also believe in nationalist and religious causes. Suicide bombing would seem to be the ultimate in violence by choice, but is it? Our feminist response is that it is violence to women and men and boys and girls when they are induced by a resistance movement to use their bodies to kill themselves and others. The nonviolence movements of Gandhi in the liberation of India and Martin Luther King Jr. in the U.S. civil rights fight were, in our view, a better form of resistance. The bodies of their followers were vulnerable to beatings, imprisonment, and murder, but the violence came from the oppressors, not the oppressed.

Violence to bodies and minds may not be spread evenly in the population, but its disastrous and ugly manifestations affect everyone and its prevalence must not be rendered invisible.

Note

1. *www.ojp.usdoj.gov/bjs/prisons.htm*

References and Recommended Readings

Armed Conflict

Adamshick, Mark. 2005. "Social Representation in the U.S. Military Services." *CIRCLE Working Paper* 32, May. *www.civicyouth.org/PopUps/WorkingPapers/WP32Adamshik.pdf*

Baum, Dan. 2004a. "The Casualty: An American Soldier Comes Home From Iraq." *New Yorker,* 9 March, 64–73.

———. 2004b. "Two Soldiers: How the Dead Come Home." *New Yorker,* 9 & 16 August, 76–95.

Dao, James. 2005. "2,000 Dead: As Iraq Tours Stretch On, a Grim Mark." *New York Times,* 26 October, A1, 14, 15.

Grady, Denise. 2006. "Struggling Back From War's Once-Deadly Wounds." *New York Times* Sunday News Section, 22 January, 1, 24.

Hynes, H. Patricia. 2004. "On the Battlefield of Women's Bodies: An Overview of the Harm of War to Women." *Women's Studies International Forum* 27 (5–6): 431–445.

Macur, Juliet. 2005. "Two Women Bound by Sports, War, and Injuries." *New York Times* Sunday News Section, 10 April, 1, 28.

Moser, Carolyn, and Fiona Clark (eds.). 2001. *Victims, Perpetrators, or Actors? Gender, Armed Conflict, and Political Violence.* London: Zed Books.

Scheper-Hughes, Nancy, and Philippe I. Bourgois (eds.). 2003. *Violence in War and Peace: An Anthology.* Oxford, UK: Blackwell.

Tavernise, Sabrina. 2005. "Rising Civilian Toll Is the Iraq War's Silent, Sinister Pulse." *New York Times,* 26 October, A12.

U.S. Department of Defense. 2002. "Population Representation in the Military Services." *www.dod.mil/prhome/poprep2002/chapter2/c2_raceth.htm*

White, Josh. 2005. "Steady Drop in Black Army Recruits." *Washington Post,* 9 March, A1.

Zarkov, Dubravka. Forthcoming. *The Fe/Male Body and the Productive Power of Violence: On "Media War" and "Ethnic War" in Former Yugoslavia.* Durham, NC: Duke University Press.

Gender and the Holocaust

Baer, Elizabeth, and Myrna Goldenberg (eds.). 2003. *Experience and Expression: Women, the Nazis, and the Holocaust.* Detroit, MI: Wayne State University Press.

Delbo, Charlotte. 1997. *Convoy to Auschwitz: Women of the French Resistance.* Boston: Northeastern University Press.

Fuchs, Esther. 1999. *Women and the Holocaust.* Lanham, MD: University Press of America.

Morrison, Jack G. 2000. *Ravensbrück: Everyday Life in a Women's Concentration Camp 1935–45.* New York: Marcus Wiener.

Ofer, Dalia, and Lenore J. Weitzman (eds.). 1998. *Women in the Holocaust.* New Haven, CT: Yale University Press.

Saidel, Rochelle G. 2004. *The Jewish Women of the Ravensbrück Concentration Camp.* Madison: University of Wisconsin Press.

Tec, Nechama. 2003. *Resilience and Courage: Women, Men, and the Holocaust.* New Haven, CT: Yale University Press.

Tydor Baumel, Judith. 1998. *Gender and the Holocaust: Double Jeopardy.* London: Valentine Mitchell.

Imprisonment

Davis, Angela Y. 1998. "Masked Racism: Reflections on the Prison Industrial Complex." *ColorLines.* Fall. *www.thirdworldtraveler.com/Prison_System/Masked_Racism_ADavis.html*

Harrison, Paige M., and Allen J. Beck. 2005. "Prison and Jail Inmates at Midyear 2004." *Bureau of Justice Statistics.* Washington, DC: U.S. Department of Justice.

Mauer, M., and T. Huling. 1995. *Young Black Americans and the Criminal Justice System: Five Years Later.* Washington, DC: The Sentencing Project.

Spohn, Cassia C. 2000. "Thirty Years of Sentencing Reform: The Quest for a Racially Neutral Sentencing Process." *Criminal Justice 2000,* Vol. 3. Washington, DC: National Institute of Justice.

Welsh-Huggins, Andrew. 2005. "Death Penalty Unequal." *Cincinnati Enquirer,* 7 May. *news.enquirer.com/apps/pbcs.dll/article?AID=/20050507/NEWS01/505070402*

Rape and Prostitution

Barry, Kathleen. 1995. *Prostitution of Sexuality: Global Exploitation of Women.* New York: New York University Press.

Barstow, Anne Llewellyn (ed.). 2000. *War's Dirty Secret: Rape, Prostitution, and Other Crimes Against Women.* Cleveland, OH: Pilgrim Press.

Brownmiller, Susan. 1975. *Against Our Will: Men, Women, and Rape.* New York: Simon & Schuster.

Engle Merry, Sally. 2003. "Rights Talk and the Experience of Law: Implementing Women's Human Rights to Protection From Violence." *Human Rights Quarterly* 25, 343–381.

Hicks, George. 1995. *The Comfort Women: Japan's Brutal Regime of Enforced Prostitution in the Second World War.* New York: W. W. Norton.

Schmidt, David Andrew. 2000. *Ianfu—The Comfort Women of the Japanese Imperial Army of the Pacific War: Broken Silence.* Lewiston, NY: Mellen.

Scoular, Jane. 2004. "The 'Subject' of Prostitution: Interpreting the Discursive, Symbolic, and Material Position of Sex/Work in Feminist Theory." *Feminist Theory* 5, 343–355.

U.N. Security Council. 2004. "Women and Peace and Security." Report of the Secretary-General S/2004/814, 13 October, 1–26.

Sexual Torture

Editorial. 2005. "The Women of Gitmo." *New York Times,* 15 July, A18.

Enda, Jodi. 2004. "Female Face of Abuse Provokes Shock." *Women's Enews,* 14 May. *www.womensenews.org/article.cfm?aid=1828*

Oosterhoff, Pauline, Prisca Zwanikken, and Evert Ketting. 2004. "Sexual Torture of Men in Croatia and Other Conflict Situations: An Open Secret." *Reproductive Health Matters* 12, 68–77.

Zarkov, Dubravka. 2001. "The Body of the Other Man: Sexual Violence and the Construction of Masculinity, Sexuality, and Ethnicity in Croatian Media." In *Victims, Perpetrators, or Actors? Gender, Armed Conflict, and Political Violence,* edited by C. Moser and F. Clark. London: Zed Books.

Suicide Bombers

Amireh, Amal. 2005. "Palestinian Women's Disappearing Act: The Suicide Bomber Through Western Feminist Eyes." *MIT Electronic Journal of Middle East Studies* 5 (Spring), 228–242; *web.mit.edu/cis/www/mitejmes*

Atran, Scott. 2004. "Mishandling Suicide Terrorism." *Washington Quarterly* 27, 67–90.

218 ✦ *Gendered Bodies*

Bennet, James. 2002a. "Arab Woman's Path to Unlikely 'Martyrdom.'" *New York Times,* 31 January, A1, 10.

———. 2002b. "Arab Press Glorifies Bomber as Heroine. *New York Times,* 11 February, A8.

Eggen, Dan, and Scott Wilson. 2005. "Suicide Bombs Potent Tools of Terrorists: Deadly Attacks Have Been Increasing and Spreading Since Sept. 11, 2001." *Washington Post,* 17 July, A1.

Gerami, Shahin. 2003. "Mullahs, Martyrs, and *men:* Conceptualizing Masculinity in the Islamic Republic of Iran." *Men & Masculinities* 5, 257–275.

Greenberg, Joel. 2002. "Portrait of an Angry Young Arab Woman." *New York Times,* 1 March, A10.

Hasso, Frances S. 2005. "Discursive and Political Deployments by/of the 2002 Palestinian Women Suicide Bombers/Martyrs." *Feminist Review* 81, 23–51.

Kimmel, Michael S. 2003. "Globalization and its Mal(e)contents: The Gendered Moral and Political Economy of Terrorism." *International Sociology* 18, 603–620.

Myers, Steven Lee. 2004. "From Dismal Chechnya, Women Turn to Bombs." *New York Times,* 10 September, A1, 6.

Internet Sources

Amnesty International
www.amnesty.org

Antiwar.com
www.antiwar.com

Arab Organization for Human Rights
www.aohr.org

Coalition Against Trafficking in Women
www.catwinternational.org

Coalition for Women's Rights in Conflict Situations
www.womensrightscoalition.org

Death Penalty Information Center
www.deathpenaltyinfo.org

Human Rights Watch
www.humanrightswatch.org

International Center for Transitional Justice
www.ictj.org

International Rehabilitation Council for Torture Victims
www.irct.org/usr/irct/home.nsf

International Service for Human Rights
www.ishr.ch

Iraq Body Count
www.iraqbodycount.net
Jewish Voice for Peace
jewishvoiceforpeace.org
Network of East West Women
www.neww.org
South Asian Women's Network
www.umiacs.umd.edu/users/sawweb/sawnet/index.html
UNIFEM Portal on Women, Peace, and Security
www.womenwarpeace.org
U.S. Department of Justice, Bureau of Justice Statistics
www.ojp.usdoj.gov/bjs/welcome.html
Vera Institute
www.vera.org
Women's Initiative for Gender Justice
www.icc.women.org
Women's International League for Peace and Freedom
www.peacewomen.org
World Organization Against Torture
www.omct.org ✦

Chapter 9

Social Bodies

Communities and Control

Key concepts: body economics, body knowledge, social bodies, symbolic bodies

In this chapter, we discuss social bodies in two different but related ways. First, a social body is the entity formed of a community of individual bodies. Second, our physical bodies become social bodies through recognition by a community and application of the community's body norms and practices. For example, New York City is a social body, a metropolis populated by heterogeneous individual bodies. These individual bodies become social bodies in interaction with other individual bodies. As social bodies, New Yorkers walk on streets crowded with other bodies, careful not to bump into them; they ride on subway cars watched by police; those in wheelchairs expect bus drivers to operate the stair lifts for them. They are strangers to each other but recognize each other's presence, and that makes them social bodies. In contrast, when a homeless person sleeps in someone's doorway, and people walk by as if that body were invisible, the person has been excluded from the community. Community inclusion makes us social bodies, which is why excommunication and exile are such harsh punishments.

221

What Makes a Body a Social Body?

Environmental, economic, and geopolitical disasters bring to the fore the ways in which physical bodies are made into social bodies. Who dies and who survives, who is mourned and who is reviled, who eats and who starves, who is helped and who is ignored, who is in control and who is vulnerable—these are all ways in which communities create social bodies out of physical bodies. Through the multiplicity of media coverage—24/7 news broadcasts, podcasts, traditional and alternate newspapers, and the internet—we can see bodies interacting in real time physically and socially. Through our viewing, these bodies enter our own social lives and become part of a global social community. We form opinions about how survivors are being aided—or not—and we may deplore and protest the conditions that led to the disaster or its magnitude. We are moved to help, through donations of money, clothing, and other material items and through volunteering to go and lend our bodies to rescue and recovery efforts.

In the first five years of the twenty-first century, bodies rammed into the Twin Towers on September 11, 2001, and bodies jumped out of them before the 110-story buildings collapsed. Fragments of bodies were carefully collected from the tons of rubble and painstakingly identified as people. The names—*symbolic bodies*—of the almost 3,000 dead are read by their kin at Ground Zero in downtown New York City on every anniversary of the event.

On December 26, 2004, a tsunami in the Indian Ocean drowned hundreds of thousands in Indonesia, Sri Lanka, India, and Thailand. The bodies of foreign tourists became people to us in the tears of the local survivors on television and photos left in cameras. In contrast, the hundreds of thousands of bodies of people who had lived in wiped-out villages and towns and who died or were displaced by the massive devastation to the terrain and economy of Southeastern Asia were rendered nearly invisible in the West, identified only by where they had once lived (Dewan 2005). The most visible survivors of the people who had lived there were the orphaned children featured in many television accounts. On the first anniversary, the stories in the media about how the survivors fared turned them into the symbolic bodies of that disaster (Bearak 2005).

On August 28, 2005, we saw the effects of Hurricane Katrina on the Gulf Coast and the flooding of New Orleans and sections of Mississippi when levees broke. The disintegration of a once vibrant community, ineptitude and apathy of government officials, and years of neglect of the physical infrastructure caused the uprooting of thousands of mostly poor and African American mothers and children, and the deaths of sick and old men and women, many with disabilities. They were very visible as people, thanks to constant television coverage and interviews in which they or their family members told what was happening to them. They became part of the national and global community, a visual indictment of America's neglect of poor African Americans.

More bodies were disabled and killed in early fall 2005 in earthquakes in Kashmir, mud slides in Managua, and because of continuing drought, civil war, and starvation in Darfur, but the further we get from our own social worlds, the less attention is paid to these disasters. Yet we are all connected in networks of social communities. In her book, *Precarious Life*, feminist philosopher Judith Butler asks, "Who counts as human? Whose lives count as lives? And, finally, What *makes for a grievable life?* . . . Loss has made a tenuous 'we' of us all" (Butler 2004, 20). In the following excerpt, she presents further thoughts on vulnerable social bodies.

Precarious Lives

Judith Butler
University of California, Berkeley

The body implies mortality, vulnerability, agency: the skin and the flesh expose us to the gaze of others, but also to touch, and to violence, and bodies put us at risk of becoming the agency and instrument of all these as well. Although we struggle for rights over our own bodies, the very bodies for which we struggle are not quite ever only our own. The body has its invariably public dimension. Constituted as a social phenomenon in the public sphere, my body is and is not mine. Given over from the start to the world of others, it bears their imprint, is formed within the crucible of social life; only later, and with some uncertainty, do I lay claim to my body as my own, if, in fact, I ever do. Indeed, if I deny that prior to the formation of my "will," my body related me to others whom I did not choose to have in proximity to myself, if I build a notion of "autonomy" on the basis of the denial of this sphere of a primary and unwilled physical proximity with others, then am I denying the social conditions of my embodiment in the name of autonomy?

At one level, this situation is literally familiar: there is bound to be some experience of humiliation for adults, who think that they are exercising judgment in matters of love, to reflect upon the fact that, as infants and young children, they loved their parents or other primary others in absolute and uncritical ways—and that something of that pattern lives on in their adult relationships. I may wish to reconstitute my "self" as if it were there all along, a tacit ego with acumen from the start; but to do so would be to deny the various forms of rapture and subjection that formed the condition of my emergence as an individuated being and that continue to haunt my adult sense of self with whatever anxiety and longing I may now feel. Individuation is an accomplishment, not a presupposition, and certainly no guarantee.

Is there a reason to apprehend and affirm this condition of my formation within the sphere of politics, a sphere monopolized by adults? If I am struggling for autonomy, do I not need to be struggling for something else as well, a conception of myself as invariably in community, impressed upon by others, impinging upon them as well, and in ways that are not fully in my control or clearly predictable?

Is there a way that we might struggle for autonomy in many spheres, yet also consider the demands that are imposed upon us by living in a world of beings who are, by definition, physically dependent on one another, physically vulnerable to one another? Is this not another way of imagining community, one in which we are alike only in having this condition separately and so having in common a condition that cannot be thought without difference? This way of imagining community affirms relationality not only as a descriptive or historical fact of our formation, but also as an ongoing normative dimension of our social and political lives, one in which we are compelled to take stock of our interdependence. According to this latter view, it would become incumbent on us to consider the place of violence in any such relation, for violence is, always, an exploitation of that primary tie, that primary way in which we are, as bodies, outside ourselves and for one another.

As social bodies, we are connected through a social contract, a recognition that individuals and local communities will help each other and that when a disaster strikes, they can count on the help of those with national and international resources (Ignatieff 2005). Young people who were not directly involved in the events of September 11, 2001, recognized this social contract and became more involved in public affairs:

The attacks and their aftermath demonstrated that our fates are highly interdependent. We learned that we need to—and can—depend on the kindness of strangers who happen to be near us in a plane, office building or subway.

Moreover, regardless of one's political leanings, it was easy to see that we needed effective governmental action: to coordinate volunteers, police national borders, design emergency response preparedness, engage in diplomacy, and train police and firefighters. Government and politics mattered. (Sander and Putnam 2005, A23)

That is the lesson of the dual meaning of social bodies: without a community, a collection of social bodies, individual bodies often don't survive.

Body Economics

When communities neglect people, the social and individual bodies suffer. Disasters may push people past their breaking point, but for those who live in poor economic conditions, their bodies have already been under constant assault. In nations that experience economic crisis, sociological and anthropological research has found that bodies, particularly of mothers who must care for children and scrounge for food for them, are increasingly fatigued, stressed, overworked, malnourished, and sick (Sutton 2005). The effects of disasters, like those of wars, fall most heavily on women and children, especially if they have few economic resources. Disasters take everyday vulnerability to a higher degree because social networks break down. According to the U.N. Population Fund,

When conflict or natural disaster strikes, women survivors usually bear the heaviest burden of relief and reconstruction. They become primary caretakers for other survivors—including children, the injured or sick, and the elderly. The vulnerability and responsibilities of women are further increased by the loss of husbands and livelihoods and the need to procure essentials for family survival.

Gender-specific needs have often been overlooked when it comes to relief and recovery planning. The vulnerability of girls and women to exploitation, trafficking and abuse has largely been ignored, as have their needs for pregnancy-related care, sanitary supplies and locally appropriate clothing. The distribution of emergency assistance has often been managed by, and delivered to, men, without attention to whether women and their dependents will benefit. (2005, chap. 8)

In another form of body exploitation that only government intervention can change, the owners of factories, mines, and plantations push workers to exhaustion. Given the global dominance of free-market capitalism and agribusinesses, bodies are drained of their physical, emotional, and procreative resources in sweatshops manufacturing cheap clothing and electronics, gold and diamond mines, slaughterhouses and food processing factories, and fruit and vegetable farms and orchards. We benefit by low prices for clothing and food and, for those who can afford them, a supply of jewelry and other luxuries.

Male bodies often take on the greatest occupational risks because men are encouraged to work at dangerous jobs and to hide injuries and illnesses (Courtenay 2000). A study of black lung disease demonstrated how the men who worked in coal mines were expected to normalize the symptoms of disease—since everybody coughed and spat black sputum, it was just part of life in coal mines. When a miner could not breathe well enough to work, he was denied compensation by physicians working for the mining industry. Instead of identifying the toxins of the work environment, the owners and the medical profession blamed the workers' lifestyles—smoking and drinking—for their ill health (Smith 1987).

Years of potential life lost (YPLL) is a statistic that estimates the number of years of life lost owing to premature death in a population. Premature death is usually defined as death at the age of less than 65 or 75 years, or less than the average life expectancy. YPPL is used as a measure of the economic burden of premature death to society, since it represents the loss of productive workers, consumers, and taxpayers. International comparative research has demonstrated that suicide and premature death due to coronary heart disease, violence, homicides, accidents, and drug and alcohol abuse are a strikingly male phenomenon, particularly in the young and middle-aged (Möller-Leimkühler 2003). Much of this research suggests that the social expectations of traditional masculinity make men and boys vulnerable to an early death.

The scourge of untreated AIDS, particularly in sub-Saharan Africa, has wiped out a whole generation of young women and men, leaving orphaned children to the care of impoverished grandparents and other relatives. Nearly two-thirds of the world's HIV-positive people live in sub-Saharan Africa, which has a little over 10 percent of the world's population. Not only are innumerable years of potential productive life lost, but family networks fall apart, and there are fewer health workers, teachers, farmers, and urban workers (Avert 2005).

HIV is mostly transmitted heterosexually in Africa, and women and girls, especially those aged 15 to 24, have higher rates of infection than men and boys (U.N. AIDS 2004). Three-quarters of the women with HIV/AIDS live in Africa. Their vulnerability comes from economic dependence, high rates of rape, migrant labor patterns that send husbands to cities to work and to find other sex partners, and "transactional sex" with older men for money or gifts. In the United States, poor and marginalized women are also highly vulnerable. African American women and Latinas are less than one-quarter of the population, but they accounted for 80 percent of the reported cases of HIV/AIDS in the United States in 2000.

In sum, the economics of the body—occupational exploitation, the toll of poverty, vulnerability in disasters and epidemics—are both gendered and classed, with much of the effects of racial ethnic social differences reflective of economic differences. Women and men suffer from poor economic conditions in different ways, men from exhaustive physical labor and women from trying to care for children with little food or adequate shelter. They scrounge for food, and, if they cannot earn some money in home-based work, they prostitute their bodies. The poorest women, men, and children become the least valued social bodies.

Bodies as Religious Symbols

Bodies are cultural as well as economic entities, and women's bodies in particular are used symbolically for family honor and religious identity, which subjects them to community control. The roots of Western culture's religious control over the body—men's as well as women's—can be found in the Hebrew Bible. In "The Problem of the Body for the People of the Book," Howard Eilberg-Schwartz (1999) said that for the priests of ancient Judaism, the human body was the source of deep-seated contradictions. Humans are created in the image of God, but God has no body. Humans are enjoined by God to be fruitful and multiply, which implies very real bodies. The tensions around the body as a "conflicted object" not only invoke preoccupation with its cleanliness and control but also turn the body into a source of symbolism.

Women's bodies are thought to be more "unruly" and in need of social control than men's. Under religious doctrines, girl's and women's bodies are controlled through covering, segregation, and rules about purification after menstruation and childbirth. Men have to purify their bodies, too, before praying or entering a sacred place, but women's bodies seem to need control by men in the family and the community all the time. In the following excerpt, Susan Farrell, a sociologist, discusses body control in Christianity, Judaism, and Islam, especially as it affects women.

Hidden Symbols: Women's Religious Bodies

Susan A. Farrell
Kingsborough Community College, City University of New York

There are more than 4,200 religions, churches, denominations, splinter sects, faith groups, tribes, cultures, movements, and other religious and spiritual forms with billions of adherents in the world today.[1] Each one has various views on the body, positive and negative, and some even have contradictory views within the same belief system. However, in almost all contemporary religious beliefs, bodies are problematic. Bodies are usually viewed with suspicion and somewhat negatively. The body is seen as a barrier to religious and spiritual fulfillment, an entity that must be tamed and controlled through fasting, or renouncing sex, or self-mutilation. Although there are occasional exceptions, such as Tantric Buddhism, where spiritual enlightenment can be achieved through sexual practices, most religions view sexuality with suspicion. Their goal is to regulate and control the body's impulses and desires.

My focus will be on the understandings of the body, gender, and sexuality associated with two of the largest world religions, Christianity and Islam, and with Judaism as a source of Christianity and Islam. In each of these religions, women's bodies seem to be most problematic and most in need of control and regulation. Some theorize that it was the move from the traditional goddess religions to the patriarchal religions in the Middle East that led to this view (Eisler 1987); others see the change coming later, influenced by Greek stoicism and Gnostic beliefs, which saw the world dualistically, creating a mind/body split yet to be healed (Brown 1988; Fox 1995; Ranke-Heinemann 1990). Or the negative view of women's bodies may be part of the development of patriarchy in most societies (Sharma 1994). We may not be able to definitively state the origins of the Judaic, Christian, and Muslim perspectives on women's bodies as potentially polluting and therefore in need of restraint, but women and their bodies always seem to be "out of order" in the religious world. According to Martha Reineke,

> religious myths, rituals, and sacred symbols that are focused on the human body are among the primary vehicles for (1) socializing women to gender roles, (2) assigning women to subservient positions within the gendered caste system, and (3) controlling women's sexuality through the use of power. (1995, 431)

Separate, Hidden, and Embattled

In the major religions, women's bodies, and particularly their hair, are seductive and must be kept out of sight by modest clothing, wigs, and veils. Fundamentalist Islam goes the furthest in covering women, veiling them head to toe in *abbayas, chadors,* or *burqas,* sometimes with only a small net around the eyes for seeing through. Christianity, although originally embracing separation and veiling, ultimately rejected almost all of the monitoring of women's bodies by way of covering. Separation during rituals and ceremonies all but disappeared early in Christianity, except for children in parochial schools. Religious views of women, their bodies, and sexuality as dangerous, polluting, and seductive are important because Christianity was, and to a certain extent remains, a major sociopolitical force and shaper of ideology throughout Western culture. Thus, even in the American legal system, there remain attitudes toward sexuality and gender that support institutionalized sexism and heterosexism. These institutionalized attitudes are the basis of much of the ongoing conflict over women's right to have an abortion and equal rights for gays and lesbians, as well as issues related to the broad spectrum of sexual practices.

According to Reineke, women's sexuality is "irrational, and potentially chaotic," needing to be "either controlled" or "in service to a Christian culture, or is dangerously out of control and is evil" (1995, 441). The most extreme manifestations of Christian misogyny were the rampant accusations of witchcraft during the "burning times" of the late Middle Ages and the early modern period in Europe (Daly 1990). Recent studies estimate that from 1400 to 1800, somewhere between 40,000 and 100,000 people accused of witchcraft were executed; 80 percent of them were women (Behringer 2004; Briggs 1996; Cawthorne 2004; Gaskill 2005).

The issue of abortion has created a bitter debate in the Catholic church, as women and men who support women's right to choose try to remain faithful while asserting a woman's right to decide what is done to her body. In traditional Roman Catholicism, the life of the fetus is sacred. Sexuality exists for procreation primarily, and every act of sexual intercourse must be open to the possibility for the transmission of life. Therefore, even artificial birth control is forbidden, as is premarital sex, masturbation, and homosexual sex, which is seen to be "intrinsically disordered" as it is not open to the possibility of new life and is therefore "unnatural." Liberal and progressive as well as feminist Roman Catholic women and men see these issues as matters of justice as well as of choice (Farrell 2005).

Judaism and Women's Bodies

Diversity is the best word to characterize issues around the body in Judaism, especially today. Conservative, Reform, and Reconstructionist Jews do not separate women and men in the synagogue and do not stipulate modest dress in public.

Separation of and maintaining boundaries between men's and women's bodies is a hallmark of Orthodox Judaism. Men and women are physically separated in all official rituals as well as in the synagogue. Men's and women's bodies need to be well-covered, and men must also cover their heads. Married Orthodox Jewish women are forbidden to show their own hair, so they must cover it with wigs, headscarves, and hats.

In traditional Judaism, women must adhere to the practices of *niddah*. A wife and husband may not touch each other while she is menstruating and until no blood is evident on the white cloth used for testing. Once free of blood, the woman must immerse her whole body and head in a ritual bath (*mikvah*) for purification before she can have intercourse with her husband. *Niddah* can be seen as a patriarchal practice of repression, subjugation, and taboo, but many of the women who observe *niddah* feel that the forced separation enhances marital sexuality (Hartman and Marmon 2004). They also use the time of purification and ritual cleansing for spiritual healing, meditation, and body renewal.

Muslim Women and Veiling

As with Catholic women and abortion and Jewish women and *niddah*, the most prominent example of women's difference and separation from men in Islam is the tradition of veiling. Women's bodies in the most traditional Islamic practices must be completely covered. Other Muslim women wear only head coverings, as do women in the Nation of Islam founded in the United States by Elijah Muhammad in the 1930s (Ammat'ullah 2005). This veiling, whether just the head or the full-body cover of *abbayas, chadors,* and *burqas,* seems to be a gendered practice held in common by most Muslims. But as with *niddah,* many interpretations of the meaning of veiling can be found throughout the Muslim world (Nyhagen Predelli 2004; Sa'ar 2005).

Veiling is a means of maintaining identity for immigrant women in European countries, the United States, and Canada. Veiling can even be seen as a survival strategy in Islamic countries torn by war and revolution, as it may protect women from sexual assault. From a postmodern perspective, sometimes the veil covers up radical and subversive practices, such as wearing cosmetics and seductive lingerie. For many Muslim women, retaining the veil is seen as resistance to colonial and postcolonial patriarchy and even a way of countering globalization (Ahmed 1992; El Saadawi 1980; Nafisi 2003; Nomani 2005).

A Revisioning: The Feminist Good Body

When we examine religious practices, we should not discount women's agency. Reinterpretation of patriarchal practices is quite common in all religions (Sharma 1994). Judaism, Christianity, and Islam have been revisioned by feminists who find more positive views celebrating women's bodies and sexuality and who accept embodiment as part of creation and therefore good (Davies and Haney 1991; Karam 2005; Nelson and Longfellow 1994; Plaskow 1990).

Some religions have a more holistic vision—transcending the dualism of spiritual man versus bodily woman. An ancient religious tradition, Tantric Buddhism, believes that enlightenment, or nirvana, can be reached through the body, especially through sexual practices. In these traditions, women are not seen as barriers to salvation but as partners and conduits to fulfillment (Mann and Lyle 1995).

Many New Age religions based on paganism and Wicca have significantly revisioned the body and sexuality (Berger 1999, 2005; Radford Ruether 1992; Starhawk 1979). Some have revived ancient Celtic beliefs. Even after being Christianized, Celtic religious beliefs survived in monasteries where married women and men clergy lived together and raised their children in monastic traditions (Condren 1989; Ellis 1998). Sexuality was celebrated, and women were respected and treated as equal partners. For many New Age religions, the goddess has become the symbol of healing the split between mind and body, men and women. In "Why Women Need the Goddess," Carol Christ said that

> as women struggle to create a new culture in which women's power, bodies, will, and bonds are celebrated, it seems natural that the Goddess would reemerge as symbol of the newfound beauty, strength, and power of women. (1979, 286)

Conclusion

However women struggle to reclaim their bodies through religion and spirituality, whatever their strategies, bargains, and practices, women in all religious belief systems are finding new ways in old traditions to do this reclaiming. Women in Orthodox Judaism may feel constrained by some of their roles and the rituals around their most intimate bodily functions, but they have important commandments to obey. Jewish heroines abound both in scripture and throughout their history.

Similarly, Christian women, particularly Roman Catholics, can look to Mary, the Mother of God, as a powerful, almost goddess-like figure. As Sojourner Truth noted in a suffrage speech: Christ was born of God and a woman, man had nothing to do with it. Both Judaism and Christianity have reform denominations where women are called to the rabbinate and ordained as priests and ministers. Even Catholicism, which has not yet ordained women, allows women pastors to run parishes (Wallace 1992), and nuns have always had a revered place in the institutional church.

Muhammed was very respectful of women, enjoyed their company, and would consult his wives and take their advice seriously. Although later developments and cultural pressures of Middle Eastern society put Islamic women in a disadvantaged status, Islamic women's status varies by geographical region and denomination, as in the other religions. Women have more freedom in the Sunni tradition and less in the Shiite, with Saudi women of the Wahhabi tradition (a conservative branch of Sunni Islam adopted by the ruling Saudi family), the least amount (Ahmed 1999; Nomani 2005). Although Sufism comes out of the more conservative Shiite tradition, women are seen as respected mystics and saints (Armstrong 2000; Smith [1994] 2001).

In sum, women's bodies may be subsumed under the demands of traditional religions, but in modern interpretations and reclamations of past religious participation, women have insisted on a respected religious status that values their bodies and their sexuality.

Note

1. *www.Adherents.com*

References

Ahmed, Akbar S. 1999. *Islam Today.* New York: St. Martin's Press.

Ahmed, Leila. 1992. *Women and Gender in Islam: Historical Roots of a Modern Debate.* New Haven, CT: Yale University Press.

Ammat'ullah, Nurah W. 2005. "The Faith of Believing." In *Still Believing: Jewish, Christian, and Muslim Women Affirm Their Faith,* edited by Victoria Lee Erickson and Susan A. Farrell. Maryknoll, NY: Orbis Books.

Armstrong, Karen. 2000. *Islam: A Short History.* New York: Modern Library.

Brown, Peter. 1988. *The Body and Society: Men, Women, and Sexual Renunciation in Early Christianity.* New York: Columbia University Press.

Behringer, Wolfgang. 2004. *Witches and Witch-Hunts.* Cambridge, UK: Polity Press.

Berger, Helen A. 1999. *A Community of Witches: Contemporary Neo-paganism and Witchcraft in the United States.* Columbia: University of South Carolina Press.

——. (ed.). 2005. *Witchcraft and Magic: Contemporary North America.* Philadelphia: University of Pennsylvania Press.

Briggs, Robin. 1996. *Witches and Neighbors: The Social and Cultural Context of European Witchcraft.* New York: Viking Penguin.

Cawthorne, Nigel. 2004. *Witch Hunt: History of a Persecution.* Secaucus, NJ: Chartwell Books.

Christ, Carol P. 1979. "Why Women Need the Goddess." In *Womanspirit Rising: A Feminist Reader in Religion,* edited by Carol P. Christ and Judith Plaskow. San Francisco: Harper & Row.

Condren, Mary. 1989. *The Serpent and the Goddess: Women, Religion, and Power in Celtic Ireland.* San Francisco: Harper & Row.

Daly, Mary. 1990. *Gyn/Ecology: The Metaethics of Radical Feminism.* Boston: Beacon Press.

Davies, Susan E., and Eleanore H. Haney (eds.). 1991. *Redefining Sexual Ethics.* Cleveland, OH: The Pilgrim Press.

Eisler, Riane. 1987. *The Chalice and the Blade: Our History, Our Future.* San Francisco: Harper & Row.

El Saadawi, Nawal. 1980. *The Hidden Face of Eve: Women in the Arab World.* New York: St. Martin's Press.

Ellis, Peter Berresford. 1998. *The Ancient World of the Celts.* London: Constable.

Farrell, Susan A. 2005. "Reframing Social Justice, Feminism, and Abortion." *Conscience* 26, 1, 42–44.

Fox, Thomas C. 1995. *Sexuality and Catholicism.* New York: George Brazillier.

Gaskill, Malcolm. 2005. *Witchfinders*. Cambridge, MA: Harvard University Press.

Hartman, Tova, and Naomi Marmon. 2004. "Lived Regulations, Systemic Attributions: Menstrual Separation and Ritual Immersion in the Experience of Orthodox Jewish Women." *Gender & Society* 18, 389–408.

Karam, Azza M. 2005. "Reclaiming God." In *Still Believing: Jewish, Christian, and Muslim Women Affirm Their Faith*, edited by Victoria Lee Erickson and Susan A. Farrell. Maryknoll, NY: Orbis Books.

Mann, A. T., and Jane Lyle. 1995. *Sacred Sexuality*. Rockport, MA: Element Books.

Nafisi, Azar. 2003. *Reading Lolita in Tehran*. New York: Random House.

Nelson, James B., and Sandra P. Longfellow (eds.). 1994. *Sexuality and the Sacred: Sources for Theological Reflection*. Louisville, KY: Westminster/John Knox Press.

Nomani, Asra Q. 2005. *Standing Alone in Mecca: An American Woman's Struggle for the Soul of Islam*. New York: HarperCollins.

Nyhagen Predelli, Line. 2004. "Interpreting Gender in Islam: A Case Study of Immigrant Muslim Women." *Gender & Society* 18, 473–493.

Plaskow, Judith. 1990. *Standing Again at Sinai: Judaism From a Feminist Perspective*. San Francisco: HarperCollins.

Radford Ruether, Rosemary. 2005. *Goddesses and the Divine Feminine: A Western Religious History*. Berkeley: University of California Press.

Ranke-Heinemann, Uta. 1990. *Eunuchs for the Kingdom of Heaven: Women, Sexuality, and the Catholic Church*. New York: Doubleday.

Reineke, Martha J. 1995. "Out of Order: A Critical Perspective on Women in Religion." In *Women: A Feminist Perspective*, edited by Jo Freeman. Mountain View, CA: Mayfield.

Sa'ar, Amalia. 2005. "Postcolonial Feminism, the Politics of Identification, and the Liberal Bargain." *Gender & Society* 19, 680–700.

Sharma, Arvind (ed.). 1994. *Today's Woman in World Religions*. Albany: State University of New York Press.

Smith, Margaret. [1994] 2001. *Muslim Women Mystics*. Oxford, UK: Oneworld Publications.

Starhawk. 1979. *The Spiral Dance: A Rebirth of the Ancient Religion of the Great Goddess*. San Francisco: Harper & Row.

Wallace, Ruth A. 1992. *They Call Her Pastor: A New Role for Catholic Women*. Albany: State University of New York Press.

Original article commissioned for this book.

Body Knowledge

We have seen that women's bodies are particularly at risk from poor economic conditions and sexual exploitation and also that their bodies are controlled in the name of religion. In the last thirty-five years, feminists have promoted knowledge of their bodies as a way of enhancing women's control over them.

In 1970, a 193-page book of stapled newsprint called *Women and Their Bodies* was published by the New England Free Press; it sold a quarter of a million copies (Jacobs 2005). In 1973, it was commercially published as *Our Bodies, Ourselves* and, after numerous editions, came out most recently as *Our Bodies, Ourselves: A New Edition for a New Era* (BWHBC 2005). This book of feminist knowledge about women's bodies has been published in many languages and adapted to the cultures of different countries. In the following excerpt, Kathy Davis, a sociologist, shows how the idea of body knowledge as power traveled over the world.

The Travels of Our Bodies, Ourselves

Kathy Davis
Utrecht University, The Netherlands

In 1969, at one of the first conferences organized by second-wave feminists in the US, a group of Boston women met in a workshop on "Women and their Bodies." Most of the participants were young, white, middle-class, college-educated women, who had been active in the Civil Rights Movement or had helped draft resisters during the Vietnam War. For many of them, it was their first encounter with feminism and it was electrifying. They talked openly about their sexuality (a burning issue for young feminists at that time), about their experiences with pregnancy and childbirth, and they shared their frustrations with physicians. The group, which later became known as the Boston Women's Health Book Collective (BWHBC), began to meet regularly. They collected information about their bodies and health and wrote discussion papers. A year later, this collection of papers was assembled and the first version of *Our Bodies, Ourselves* was born. Originally printed on newsprint by an underground publisher and selling for 75¢, *Our Bodies, Ourselves* (*OBOS*) was a lively and accessible manual on women's bodies and health. It was full of personal experiences and contained useful information on issues ranging from masturbation (how to do it) to birth control (which methods were available and how to access them) to vaginal infections, pregnancy and nursing. It combined a scathing critique of patriarchal medicine and the medicalization of women's bodies as well as an analysis of the political economics of the health and pharmaceutical industries. But, above all, *OBOS* validated women's embodied experiences as a resource for challenging medical dogmas about women's bodies and, consequently, as a strategy for personal and collective empowerment. . . .

Despite being a North American artefact, *OBOS* has, by no means, remained within the borders of the US. From the beginning, it has crossed borders to become an international bestseller. As of 2002, *OBOS* has been translated into 20 languages, including five other-language versions which have been openly inspired by and/or acknowledge *OBOS,* and an additional five groups or individuals are actively working on a translation/adaptation.[1]

The worldwide success of the book raises several sets of questions.

First, how could such a distinctively North American book become so popular in so many different contexts? What was its appeal for women in such different parts of the world?

Second, how was the book translated and adapted to address the specific concerns of women in different contexts? What did the translations leave out, what was added, and, more generally, what does the process of translation say about how feminist knowledge circulates?

Third, to what extent does the dissemination of *OBOS* around the world, but particularly in the so-called "third world," make it just another western product (not unlike Nestlé's milk or Coca Cola) which has inundated less affluent nations, undermining indigenous women's struggles to improve their circumstances? . . .

OBOS Abroad

The BWHBC's main concern was to ensure that feminists would have editorial control over the translation and could adapt the book to fit their own social, political, and cultural context. Mindful of their own experiences with censorship in the US, they were also concerned that the "problem" chapters on controversial subjects like abortion, lesbian relationships, or masturbation would not be deleted by conservative, male-dominated publishing houses. To this end, they began to establish guidelines, which stated that no foreign adaptation could use their title if it did not include at least some part of every chapter from the original book. . . .

Strictly speaking, very few of the foreign editions could even be considered a direct translation—that is, a verbatim rendition of the original in another language. Even the early books initiated by foreign publishing houses tended to delete or "sanitize" parts of the original book (usually the controversial chapters on lesbian sexuality, masturbation and abortion). For example, the Taiwan edition (1973) not only omitted the lesbian chapter, but also toned down all references to homosexuality in other chapters.[2] In Japan, as late as 1990, customs officials seized copies of the book as "pornography" (representations of genitalia and pubic hair were cited as particularly offensive), sparking a lively debate in the local newspapers against "western-style feminism."[3] Chinese publishers were concerned about topics like prostitution and safe sex, which they considered obscene under Chinese law. Moreover, they found it difficult to square China's "one child policy" with the women's rights orientation of *OBOS*—a critique which the translators strategically countered with the argument that the book was not *against* family planning, but rather *for* a more "patient-centered" policy which was "compatible with women's needs."[4] . . .

In contrast to direct translations, the majority of the foreign editions fell under the category translation/adaptation. The original *OBOS* was reworked and contextualized in accordance with the translators' notions of what was appropriate, useful, or necessary in their particular situation. Throughout the 1970s and 1980s, changes in *OBOS* were fairly minimal, thus reflecting a similarity in feminist issues between the US and Western Europe. For example, the Swedish translators felt that *OBOS* placed too much emphasis on sexuality. "We had a ten-year advantage over the US where the sexuality debate only began in the late sixties."[5] The Dutch translators rejected the division between lesbian and heterosexual relationships as too "strict." It did not fit the Dutch context, nor did it correspond with their own feeling that homosexuality and heterosexuality are a "continuum with lots of feelings in between."[6] The Dutch edition also includes lengthy passages on feminist therapy—a subject which was considered of particular relevance in the Netherlands.[7] The German adaptation, *Unser Körper, Unser Leben,* was the subject of considerable dispute among feminist groups who felt the book wasn't "radical" enough. It was much too "fixated" on childbearing and breastfeeding. As one translator notes in a letter to the BWHBC, "we prefer to influence debates in the direction of HOW we have our children and IF we choose to have any. But this is not the only destiny for us. Don't you agree?"[8]

The foreign versions invariably had to take differences in abortion laws and histories of feminist struggle around reproductive health issues into account. In some countries, abortion was still illegal or controversial for religious reasons. The context not only affected how information was presented, but which issues needed to be emphasized. For example, the Japanese translators were especially concerned with unnecessary gynecological surgery, given a recent spate of Caesarian sections in hospitals, or a long tradition of pronatalist policies made infertility an important concern for the Romanian adaptation. . . .

The Egyptian Case

Hayāt al-mar'a wa'sihatuhā (translated as "The Life of a Woman and Her Health") was explicitly written for a non-western audience. The authors assumed not only that Egyptian women, in particular, and Arab women, in general, have their own health problems, but also that feminist movements have their own histories of struggle and battles to fight, making both the issues and the rhetoric in which they are framed different from one context to another.

Many Egyptian women see themselves as fighting not so much against patriarchy or local oppressors, but against the Egyptian government, Western cultural and economic domination, and global forces, which impose harsh economic policies and alien life styles (El Dawla et al., 1998: 103). While the Cairo Women's Health Book Collective clearly wanted to borrow from US feminism, they were also shaped by the prevailing sentiment of anti-imperialism and anti-Americanism of contemporary political movements in Egypt (Al-Ali, 2000). Secular in orientation, they were also part of a culture where the Islamist movement enjoys considerable popularity and where most women, whether Muslim or Copt, were religious and where tradition is the locus of the most salient norms by which women are judged (El Dawla et al., 1998: 75).

In this context, the book was bound to be controversial, and it required considerable juggling to make a book which would be culturally sensitive, not offend religious feelings, but would still sustain a strong commitment to women's rights (Ibrahim and Farah, 1992: 7). The result was a delicate balancing act whereby contradictory messages were presented, often side-by-side. The flexible strategy adopted by the Cairo group in deciding whether or not to include issues and how to address them is illustrated by the following three examples.

The first concerns the Cairo group's stance toward medicine. Like the original *OBOS*, the Egyptian book was critical of medical knowledge and practice. However, they described medicine explicitly as "western." While the authors support women's right to have access to all medical knowledge about their bodies and health (the cover of the book shows a young woman with bare arms, western attire, and flowing hair peering intently through a microscope), they are also critical of western medicine, which is often authoritarian and disrespectful to women's needs. Underprivileged women often experience demeaning treatment when they enter a "modern" clinic in Egypt. Physicians trained in western medicine are often contemptuous of Islamic codes of modesty which make women reluctant to be examined by male doctors, or discount the importance of virginity for many unmarried women, who fear that their hymen will break during a gynecological exam (Hill, 1994: 4–5).

The second example concerned the authors' treatment of sexuality. While the explicit mention of sexuality and sexual enjoyment was a revolutionary eye-opener for the US readers of *OBOS*, sexuality was not a particularly controversial subject in Egypt, where women's sexual pleasure is taken for granted and where women's networks have always allowed extensive talk about the details of sex. However, sexuality outside of marriage is entirely off limits, let alone between women. Although the Cairo group took up the issue of lesbianism because it is "regarded as a path toward liberation by many women in the west," they ultimately decided not to include it in their book, as it would have invoked certain censure from religious authorities for something which was not a "viable life style" in Egypt (Farah, 1991: 17). Another "hot item"—masturbation—was treated in a similarly ambivalent way. On the one hand, Egyptian readers were reassured that it was "natural" for their children to masturbate. On the other hand, mothers were encouraged to tell their children to go out and play ("do something worthwhile") rather than masturbate. Rape was also controversial. Some group members felt that women brought rape upon themselves through immodest clothing, while others did not like the idea of attributing violence against women only to men (what about daughter-in-law abuse or female genital mutilation?). Ultimately, rape was included, but in a comprehensive chapter on violence against women perpetrated by both sexes.

The third example was female genital excision and, more generally, the issue of how to deal with "cultural traditions." The issue of female genital excision has, not surprisingly, stirred considerable debate both within and outside Egypt. As the issue which western feminists invariably focus on in connection with Muslim women, the Cairo group agonized about how to take a stand against it without alienating their readers who had an understandable aversion to the attitude of western feminists. After much discussion, they took a stand against the practice, providing information on the psychological and social damage which it entails. However, they also explained the cultural context, which allows for the continuation of the practice among Egyptian women, particularly in rural settings.[9] As the book was being tested on different groups of Egyptian women, the authors routinely took along an imam who, in the course of the discussion, would stand up and announce that there was nothing in the *Q'uran* which required female genital excision, thereby lending the book legitimacy among religious women.

Rearticulating Feminist Body/Politics

. . . Although early versions of *OBOS* were written in the spirit of universal sisterhood which belonged to the US second-wave feminist discourse of the time, the universalism inherent in this model was also undercut by the book's claim that each woman was the ultimate authority over her own bodily experiences. The authors of *OBOS* were, to be sure, all white, middle-class feminists who, in their own words, could not pretend to "speak for" all women. Their intention was rather to "inspire" other women to write their own books. The translations which emerged in the three decades following the first edition of *OBOS* indicate that it was not the notion of "global sisterhood" which travelled (although some of the translation projects, as for example, the Egyptian collective, did refer to the BWHBC as their "US sisters"). On the contrary, what travelled was *how* the original collective wrote the book. The image of a group of (lay)women collectively sharing knowledge about their embodied experiences seems to be what fired the imagination of women in different parts of the world and served as an invitation to do the same. While the notion of "global sisterhood" creates a spurious universality, which denies differences among women, the process by which the original collective wrote their book could be taken up fairly easily by a diversity of women and adapted to their specific circumstances. It was the method of knowledge sharing and not a shared identity as women which appeared to have a global appeal, making *OBOS* a case in point for a transnational feminist body/politics based on oppositional practices rather than identity politics (Grewal and Kaplan, 1994). . . .

While the original *OBOS* was a decidedly North American book, firmly wedded to modernist notions of individualism and equal rights feminism, in the process of travelling it underwent continuous and often dramatic revisions. *OBOS* was not simply "consumed" by non-western feminists as a US export product. Despite limited finances and difficult working conditions, translators reframed and adapted *OBOS* to make it culturally and politically appropriate to their local circumstances. They were critical of the content and did not hesitate to make the book less individualistic or more explicitly political (as in the adaptation for Latin America). If the cultural discrepancies were too great—as was the case with the Egyptian version—the translation collective simply made their own book. This resulted in what Ahmed (2000) would call a "strange encounter": the "American-ness" of the book was explicitly drawn upon to promote women's rights locally, while the pervasive anti-American sentiment in the Arab world was acknowledged as a valid response to oppressive or paternalist foreign intervention. Each project, in fact, attested to the creative agency of translators in developing flexible and effective strategies for making their version of *OBOS* sensitive to the local political and cultural climate as well as to differences and schisms within their own feminist movements. The diversity in the translation projects show that feminist knowledge is not simply transferred from one context to another. It invariably requires re-working and contextualization. What is empowering or disempowering in one context is not necessarily so in another.

Notes

1. Much of the information on the translation/adaptations projects is taken from *Our Bodies, Ourselves in Many Languages: A Global History and Status Report,* which was compiled by the BWHBC in July 1998, the BWHBC website, and updates from various staff members.
2. A sentence like "we don't all want to sleep together, but we don't want to limit our friendships because of fear of homosexuality . . ." in the original became "We don't say we agree with homosexuality . . ." Or, an anecdote of a woman in a bathtub touching her clitoris (in the section "Lovemaking") was cut, along with other references to touching—apparently a taboo subject.
3. Critics of censorship argued that the controversy should be seen as a symptom of Japan's history of isolationism and a denial of women's rights to communicate internationally (*Japan Times,* 3 September 1990).
4. Interview with Liu Bohong, coordinator and major translator of the Chinese translation, in the *Boston Globe* 12 December, 1998.
5. BWHBC minutes, September–December 1978.
6. In the preface of *Je lichaam je leven* (1975: 12).
7. Interestingly, therapy was a bone of contention in the BWHBC. Many of the members of the collective did not want to include information on psychotherapy at all as they felt it depoliticized women's problems and, therefore, had no place in a book aimed at empowering women.
8. BWHBC correspondence, 5 August 1977.
9. Female circumcision was officially banned in Egypt in 1959, but continues to be performed, particularly in rural settings, where it is estimated that 90 percent of women are circumcised, whether they are Christian or Muslim. The reasons women give for engaging in the practice range from wanting to be "pure" to the belief that it is more "aesthetic" to not wanting to become dependent on a man through sexual desire.

References

Ahmed, Sara (2000) *Strange Encounters: Embodied Others in Post-Coloniality.* London and New York: Routledge.

Al-Ali, Nadje (2000) *Secularism, Gender and the State in the Middle East: The Egyptian Women's Movement.* Cambridge: Cambridge University Press.

El Dawla, Aida Seif, Amal Abdel Hadi, and Nadia Abdel Wahab (1998) "Women's Wit Over Men's: Trade-offs and Strategic Accommodations in Egyptian Women's Reproductive Lives," pp. 69–107 in R. P. Petchesky and K. Judd (eds.) *Negotiating Reproductive Rights.* London: Zed Books.

Farah, Nadia (1991) "The Egyptian Women's Health Book Collective," *Middle East Report,* November–December: 16–25.

Grewal, Inderpal and Caren Kaplan (1994) "Introduction: Transnational Feminist Practices and Questions of Postmodernity," pp. 1–33 in I. Grewal and C. Kaplan (eds.) *Scattered Hegemonies: Postmodernity and Transnational Feminist Practices.* Minneapolis: University of Minnesota Press.

Hill, Nancy (1994) "An Egyptian Women's Health Book Inspired by Our Bodies, Ourselves: Is Global Sisterhood Possible After All?," Paper presented at the Eastern Sociological Society, 18 March.
Ibrahim, Barbara and Nadia Farah (1992) "Women's Lives and Health: The Cairo Women's Health Book Collective," *Quality/Calidad/Qualité*, 4: 4–11.

Critical Summary

Our bodies are material; they are flesh and blood. Our bodies are invested with social meaning when we are part of a community; then we become people with biographies, stories of our personal social bodies. Community norms and expectations determine the meanings of bodies and their relative value. Whether a body is handled with reverence or contempt, whether it is nourished or starved, whether its owner has control over it or must succumb to others' control—these are all determined by the intertwining of communities, families, and individuals.

In this book, we have seen the extent to which bodies are shaped according to gendered norms and ideals of masculinity and femininity. We have explored the resistances and revolution in meanings of bodies with impairments, the battles by and about intersexed and transgendered people, and the horrors of body violations in war, disasters, and imprisonment. The major themes of this book are that bodies become social entities through membership in a community and are valued according to their gender, social class, religion, racial ethnic, and national status; that bodies survive and thrive depending upon economic resources and social power; that men's bodies are at risk of military, athletic, and industrial exploitation, and, for disadvantaged men, imprisonment; that women's bodies are controlled by institutions dominated by men, namely, medicine and religion, but that knowledge gives women increased autonomy; and finally, that it is possible for the marginalized—the elderly, those with disabilities, intersexed and transgendered people—to forge communities that give their bodies value.

Bodies are shaped by conforming to norms and expectations, but bodies can also be used to rebel, to flaunt differences and celebrate them. Bodies have been used as weapons, but bodies are also used as a means of non-violent resistance—in civil rights and anti-war demonstrations, hunger strikes, picket lines, and sit-ins.

What this adds up to is that our gendered bodies are material, physical, and biological, but it is communities that give us humanity. From birth to death, we are social bodies in social worlds.

References and Recommended Readings

Avert. 2005. "The Impact of HIV and AIDS on Africa." *www.avert.org/aidsimpact.htm*

Bearak, Barry. 2005. "The Day the Sea Came." *New York Times Magazine,* 27 November, 46–66, 70, 97, 101.

Butler, Judith. 2004. *Precarious Life: The Powers of Mourning and Violence.* New York: Verso.

BWHBC (Boston Women's Health Book Collective). 2005. *Our Bodies, Ourselves: A New Edition for a New Era.* New York: Touchstone/Simon & Schuster.

Courtenay, W. H. 2000. "Constructions of Masculinity and Their Influence on Men's Well-Being: A Theory of Gender and Health." *Social Science and Medicine* 50, 1385–1401.

Dewan, Shaila. 2005. "Disasters and Their Dead." *New York Times Week in Review,* 16 October, 4.

Eilberg-Schwartz, Howard. 1999. "The Problem of the Body for the People of the Book." In *Women in the Hebrew Bible,* edited by Alice Bach. New York: Routledge.

Enarson, Elaine, and Betty Hearn Morrow (eds.). 1998. *The Gendered Terrain of Disaster: Through Women's Eyes.* Miami: Florida International University Press.

Gallagher, Catherine, and Thomas Laqueur (eds.). 1987. *The Making of the Modern Body.* Berkeley: University of California Press.

Gatens, Moira. 1997. *Imaginary Bodies: Ethics, Power, and Corporeality.* New York: Routledge.

Grosz, Elizabeth. 1994. *Volatile Bodies: Toward a Corporeal Feminism.* Bloomington: Indiana University Press.

———. 1996. *Space, Time, and Perversion: Essays on the Politics of the Body.* New York: Routledge.

Hawthorne, Susan, and Bronwyn Winter (eds.). 2002. *September 11, 2001: Feminist Perspectives.* North Melbourne, Australia: Spinifex.

Ignatieff, Michael. 2005. "The Broken Contract." *New York Times Magazine,* 25 September, 15–17.

Jacobs, Alexandra. 2005. "A Feminist Classic Gets a Makeover." *New York Times Book Review,* 17 July, 27.

Mernissi, Fatima. 1987. *Beyond the Veil: Male-Female Dynamics in Modern Muslim Society.* Bloomington: Indiana University Press.

———. 1991. *The Veil and the Male Elite: A Feminist Interpretation of Women's Rights in Islam* (trans. Mary Jo Lakeland). Cambridge, MA: Perseus Books.

Möller-Leimkühler, Anne Maria. 2003. "The Gender Gap in Suicide and Premature Death or: Why Are Men So Vulnerable?" *European Archives of Psychiatry & Clinical Neuroscience* 253, 1–9.

Price, Janet, and Margrit Shildrick (eds.). 1999. *Feminist Theory and the Body.* New York: Routledge.

Rahman, Momin, and Anne Witz. 2003. "What Really Matters? The Elusive Quality of the Material in Feminist Thought." *Feminist Theory* 4, 243–261.

Riska, Elianne. 2004. *Masculinity and Men's Health: Coronary Heart Disease in Medical and Public Discourse.* Lanham, MD: Rowman and Littlefield.

Rosenfeld, Dana, and Christopher Faircloth (eds.). 2006. *Medicalized Masculinities.* Philadelphia: Temple University Press.

Salzinger, Leslie. 2003. *Genders in Production: Making Workers in Mexico's Global Factories.* Berkeley: University of California Press.

Sander, Thomas H., and Robert D. Putnam. 2005. "Sept. 11 as Civics Lesson." *Washington Post,* 10 September, A23.

Scheper-Hughes, Nancy, and Loïc Wacquant (eds.). 2004. *Commodifying Bodies.* Thousand Oaks, CA: Sage.

Sered, Susan. 2000. *What Makes Women Sick? Maternity, Modesty, and Militarism in Israeli Society.* Hanover, NH: University Press of New England.

Shilling, Chris. 2005. *The Body in Culture, Technology, and Society.* Thousand Oaks, CA: Sage.

Smith, Barbara Ellen. 1987. *Digging Our Own Graves: Coal Miners and the Struggle Over Black Lung Disease.* Philadelphia: Temple University Press.

Sutton, Barbara. 2005. "The Bodily Scars of Neoliberal Economics: A Feminist Analysis." Paper presented at the American Sociological Association Annual Meeting, Philadelphia.

Turner, Bryan S. 1996. *The Body and Society: Explorations in Social Theory* (second edition). Thousand Oaks, CA: Sage.

U.N. AIDS. 2004. "AIDS Epidemic Update: December 2004." *www.unaids.org/wad2004/EPI_1204_pdf_en/Chapter2_women+aids_en.pdf*

U.N. Population Fund. 2005. "State of World Population 2005." *www.unfpa.org/swp/2005/english/ch8/index.htm*

Weiss, Meira. 2002. *The Chosen Body: The Politics of the Body in Israeli Society.* Stanford, CA: Stanford University Press.

Internet Sources

Carpenter Program in Religion, Gender, and Sexuality
www.vanderbilt.edu/divinity/carpenter

Disaster Watch
www.disasterwatch.net

Gender and Disaster Network
www.gdnonline.org

Gender and Globalization
gpeig.org/gender/2004/11/gender-in-global-perspective.html

Globalization, Gender, and Health
www.crwh.org/programs/globalization.php

Our Bodies, Ourselves
www.ourbodiesourselves.org/default.asp

UNAIDS
www.unaids.org/en/default.asp

U.N. International Strategy for Disaster Reduction
www.unisdr.org/eng/risk-reduction/gender/rd-gender-eng.htm

U.N. Population Fund
www.unfpa.org/index.htm ✦

Class Exercises

Lisa Jean Moore

Exercise I

Body Variables

Procedure: Hand out charts to all students and ask them to fill them in to the best of their abilities for about 10 minutes. Then go over them in class together using the board or an overhead projector. After students have filled in their charts, ask them if there are people who do *not* have the assumed correspondence of categories. For example, they can begin with themselves. Do they fit the logic of an entire column? Do they know anyone else who doesn't?

Aim: This exercise is intended to demonstrate to students the ways in which binary thinking about human bodies forces us to think in pre-existing dichotomous categories. By placing terms in each box, students start to follow what seems to be a logical progression. There are assumptions we make about individuals from their gendered performances—these assumptions are often about some "natural" or biological facts. Although we do not see penises or vaginas, we assume they are lurking beneath clothing and that is what drives certain gendered performances. But when students confront real-life experiences of individuals who do not neatly fit into the categories, the class can begin discussions of how social structures work to re-insert or force people into categories or to shun them. Students can then discuss how the naturalness of the body is really a fiction or an imaginary that we construct as real and use for our perceptions of others.

Instructions for Students
Please fill in the chart to the best of your ability. You have 10 minutes to complete the chart.

Table E-1
Body Variables Sex and Gender Chart

Category— Note: These are Binary and Dichotomous	Normative Sex/Gender Assumptions	Normative Sex/Gender Assumptions
Descriptor	Feminine	Masculine
Hormones		
Chromosomes		
Genitalia		
Symbols		
Childhood Term		
Sphere		
Labels/Slang		
Social Behavior		
Gender Performance		
Sexual Attraction to—		
Adjectives to Describe		

Exercise II

What Are Normal Bodies?

Procedure: Hand out charts to all students and ask them to fill them in to the best of their abilities for about 10 minutes. Then go over them in class together using the board or an overhead projector. In a discussion, ask them to focus on the social construction and purpose of "normal bodies."

Aim: This exercise is designed to demonstrate how becoming normal is a social process of managing one's performance through the consumption of discourses, products, and practices. Although people often say that "being normal is natural," this exercise aims to deconstruct that notion and get students to begin to look at the ways the "range of normal" is quite limited and used to control individuals' body practices and appearances.

Questions for Discussion
1. How are normal bodies made?
2. What is normal for women and men?
3. Why is it important for women/men to have these normal body characteristics?
4. How do normal and natural become interchangeable terms?
5. What happens when they are used interchangeably?
6. What are the consequences of "abnormality"?

Instructions for Students
For this exercise, go through column one and describe the social and individual expectations for the normal body for men and for women. Second column—give one example of how people attempt to attain it. Third column—think of what is considered abnormal. Fourth col-

247

umn—list some consequences of abnormality. Please fill in the chart to the best of your ability. You have 10 minutes to complete the chart.

Table E-2
What Is the Normal Body?

Topic	Description of the appropriate range of normal		How do people attempt to attain the normal?		What is "abnormal"?	What are the consequences of "abnormality"?
	Men	Women	Men	Women		
Normal Weight						
Normal Height						
Normal Physical Appearance						
Normal Health						
Normal Gender						
Normal Sex						
Normal Sexuality						
Normal Future Body: Middle Age Elderly						

Exercise III

Body Projects

Procedure: Students conduct informal interviews with 1 to 5 individuals outside of class over two weeks. (The number interviewed depends on the class size.) The first week, students interview girls/women, and the second week students interview boys/men. If students are interviewing more than one person, it is important that they try to vary the sexual orientation, religion, ability, age, and/or racial or ethnic group of those they are interviewing. They ask a series of six questions and bring the data back to class the next session. These data are then aggregated on the board for students to make some general sociological observations about gendered body projects. Generally, despite sampling from a diverse group, certain trends emerge in the aggregated data, which leads to interesting discussions about what types of body projects exist and how they are gendered.

Aim: This exercise is designed to demonstrate similarities and differences in contemporary body projects of women and men. During an in-class discussion, students are asked to consider these questions:

- What patterns do they see?
- What is the range of variation for women/men's ideal bodies and body projects?
- In what ways are they similar? In what ways are the different?

Additionally, the professor can ask students to discuss

- Difficulties of informants discussing their bodies
- Interviewing across gender lines
- Truth-telling regarding potentially stigmatizing body analysis

Instructions for Students

Please interview X individual women/men about their bodies. After establishing the demographic variables, ask each person the following six questions. Please bring this data in to class for a group exercise.

Table E-3
Body Projects Interview Schedule

Demographics:

Age

Racial Ethnic Identity

Religion

Sexual Orientation

QUESTIONS:

a. In your opinion, what is the ideal female/male body?

b. How do you feel about your own body?

c. What is one thing you would like to change about your body?

d. How would you change this?

e. What is one thing you love about your body?

f. Is there anything you are currently doing to fit into the ideal female/male body?

Exercise IV

Taking Care of Bodies

Procedure: For this exercise, students are provided with a sheet to tally their labor performed in the service of the body. Be clear that this labor is unpaid and often invisible until noted. In a weeklong journal, students are asked to keep track of tasks that they themselves do in the service of their own bodies and those of their children, their parents, and other loved ones. After creating a log of unpaid or (in)visible labor for the body, students are asked to determine a salary for their time for the tasks and to calculate the amount of money that is saved by doing these tasks themselves.

These websites provide some version of wages that can be modified to help students to determine their hourly wage had they been compensated for their labor:
WebWage—*www.wageweb.com/health1.htm*
U.S. Bureau of Labor Statistics—*www.bls.gov/cps/home.htm*

Aim: The purpose of this assignment is threefold. First, it is an accounting of unpaid, informal labor routinely done in service of the body. Second, it is a mathematical calculation of cost savings because the labor is done in the private and unpaid sector. Finally, it leads to a gender analysis of childcare and eldercare that women are often expected to perform in the service of bodies. It provides students with an opportunity to see the effects of deskilling, the labored division of caregiving and informal, unpaid care work, and the state/corporate benefit from informal, unpaid caregivers. In particular, older women seem to be very affected by the consciousness-raising about their work and its worth.

Instructions for Students
Please create a log of your informal, unpaid labor that you perform in the service of bodies—your own, children, parents, lovers: cleaning,

grooming, dressing, applying cosmetics, giving/taking injections or medications, changing diapers or bandages, and so on. Do this log for a week and bring it to class. This chart can be used as a model. Feel free to modify it to fit your needs. We will fill in the columns with the wages in class together. Three examples have been provided for you. ✦

Table E-4
Taking Care of Bodies: Chart

Task	Time in Week	Professional Career if Paid	Hourly Wage	Yearly Wage	Total Wages
Diaper Changing/Diaper Rash Treatment	5 hours	Childcare Provider			
Purchasing/Preparing/ Cooking for Family	22 hours	Chef			
Administer Meds/ Vitamins to Children and Mother	1 hour	Pediatrican/Pharmacist/ Case Worker			
TOTAL					

Films With Somatic Themes

Big Enough (2004)—Explorations of "otherness" in 20-year documentary follow-up to *Little People*. Available from Fanlight Productions, *www.fanlight.com*

Boys Don't Cry (1999)—Teena Brandon story of transgender identity and violent reactions

Casa de los Babies (2003)—Western women waiting to adopt babies in South America

Chutney Popcorn (2000)—Interracial lesbian couple and pregnancy

The Crying Game (1992)—Transgendered person in IRA psychological thriller

Dare to Dream: The Story of the U.S. Women's Soccer Team (2005)—From their beginning in the 1980s as "the red-headed stepchild" of sports through four World Cups and three Olympic games (HBO documentary)

The Day I Will Never Forget (2002)—Ritual genital cutting in Kenya

The Deer Hunter (1978)—Expendable working-class male bodies and minds in Vietnam

Dirty Pretty Things (2002)—Organ donation for travel documents

Dying to Be Thin (2000)—Eating disorders and the American obsession with thin women

The Elephant Man (1980)—Carnivalesque use of body for freak show

Gattaca (1997)—Two men exchange genetic identity in a DNA future

Girlfight (2000)—Young Brooklyn woman trains as a boxer

Growing Up and Liking It: The Menstruation Myth (1992)—Women share stories of "coming of age"

Hotel Rwanda (2005)—Genocide in Rwanda

Is It a Boy or a Girl? (2000)—Controversy surrounding intersex medical treatment. Video available at *www.isna.org/videos/boy_or_girl*

Junior (1994)—Male scientist (Arnold Schwartzenegger) experimentally carries a fetus in his own body

The Killing Fields (1984)—Cambodian genocide under Pol Pot

Killing Us Softly 3 (2000)—Women's bodies portrayed in advertising

The Life and Times of Sara Baartman: "The Hottentot Venus" (1998)—The life of a Khoikhoi woman who was taken from South Africa in 1810 and exhibited in Britain as a freak

Little Man (2005)—Lesbian couple adopt a seriously ill premature baby (documentary)

Ma Vie en Rose (1997)—Transgender child in Western Europe

Maria Full of Grace (2004)—Female Colombian drug "mules"

Million Dollar Baby (2004)—Female empowerment in athletics and euthanasia

Miss Evers' Boys (1997)—U.S. government's 1932 Tuskeegee syphilis experiments, in which a group of Black men who were test subjects were left untreated, despite the development of a cure

Moolaade (2004)—Female genital cutting in Burkina Faso

Murderball (2002)—Wheelchair Rugby World Championships

My Left Foot (1989)—Christy Brown, born with cerebral palsy, learned to paint and write with his only controllable limb, his left foot

Paradise Now (2005)—Two Palestinian best friends in a suicide mission

Paternal Instinct (2003)—Gay male couple establish a relationship with a surrogate to start a family

Pumping Iron (1977)—Arnold Schwartzenegger's first film

Pumping Iron II: The Women (1985)—Female body-builders and the sexism in the competitive world

Real Women Have Curves (2002)—Mexican American woman and sweatshops in U.S.

Schindler's List (1993)—Holocaust victims saved through working for an Austrian benefactor

The Sea Inside (2004)—Completely paralyzed man in 30-year fight to end his own life

Silence Broken: Korean Comfort Women (1999)—historical footage, interviews, and dramatic reenactments tell the true story of Korean women forced to work as prostitutes for the Japanese Army during World War II

Silkwood (1983)—Occupational toxic exposure and whistle blower

Southern Comfort (2001)—Struggle of an FtM who is dying from ovarian cancer and can't get medical treatment (documentary)

Super Size Me (2004)—Fast food industry and nutritional consequences

Switch (1991)—As punishment for his misogyny, a male is transferred into a sexy female body

Thirteen (2003)—Adolescent girls and self-injury

Toilet Training (2003)—Persistent discrimination, harassment, and violence that transgender people face in gender-segregated bathrooms. Video available at *www.srlp.org/index.php?sec=05A&page=toilettraining*

Transamerica (2005)—Pre-op MtF transgender must care for the son she never knew she had fathered

The Twilight of the Golds (1997)—Fictional family confronted with gay gene in fetus

Vera Drake (2004)—Abortionist in 1950s England

Warm Springs (2005)—President Franklin D. Roosevelt learning to live with paralysis from polio in the late 1920s. Cable film available at *www.hbo.com* ✦

Subject Index

categories, racial, 13, 138, 139, 156–161
Catholicism
  abortion and, 229–230
  female circumcision, 95, 97
  Virgin Mary, 231
Caucasians. *See* Whites
Celtic religions, 231
cerebral palsy, 182–183, 189, 254
Chase, Cheryl, 150
Chechnyan suicide bombers, 206
cheerleading, radical, 90
child care
  class exercises, 251–252
  disabilities and, 174
  gender norms, 2, 3, 19, 29–30, 55
  hormones, impact on, 14
  maternal instinct, 18
  natural disasters, 225, 227
  work-family balance, 18, 19
childbirth. *See also* pregnancy; procreation
  Africa, health care in, 56
  feminist studies of, 4
  hormones, 14
  medicalization of, 42, 43–49, 55–56
  Our Bodies, Ourselves, 234, 236
  patriarchal control of, 29, 41
  religious purification, 228
  suicide bomber imagery, 205
children
  adopted, 34, 35
  books on procreation, 51–54
  communities, 181
  cultural status, 6, 19, 96
  custody disputes, 41
  donor and surrogate parents, 34–35, 39–41
  gender categorization, 2–3
  gender norms, 55, 62
  genetic testing, 32–38
  genocide, 31
  intersex, 138, 140, 149–151, 154, 155, 157, 159, 160, 162
  Joan/John case study, 20–23
  love for parents, 224
  multiracial, 156–161
  orphans, 222, 226
  prostitutes, 209–210
  sports and gender development, 63–68, 80
  toys and gender development, 61, 63–64
  value as social bodies, 227
  war casualties, 198, 209
Chile, military draft, 196, 214

China
  Korean occupation, 210
  male birth control pill, 50
  Our Bodies, Ourselves, 235
  procreation policies, 30, 235
  sex selection, 36
  sexual torture in, 200
Cho, Grace, 210–214
Christianity
  Adam and Eve, 85
  children's books on procreation, 54
  circumcision, 95, 97, 131
  women's bodies, control of, 227–230, 231
chromosomes
  assumptions about, 139
  defined, 5
  disease and, 23
  films about, 253
  genetic testing, 32–38
  intersex, 6, 21, 23, 138, 149
  sex selection, 31–34, 36
  sex/gender differences, 12, 18–20, 23–24
  social engineering, 31
chronic fatigue syndrome, 185–188
chronic pain
  euthanasia, 182–183
  living with, 185–188
circumcision
  botched, 20–23
  female, 94–99, 106, 237–238
  films about, 253, 254
  male, 95–97, 127–132, 134–135, 136
  readings, recommended, 110
Clare, Eli, 181–185
clarifying surgery, 138, 140, 149–151, 154, 155, 157, 159, 160, 162
class
  AIDS, 226–227
  appearance and, 1, 114–115
  bear subculture, 119–122, 132
  brain development studies, 15–16
  breast cancer, 103–104
  categorizing people, 11
  cool walk, 115–118
  cosmetic surgery, 99
  diet, 11–12
  disabilities and, 183–184
  eating disorders, 104–105, 106–107
  feminist solidarity, 208
  gendered divisions of labor, 2–3

health care and, 30, 55–56
hierarchy, 115, 163
homosexuality and, 183–184
incarceration rates, 199
labor exploitation, 226
medical testing, unethical, 30, 254
military service, 195–197
natural disasters, 222–223, 225
nature *vs.* nurture, 13
Our Bodies, Ourselves, 234, 238
procreation and, 30, 40, 41, 55–56
relationship with gender, 2, 4, 15–16, 24, 115, 240
social engineering, 31
sports and, 68, 79
sterilization programs, 31
surrogate mothers, 40
transgender individuals, 142
class exercises, 245–252
clitoris
  circumcision, 94–99, 237–238
  historical views of, 92–94
  intersex "clarifying" surgery, 149–150
  masturbation and, 128
  orgasms and, 92–94, 98
clothing
  disaster relief, 225
  Dove "real women" campaign, 85
  feminine, 140–141
  gender display, defined, 6
  intersex individuals and, 153, 154
  Islamic women, 206, 207, 229, 230, 237
  metrosexuals, 119, 132
  queer gendering, 142
  rape and, 230, 237
coal mines, 226
Colombo, Realdo, 92
communities
  bear subculture, 119–122
  boxing, 75–78
  disabilities and, 181–185
  female circumcision, 94–99
  homosexual, 181–185
  intersex support groups, 151–154
  male circumcision, 129–132
  religion and control, 227–232
  social bodies, 221–225, 240–241
  transgender individuals, 139, 145, 146
computer-assisted speech, 170–171
connections. *See* communities
Connel, R.W., 115, 132–133
conscripted military service, 196, 214